| DATE DUE | | | |
|---|---|---|---|
| | | | |
| | | | |
| | | | |
| | | | |
| | | | |
| | | | |
| | | | |
| | | | |
| | | | |
| | | | |
| | | | |
| | | | |

# THE CONSTITUTION AND THE REGULATION ★ ★ ★ OF SOCIETY ★ ★ ★

EDITED BY

*Gary C. Bryner and Dennis L Thompson*

BRIGHAM YOUNG UNIVERSITY

Library of Congress Cataloging-in-Publication Data

The Constitution and the regulation of society / edited by Gary C.
 Bryner, Dennis L Thompson.

 Includes index.
  1. Interstate commerce. 2. United States—Constitutional law.
 I. Bryner, Gary C., 1951–    . II. Thompson, Dennis L
 KF4606.C55    1988
 342.73'02—dc19
 [347.3022]                                                    88.457
                                                                CIP

 ISBN 0-88706-851-0
 ISBN 0-88706-852-0 pbk.

Brigham Young University, Provo, Utah 84602
© 1988 by Brigham Young University. All rights reserved
Printed in the United States of America

Distributed by State University of New York Press,
State University Plaza, Albany, New York
12446-0001

# Contents

# Introduction

G overnment regulation reaches virtually every area of social and economic activity. Governmental efforts to control and direct decisions range from the content of the food we eat to the environmental systems in which we live. The regulatory authority of government includes the power to issue administrative rules and regulations that have the force of law, to enforce these legal requirements on individuals and firms, and to adjudicate the claims and complaints of those to whom the regulatory activity is directed.

The great burst of regulatory activity in the 1970s was greater than in any other period of American history. In that decade, twenty-one new regulatory agencies were created and some 120 major regulatory laws were enacted. The number of employees in regulatory agencies grew from 27,600 in 1970 to 87,500 in 1979. Spending in these agencies increased from $866 million to $6.94 billion, an increase of 800 percent. The number of pages in the *Federal Register* that records all proposed and final regulations mushroomed from 9,562 in 1960 to 74,120 in 1980. By 1980, according to one count, there were 116 federal agencies involved in regulatory activities.*

This growth in regulatory activity has prompted numerous efforts to evaluate and reform regulation, to make regulation more efficient and effective, or to reduce the costs of compliance. Both the Carter and Reagan administrations, while fundamen-

---

*See Ronald Penoyer, comp., *Directory of Federal Regulatory Agencies* (St. Louis: Center for the Study of American Business, Washington University, 1980), and Congressional Quarterly, *Federal Regulatory Directory* (Washington D.C.: Congressional Quarterly, Inc., 1986).

tally reflecting commitments to regulation, sought to reduce regulatory burdens. The Carter approach emphasized the rewriting of statutes that provided the basis for regulating specific sectors of the economy, while efforts of the Reagan administration have focused on providing relief from environmental, health, and safety regulations through administrative adjustments in budgets, personnel, and enforcement priorities. Regulation continues to be enveloped in controversy as regulatory costs compete with other concerns of reducing unemployment, increasing productivity, and improving the competitive position of United States firms in international markets.

Regulation poses challenges to the American political system that go beyond current economic and political debate and touch its constitutional underpinnings. The growth of regulatory power threatens expectations of limited government. The discretionary authority of regulatory bureaucracies appears to violate the rule of law, individual rights, and other values that are at the heart of consitutional government. The fusion of legislative, executive, and judicial-like powers in regulatory agencies is inconsistent with the separation of powers, one of the central concepts on which the constitutional structure rests.

The Constitution does not outline the express regulatory power of the national government in any detail; it merely authorizes Congress to "regulate Commerce with foreign Nations, and among the several States." The Framers assumed that most of the regulatory power of government would be exercised at the state level. Indeed, until the twentieth century, most of the regulation of economic and business activity, public health, marriage and family arrangements and decisions, politics and elections, and natural resources and the environment was a function of state and local governments.

The bicentennial of the Constitution provides a particularly useful occasion to provide a constitutional perspective on the government regulation of individuals and institutions in society. Two characteristics of our constitutional polity are useful to us in attempting to understand and evaluate government regulation. First, the Constitution provides some substantive guidelines for the scope and content of regulatory initiatives as well as some structural and procedural provisions. It imposes standards for the skirmish in which regulatory decisions are to be formulated and applied and indicates areas of activity where regulatory intervention is to be limited. Second, the Constitution reflects a broader concern with political culture, national ideology, and societal norms and values that produce our expectations concerning the extent and direction of regulatory power.

The essays in this volume explore and analyze contemporary developments and characteristics of government regulation from a constitutional perspective. They reflect the variety of definitions of regulation that exist and rely on different theoretical approaches and concerns. They do, however, share a common purpose of broadening and deepening our understanding of regulation from the perspective of constitutional principles, political culture and ideology, and political philosophy. The first two essays provide an overview of the scope and range of regulation and offer explanations for its dramatic growth. Theodore Lowi's "Liberal and Conservative Theories of Regulation" begins from the position that the Constitution has set the terms of discourse for American politics and public policies and reflects a fundamental commitment to liberalism as a public philosophy. Professor Lowi argues that the logic of liberalism contains a fatal flaw that has led to its decline. Liberalism requires that behavior whose consequences are undesirable be prohibited. Since all behavior, however, can be interpreted to have some negative effects at some point and for some interests, liberalism provides no limits to the regulatory reach of government. He compares liberal and conservative notions of regulation and examines the future of government regulation in terms of its conservative manifestation in the Reagan administration.

In "The Secret of Safety Lies in Danger," Aaron Wildavsky focuses on the way in which the American political system has responded to environmental and health risks. Professor Wildavsky contends that societies can organize themselves in at least two ways: they can try to anticipate hazards and do everything possible to prevent them, or they can employ their resources in developing the capability to respond and adjust to risks as they arise. He finds in the Constitution acceptance of the idea of resiliency, that political power be divided and dispersed to permit and even encourage innovation and flexibility. Excessive concern with anticipating and preventing risks that are not well understood actually increases the likelihood of harm and gives insufficient attention to the opportunity costs such cautionary efforts impose. Markets, voluntary associations, and freedom of individuals to bargain, Professor Wildavsky argues, are more likely to provide the basis for environmental protection and human health.

The next four essays pursue, in quite different ways, the relationship between the Constitution and the primary values and concerns of the political culture in which it functions.

Don Sorensen's essay entitled "Freedom and Regulation in a Free Society" provides a discussion of the preconditions for a free society, the set of principles that must be satisfied in order for freedom to flourish. His discussion rests on an analytic, philosophical approach to identifying the core characteristics of human nature and the way in which governments must take human nature into account when pursuing regulatory policies.

Sheldon Wolin, in his essay "Collective Identity and Constitutional Power," also addresses the distinction between public and private spheres within the context of the exercise of political and economic power. According to Professor Wolin, a concern with constitutional government focuses our attention on the nature of public power. He examines the changes that have taken place in our understanding of the power of the state, from the New Deal to Ronald Reagan's New Federalism, and argues that the Reagan revolution is primarily an attempt to expand public power, to collapse the distinctions between public and private, without fostering the kind of democratic participation that permits us to place some limits on that power. It has brought together public and corporate authority that has resulted in more centralized power and less democratic accountability and control.

Owen Fiss's essay, "The New Procedure," examines the role of constitutional litigation in giving meaning to the values embodied in the Constitution. The courts go beyond their traditional role of dispute resolution to identify and promote public values and purposes. Courts assume primary responsibility for reforming the large institutions of society in assuring that individual rights are protected. For Professor Fiss, these constitutional rights come from our commitment to equality, from our commonly shared values rather than our individuality. Large-scale social structures appear less and less able to satisfy public ends, and judicial intervention on behalf of those purposes and values has become a constitutional imperative.

In "The Regulation of Mediating Structures," Bruce Hafen examines the relationship between the public and private spheres assumed by the Constitution, and also emphasizes the importance of assuring freedom and the development of individual meaning and identity. For Hafen, private institutions such as the family, religions, and private and locally controlled educational institutions are the value-generating units of society and their autonomy must be protected. These institutions cultivate and foster the values that are essential to personal development and to democratic participation, yet their autonomy is increasingly coming under attack. The Constitution is at the heart of this conflict: while it assumes the value-generating role of private institutions, constitutional rights are also invoked that serve as the basis for governmental intervention in these institutions. Hafen argues for a more careful consideration of the impact of claims of individual rights, and the regulatory power exercised in their behalf, on the freedom of other individuals to define and pursue the purposes of their lives within the familial and religious environment they choose.

The final two essays focus on the administrative branch of government and the constitutional issues presented by the exercise of administrative power in regulatory and other policy areas. Louis Gawthrop's essay, "Bureaucracy and Constitutional Government: The Duty to Risk," examines the political culture of administrative power. For Gawthrop, the federal bureaucracy has been the primary vehicle by which regulatory and other public policies have been undertaken and has become the central institution of governance. His discussion of the evolution of public administration emphasizes the importance of constitutional-democratic norms and expectations for public administrators and argues that they are more important than the structures and procedures outlined in the Constitution itself. For Professor Gawthrop, the primary constitutional principle relevant to bureaucratic government is duty—the duty public officials have to the citizens they serve. A sense of duty and the other public service virtues of hard work, enthusiasm, moral integrity, and common sense are central to bringing together constitutional democracy and bureaucratic government.

Martin Shapiro, in his essay "Prudence and Rationality under the Constitution," also examines administration as a central element of the constitutional system and the regulatory process. Administrative law is the means by which the Constitution and constitutional principles are applied to public administration, and judicial review of agency actions is central to reconciling the Constitution and administration. Shapiro discusses two competing "family circles" of thought concerning the nature of constitutional interpretation and its application in administrative decision making. The rationalist vision sees the Constitution as a formal blueprint for the mechanics of government and a set of principles and rights that are to be discovered and applied by administrators and judges. The prudential ideal finds the constitutional system a set of organic, flexible, political arrangements and processes and a melange of values and aspirations. The tension between these competing visions is focused on the federal courts as they have sought to satisfy both sets of expectations in reviewing agency decisions. As courts impose rationalist expectations on agencies, they lose their ability to provide a commonsense, lay review of administrative decision making and end up deferring to expertise rather than providing an independent check on regulatory and administrative power.

These essays were all originally presented at a conference held at Brigham Young University on January 16 and 17, 1986. The conference was held in several sessions, during which one or two of the essays in this volume were presented. Following presentation of the essay or essays, all the principal scholars at the conference formed as a panel to discuss the essay or essays just presented and to respond to each other. These discussions, although informal, were very informative—to the extent that we determined to include edited transcripts of them in this volume.

The conference was made possible through the generous support of the College of Family, Home, and Social Sciences; the Department of Political Science; the Associated Students; and the Office of Scholarly Publications at Brigham Young University.

GARY C. BRYNER
DENNIS L THOMPSON
August 1987

# I

# LIBERAL AND CONSERVATIVE THEORIES OF REGULATION

★

*Theodore J. Lowi*

The bicentennial has America in a constitutional mood. But what, after all, is a constitution, what is it for, what is special about ours, and what bearing does it have on what we are doing in 1987?

Constitution refers to the composition or makeup of a thing. Our bodies have a constitution of skin and bones, flesh and blood. Governmentally, a constitution provides for the structure and the allocation of powers, obligations, and functions. Politically, a constitution is a particular means for legitimizing those structures, powers, obligations, and functions. Although most governments throughout history have ruled by force, governments in the past two to three centuries have found ruling less costly as the force is backed, or fronted, by legitimacy. Rulers seek legitimacy through such social aspects as religion, tradition, and heroism and sacrifice.

The United States is unique in its attempt to legitimize its government through none of the above but through contract. The

*Theodore Lowi is the John L. Senior Professor of American Institutions at Cornell University.*

most important large-scale application of the philosophy of Hobbes, Locke, and Rousseau, the American Constitution was founded on an exchange whereby limits on power were imposed in return for consent of the people. The appeal was to self-interest, to greed, otherwise known as the pursuit of happiness. Limits on the power of the national government in the form of federalism, the separation of powers, and the Bill of Rights implied a sphere within which individuals could realize their own satisfactions. Some important powers were retained and were expected to be used, but even there the appeal of the Constitution was in terms of what these powers could do for the realization of individual satisfactions. One of the few principles carried over from the Declaration of Independence to the Constitution was that the unalienable rights were life, liberty, and the pursuit of happiness, and "that to secure these rights, Governments are instituted among men." The Preamble of the Constitution more conservatively states that the purpose of the Constitution is to form a more perfect union and to establish justice, but it also stresses promotion of the general welfare and securing the blessings of liberty. Both the eloquence and the significance of these phrases have been lost by repetition. But they bear repeating here at the outset because they so clearly point to the nature of the appeal to legitimacy and consent in the American system of government beginning with the founding and extending through until our own day. The appeal is to self-interest. The appeal is to free oneself from the shackles of guilt about one's wants. To the moralist it is greed. To the American constitutionalist it is the pursuit of happiness.

The point of this exercise is to define the Constitution for what it is and then to define the prevailing political discourse in those terms, because the American Constitution—the more so because it was a written constitution—set the terms of discourse for the important politics of most of the ensuing two centuries.[1]

Out of this contractual approach to legitimacy arose the American antistatist tradition. Sovereignty was not to be feared and worshiped as the Leviathan but resisted and checked. This was not anarchy. Power was granted and was expected to be used, but in relation to limits bounded by consent.

Out of this also arose the individualist tradition. All individuals were ends in themselves, and it was only for this reason that individuals could actually be considered possessors of rights.

Out of this also arose the liberal tradition. The American Constitution is a liberal document. Individualism is virtually the essence of liberalism because, since each individual is presumed to have a moral code, and since there are many different moral codes, moral relativism is a necessary condition of any constitution. Since there are many different moral codes and insufficient knowledge or consensus regarding the one best code, the American Constitution embraces means, not ends.

These are the sources of the prevailing American public philosophy: liberalism. Liberalism is the starting point for American political discourse as well as the study of that discourse. Liberalism is here defined within the context of its constitutional origins and applied to contemporary liberal policies, their strength and their fallacies. Then conservatism is defined in relation, or reaction, to liberalism. The differences between the two and the future of political discourse is then explored and evaluated through examination of regulatory policies. Differences between them on welfare and other policies must await another time and place.

Except for a few radical libertarians, Utopians, and anarchists, everyone wants regulation. The only question is, what kind? Liberals prefer one kind, conservatives another. The differences are not trivial and are rarely matters of easy compromise. The differences between them arise out of constitutionally defined alternatives. That is precisely why the new liberal/conservative dialogue of the 1980s will shape the future of American political discourse and will very probably alter permanently the course of the mainstream of American politics.

## LIBERALISM—STRENGTH AND FALLACIES

### *Liberalism Defined*

Liberalism in the United States has taken several forms, including the constitutional arguments of James Madison; the defense of the union arguments of Abraham Lincoln; the market liberalism of the nineteenth century as well as its contemporary counterpart, libertarianism; and the early twentieth-century reaction to market liberalism called progressivism. The liberal tradition is found not only in politics and government but in virtually all social institutions—as in liberal education, liberal marriage, and religious liberalism.

The one thing all these liberalisms have in common is their grounding in individualism and what flows from individualism, a tentativeness about moral absolutes. As proposed above, although each individual is presumed to have a moral code, there are so many definitions of goodness that no one moral code can be set too far above another. Since there is no objective, substantive definition of goodness or of justice, liberals are forced to embrace procedures over ends, means over morality. Morality has its place in liberalism, but only in private life. In the public sphere, liberalism takes a moral position against morality.[2]

Liberalism would seem to be a flimsy public philosophy from which to draw justification for the use of government power. Government is a moral force; liberalism avoids morality. Government is a collective phenomenon; liberalism exists for the individual. Government is built on coercion; liberalism is antagonistic to any such limit on liberty. But appearances are deceiving. Liberalism has turned out to provide solid support for strong, positive government, especially because of still another feature of liberalism: Liberalism asserts a justification, indeed an obligation, to use government authority over *any conduct deemed to have harmful consequences*. Harm is an empirical concept; it is measurable and demonstrable in terms of pleasure and pain, loss and gain, dependence and independence. Thus, any theory alleging injury, if that theory is supported by plausible evidence, must be taken seriously as a cause for public policy. This helps explain the strong kinship between liberalism and science.

Liberalism would appear to be providentially designed for rationalizing the government of so heterogeneous a nation. Madison's statement in *Federalist* No. 10 is the classic statement of the theory—classic in the dictionary sense of providing the model and setting the terms of discourse for all that was to come, for dissenters as well as adherents. And there were indeed few dissenters. Socialism made so little headway that, beginning with Engels himself, there developed a cottage industry of efforts to explain "Why is there no socialism in America?" There were also few dissents from true conservatism, which, until our own decade, existed only in the localities. (More below.) By and large, the majorities of both the major parties espoused variants of liberalism—a fact appreciated more by European observers than Americans. Liberalism remained even as it was transformed from the market liberalism of the nineteenth century into the progressive and the corporate liberalisms of the New Deal. There may have been a New Deal coalition, but there was a much broader liberal consensus.

Yet, for all its success and for all its influence on public policy and for all its popularity, liberalism came unstuck in the 1960s and collapsed in the 1970s. Why?

## *Liberalism and the Regulation Binge, 1969–1979*

Rather than go directly to an explanation, let me examine first the application of liberal theory to regulation in the real world of public policies. The decade between 1969 and 1979, most particularly the half decade of 1969–75, constitutes the limiting case of liberalism. This can be called a binge, and a brief review of the binge will lead toward a more concrete explanation of how so strong (ethically) and entrenched (politically) a theory could essentially undermine itself. I take no particular pleasure in claiming that this is precisely how I envisioned "The End of Liberalism" in 1969.

Between 1969 and 1979, Congress enacted and Presidents Nixon, Ford, and Carter signed into law over 120 regulatory programs (by conservative count). Table 1 includes only the highlights.[3]

This equals or exceeds the Kennedy-Johnson record and (depending on who is doing the counting) could be said to exceed even the domestic seven years of the New Deal. In 1960 there were twenty-eight major federal regulatory agencies; in 1980 there were fifty-six, and all but one of those were created after 1969. (The exception was the National Highway Traffic Safety Administration, established in 1966.) Between 1970 and 1980, the budgets for the federal regulatory agencies increased by 300 percent measured in real dollars. And, although many kinds of announcements are printed in the *Federal Register,* it is nevertheless indicative of the growth of regulation that the number of pages in the *Federal Register* increased from 14,479 in 1960 to just

Table 1
Federal Regulatory Laws and Programs Enacted since 1970

| Year Enacted | Title of Statute |
|---|---|
| 1969–70 | Child Protection and Toy Safety Act |
| | Clear Air Amendments |
| | Egg Products Inspection Act |
| | Economic Stabilization Act |
| | Fair Credit Reporting Act |
| | Occupational Safety and Health Act |
| | Poison Prevention Packaging Act |
| | Securities Investor Protection Act |
| 1971 | Economic Stabilization Act Amendments |
| | Federal Boat Safety Act |
| | Lead-Based Paint Elimination Act |
| | Wholesome Fish and Fisheries Act |
| 1972 | Consumer Product Safety Act |
| | Equal Employment Opportunity Act |
| | Federal Election Campaign Act |
| | Federal Environmental Pesticide Control Act |
| | Federal Water Pollution Control Act Amendments |
| | Motor Vehicle Information and Cost Savings Act |
| | Noise Control Act |
| | Ports and Waterways Safety Act |
| 1973 | Agriculture and Consumer Protection Act |
| | Economic Stabilization Act Amendments |
| | Emergency Petroleum Allocation Act |
| | Flood Disaster Protection Act |
| 1974 | Atomic Energy Act |
| | Commodity Futures Trading Commission Act |
| | Consumer Product Warranties/FTL Improvement Act |
| | Council on Wage and Price Stability Act |
| | Employee Retirement Income Security Act |
| | Federal Energy Administration Act |
| | Hazardous Materials Transportation Act |
| | Housing and Community Development Act |
| | Pension Reform Act |
| | Privacy Act |
| | Safe Drinking Water Act |
| 1975 | Energy Policy and Conservation Act |
| | Equal Credit Opportunity Act |
| 1976 | Consumer Leasing Act |
| | Medical Device Safety Act |
| | Toxic Substances Control Act |

20,000 in the whole decade of the 1960s, and then jumped by 300 percent to 60,000 pages in 1975. By the end of 1979, the number of pages had increased to 86,000.

Not only did the numbers of regulatory laws and agencies and their rules increase. The scale of coverage of many of these new regulatory programs exceeded by an immeasurable degree the scale and coverage of any of the most important programs of the 1930s. Whereas the older regulatory programs were designed to cover one sector or category of the economy, the "new regulation" of the decade of the regulation binge covered some aspect of the entire economy or society. For example, the Occupational Safety and Health Act took as its purpose "to assure so far as possible every working man and woman in the nation safe and healthful working conditions and to preserve human resources." Another example, which also dramatizes the extent to which the binge was bipartisan, will be found in the language of President Nixon's message to Congress proposing establishment of the Environmental Protection Agency, stressing that the purpose of the agency was to respond to the "system in its entirety" and went on to say that "we need to know more about the *total environment*" if we are effectively to "ensure the protection, development, and enhancement of the total environment."

Five factors combine to make the regulatory binge of the 1970s so significant. First, this was a period of unusually weak presidential leadership, split partisan control between White House and Congress, and general distrust and demoralization in Congress and among large segments of the public rising out of the Vietnam War. Second, the three presidents, although liberal by the definition provided here, were right-of-center and, more importantly, were sincerely concerned about the expansion of the national government especially in the regulatory area. Third, most proposals for regulatory programs nevertheless got bipartisan majorities in the House and Senate. In other words, there is ample evidence of consensus. Fourth, many of these programs were, as observed above, significantly larger in scope than any previous regulatory programs and added significantly greater direct burdens on regulated companies and people. Late in the 1970s, when reactions began to set in against regulation, there was a lot of serious discussion and some actual application of cost/benefit analysis to regulatory programs, culminating in the requirement for a "regulatory impact statement" for each and every rule proposed by a regulatory agency. But virtually all the regulatory programs adopted in the early 1970s were "cost oblivious."

Fifth, despite the tremendously strong and bipartisan *anti*-regulation movement beginning in the late 1970s, and intensifying in the 1980s, the regulatory programs of the 1970s seem to have been a good deal less affected than the traditional and older regulatory programs. Thus, although such older regulatory policies as those concerning telephone services, commercial airlines, intercity buses, railroads, banking, and broadcasting were wholly or partially deregulated, the regulatory programs adopted in the early 1970s escaped deregulation almost altogether, despite the fact that far more complaints were registered against them than the older programs. As we shall see in more detail later, even the most ideologically antiregulatory President Reagan made no serious effort to confront Congress with legislation seeking to repeal any of the newer regulatory programs.

### Explaining the Binge: The Seed of Self-Destruction

One hypothesis would be that the new regulation is an expression of the New Politics, which is at bottom antagonistic to the capitalist system. This is why some would label the new regulation "social regulation." The argument would be that the New Politics is a movement seeking to alter relations among the basic social classes in America, with regulation and regulatory agencies being the primary leverage. Tantalizing as is this hypothesis, it has very limited confirmation. Environmental protection programs, for example, have enjoyed the opposition of large segments of organized labor as well as capital. And on the one piece of legislation most likely to yield to a class interpretation, OSHA, one sympathetic analyst observed that "state intervention into the workplace has not galvanized workers around the politics of working conditions."[4]

A second hypothesis would be that the New Politics is the explanation but that the dynamic is not class consciousness but really an aspect of a "new morality" about the quality of life and the danger to that quality of life coming from any and all big institutions, whether capitalist or not. Such visions as "small is beautiful" and "limits to growth" are part and parcel of this hypothesis. Here again, some cases confirm the hypothesis but too few to constitute a satisfactory explanation of the regulatory binge. The New Politics is too small a minority with too narrow a range of interests to have played a major role in more than a scant few of all the regulatory programs adopted in the period in question.

My own explanation is composed of two related hypotheses. First, the 1970s regulation binge was one part of the maturation and crisis of the welfare state. Second, the programs of welfare and regulation expanded and then fed upon each other for a kind of spiral of expansion because of something inherent in the logic of liberalism. Each of these will be taken in its turn.

**New regulation as response to the welfare binge.** The regulation binge followed and overlapped an expansion of welfare programs and benefits between 1965 and 1972 that might well also qualify as a binge. In 1965, Congress adopted Medicare and Medicaid. These were the two largest expansions since 1935, and they were going to continue expanding very fast because of the method of third-party financing whereby the doctor and the patient agreed on the service and the government underwrote the charges. In 1969 Congress expanded the Food Stamp Program and made it a regular rather than an experimental part of the system of comprehensive social support. This meant that three of the largest commitments ever made in the United States to the welfare state (1) were made as maturity was approaching (which for any pension or insurance system is roughly thirty to forty years); (2) were commitments to persons structurally outside the work force; and (3) were made at the moment when the ratio of taxpayers to welfare beneficiaries had dropped from eighteen to one to less than four to one.

In 1972 Congress passed an across-the-board 20 percent increase in the social security benefit base and then made benefit increases automatic rather than subject to annual reconsideration by Congress, through the enactment of the cost-of-living index (COLA). Two years later, President Nixon's Supplemental Security Income (SSI) was adopted, nationalizing a uniform minimum benefit. In 1973, the Annual Report of the Board of Trustees of the Federal Old-Age and Survivor's Insurance and Disability Insurance Trust Funds forecast long-range deficits in trust funds, thereby officially recognizing what came to be known as the "social security crisis."

The welfare state commitment had become so extensive that every personal injury became a "social cost," because every private injury was a probable link in a chain of system responsibility or "socialized risk." There are few ways to control costs in such a chain of causation. One way is to regulate directly what doctors can charge. But that alters the historic position of medicine as a free profession, it would only come slowly, and it would not be adequate. Another way to hold down costs is to regulate the dependents themselves, by close surveillance and regular cleansing of the eligibility rolls. But this can be a solution that is almost as costly as the problem. Another way to control costs is to cut down drastically on coverage and hold down severely the benefit payments. But as long as the system holds itself responsible for all injuries, then the operators of that system are likely to view coverage and benefit limits as a false economy, because an injury inadequately indemnified today may become a still more costly problem of dependency or rehabilitation later—as in "a stitch in time saves nine."

Any and all of those approaches can help marginally, but a much more substantial approach to cost control in the welfare state is the prevention of injuries and dependencies in the first place. This is how regulation became coextensive with the welfare state and, thus, with the society itself. No wonder people instinctively began to refer to the new regulation as "social regulation." Fear of the immense scale or of the direct costs of regulation was not much restraint because, no matter how burdensome, these 1970s programs would be far less burdensome than the long-run costs to society if injuries and other sources of dependency were allowed to mount—as surely they must in a society so filled with dangers of carelessness, faulty mechanisms, and artificially produced environmental dangers.

**New regulation as a pathological fruit of the liberal seed.** The second hypothesis provides an explanation which subsumes the first: The programs of welfare and of regulation of the 1960s and the 1970s expanded to the entire society because of an inherent flaw in liberalism, a flaw that produced a crisis because it was not appreciated by the liberal practitioners themselves. The self-destructive seed of liberalism can be identified fairly readily by a brief reexamination of the definition of liberalism, in particular its justification of regulatory policy by its stress on controlling the *harmful consequences of conduct.* There is great strength in this position, but the problem is that under some conditions, any and all conduct can have harmful consequences. And this means that ultimately *all* conduct comes under the responsibility and therefore the surveillance of the state. Not every activity is being watched or controlled at a given point, but whether it is depends mainly on whether someone has proposed a theory connecting that action with a preventable harm. Take the homely example of a pig farmer. Raising pigs for commercial purposes is a morally neutral activity, and Farmer Brown has been raising pigs for, say, twenty years. During the course of that twenty years, let us say two things happen. One, where once Farmer Brown lived in an isolated area, other residences are now built nearby. Two, someone advances a theory that pig farming is associated with a certain disease. The conduct remains morally neutral, but suddenly there is reason to believe this particular pig farm is the source of harm, and the people who are now Farmer Brown's neighbors are too likely to catch the disease. A public health or zoning ordinance is likely to be proposed and adopted requiring that Farmer Brown cease and desist or sell his property and find another isolated place to engage in pig farming.

In the liberal regime of the 1960s, any theory about the cause of injury, if backed by some evidence, was seriously considered as a claim to public policy. Consequently almost *everything became good to do.* There were no priorities. The liberalism of the 1960s declined into what I have called "interest-group liberalism," because, without priorities, it was logical to let the participants determine what ought to be done. It had all the trappings of rational policy making because the question of making a policy could rest on the morally neutral test of the plausibility of the evidence and arguments about causation. Moreover, the actual choice embodied in the public policy could be written in language broad enough to be implemented later through a continuing process of interest-group claims and bargaining, validated by decisions in the form of rules formulated and implemented by expert, professional officials in the responsible agency.

This logic of liberalism, fed by the unexamined tendency to expand toward coverage of all conduct and all injuries, explains more than any other factor the irresistible expansion of national regulatory and welfare programs into the 1970s despite evidence officially recognized by 1973 of approaching insolvency. This irresistible expansion was ultimately going to undermine the political constituency of liberalism. There had long been an acceptance of regulation and welfare programs by a more than sufficient number of important and well-organized corporate interests. This acceptance was undermined by an unenlightened liberalism that produced the sense of a spiraling expansion of regulation and welfare, each seeming to feed the other. Undermining the political constituency of liberalism was but the first step toward undermining liberalism itself, not because the programs were failures but because liberalism was failing from within to provide sufficient justification for continuing expansion.[5]

## THE CONSERVATIVE REACTION

### Awakening of Local Moral Forces

As liberalism was undoing itself, losing its own battle without even the alibi of serious adversaries, something else was beginning to happen. Many of the policies of the liberal national government were beginning to intrude on local moral codes. This was not just a question of "intervention." There had already been plenty of that before the 1960s, and most people, even those most heavily regulated, had grown accustomed to it. The difference was precisely that the liberal national government of the 1960s began to impinge on conduct and values traditionally defined as private or local, or both.

For example, federal courts, definitively after 1954, then Congress by 1960, began to intervene against state and local racial policies. Race relations were considered part of the domain of private morality. Now, private morality in fact requires a lot of public regulation. And state laws and local ordinances have overflowed with regulatory policies. But except for some transitory post–Civil War laws, the *national* government had not entered this realm, and, whatever the merits of the intervention, it was considered intrusive. As Ronald Reagan said during the 1980 campaign, when he was a youngster, race was not a problem. The implication of that is that the Supreme Court and the U.S. Congress had made it a problem.

National welfare policies also began to be felt as an intrusion on local moral codes. The 1935 categories of social security were quick to be accepted as facilitative, but the more recent discretionary public assistance programs got professional welfare workers involved in local family and community practices, in regard to means testing, juvenile delinquency, child custody, and institutionalization/deinstitutionalization in the hitherto very local or private mental health field.

Federal education policies also became more intrusive. The most intrusive were simply extensions of civil rights policies, but other national policies were added in the late 1950s, and, although education grants-in-aid were accepted as facilitative, they became increasingly intrusive as local and state administrators and politicians found it increasingly necessary to join together for intensive lobbying for more of the grants-in-aid and for a share in influencing the criteria established for giving the grants-in-aid. Never before had the national government established substantive criteria for grants to state and local governments.

The most important and the most irritating of the impacts of federal policy were in the general category of civil liberties. This included criminal justice, election and reapportionment, privacy (especially women's) rights, and church/state relationships. This area is so important that some constitutional historians refer to it as the "second constitutional revolution," comparing its significance to the change in interstate commerce power and practices in the 1930s, which they call the "first constitutional revolution." This revolutionary expansion in public policy was of course led by the federal courts, and the full measure of local irritation against intervention into local moral codes was epitomized in the demand that moved from the constituencies to Congress—"Impeach Earl Warren." Although these policies were court-led and to an overwhelming extent court-made, that does not reduce their association with the national government. In fact, it was during the 1950s and 1960s that people began to recognize that the courts are part of the government and not part of the private sector.[6]

These categories of national governmental policy actually came to be grouped together under the new label of "social policy." There is nothing inherently prejudicial about the category "social policy," but it does emphasize not only the novelty of the policies in the category but also the tendency of these policies to deal with private values and not simply civil practices. This is certainly the

*19*

meaning of the unfortunate remark made by President Eisenhower around the time of the 1957 Civil Rights debate in Congress that "you can't legislate morality." Of course you can legislate morality. Thousands upon thousands of state statutes and local ordinances testify to that fact. What he was really saying is that the *national* government shouldn't legislate morality. But it was doing so in the area that came to be labeled "social policy." And it was inevitable. Despite our failures to accomplish very much, few people today can imagine the national government *not* having policies aimed directly and coercively at a number of social issues and moral codes, but their novelty in the 1950s and 1960s contributed directly to two unanticipated consequences. First, these policies weakened the liberal constituency, driving a wedge between northern liberal Democrats and southern conservative Democrats, eventually laying waste the New Deal coalition that had depended mightily upon tacit agreement not to put issues of north/south conflict on the national agenda. The lesson of the 1948 Dixiecrat walkout had been rejected before a decade had passed. The second unintended consequence was the mobilization of what has been called the Conservative Reaction. It is unfortunate that the label "new politics" was given over to the post–civil rights, public-interest liberal movements, which were (and are) remarkably adroit but not really new. This prevents us from using it on what is truly new at the national level, the conservative movement.

## Defining Conservatism and the Conservative Tradition

There is today a widespread misconception that conservatism and libertarianism are one and the same. Libertarianism is actually a modern name for market or laissez-faire liberalism predominant in the late nineteenth century. It came to be identified as conservative only because there was no real conservatism at the national level virtually until the 1970s. The current tendency to confuse libertarianism and conservatism is based upon the fact that libertarians and conservatives have been making common cause against certain important national policies. But they have been opposed to the same policies for very different reasons. Libertarians are truly antistatist in the liberal tradition. Conservatives, on the other hand, are prostatist.

In contrast to liberalism (including libertarianism), conservativism is much more confident that moral absolutes can be known and, once known, ought to be imposed by law. Nothing is more irksome to genuine conservatives than the moral uncertainty and relativism of liberals.

The most salient contrast between the two public philosophies is in their justification for the use of government coercion. Whereas liberalism avoids taking a moral position toward conduct and tries to limit itself to controlling the consequences of conduct, conservatism does take a moral position toward conduct and justifies the extension of government authority over *conduct deemed good or evil in itself*. Conservatives are not averse to considering consequences. Conservatives can be pragmatic—prudence is a favorite word among conservatives—but the essential feature of conservatism in government is moral guidance. "Statecraft as soulcraft," says genuine conservative author George Will. Two brief selections from Will's book can help characterize genuine conservatism.

> I am often asked: "Why do you call yourself a conservative if you believe" this or that? The question usually pertains to my belief in strong government, including the essentials of the welfare state.
>
> In a famous opinion in a famous case (one concerning compulsory flag salutes in schools), Justice Felix Frankfurter wrote: "Law is concerned with external behavior and not with the inner life of man." I am not sure what Frankfurter meant. I am sure that what he said cannot be true. The purpose of this book is to say why that proposition is radically wrong.[7]

Defined this way, conservatism is as American as liberalism and has as long a tradition. A British colleague in a personal letter expressed to me his fascination with my contention that American conservatism has a long tradition but is just emerging to national respectability. He asked, however, "Where is your equivalent of Burke?" Burke is as much a source of American conservatism as Locke is a source of American liberalism. Neither was self-consciously copied, but the writings of each are in direct line of continuity with the respective American variants. As individualism and contract were basic to liberalism, so were the same two values a problem for Burke and the American conservatives. Let one brief passage from Burke suffice to characterize the attitude.

> Society is indeed a contract . . . but the state ought not to be considered as nothing better than a partnership agreement in a trade of pepper and coffee, calico or tobacco, or some other such low concern, to be taken up for a little temporary interest, and to be dissolved by the fancy of the parties. It is to be looked on with . . . reverence; because it is not a partnership in things subservient only to the gross animal existence of a temporary and perishable nature . . . As the ends of such a partnership cannot be obtained in many generations, it becomes a partnership not only between those who are living, but between those who are living, those who are dead, and those who are to be born. Each contract of eternal society, linking the lower with the higher natures, . . . [is] according to a fixed compact sanctioned by the inviolable oath which holds all physical and all moral natures, each in their appointed place.

George Sabine, from whose masterful work that famous Burke passage is drawn, was moved to observe that for Burke, "No clear line is drawn between society at large and the state, and the latter is named as in a special sense the guardian of all the higher interests of civilization. . . . Burke's reverential attitude toward the state distinguished him absolutely from Hume and the utilitarians; . . . he practically united politics with religion."[8]

Genuine conservatism received little attention in the United States until virtually the late 1970s because it had almost no place in national politics. This is why market liberalism was saddled with the label of conservatism, merely because it was the only important source of dissent against the modern, statist liberalism of the Wilson and Roosevelt variety that continued to dominate on into the 1970s. The home of conservatism has always been in the states and localities.

This is completely understandable and most meaningful in light of the American Constitution, federalism in particular. Table 2 is a visualization of the consequences of a Constitution that delegated a specific set of powers to national government and *reserved* all the rest to the states, or to the people, who, within their respective states, have the power to delegate any authority they wish to the state government, through the state legislature.

Table 2
The Federal System:
Specialization of Functions
among the Three Levels of Government—
The Traditional System, c. 1800–1933

| National Govern-ment Policies; (domestic) | State Government Policies | Local Government Policies |
|---|---|---|
| Internal Improve-ments | Property Laws (incl. slavery) | Adaptation of state laws to local condi-tions ("variances") |
| Subsidies (mainly to shipping) | Estate & Inheritance Laws | Public Works |
| Tariffs | Commerce Laws (Ownership & Exchange) | Contracts for Public Works |
| Public Lands Dis-posal | Banking & Credit Laws | Licensing of public accommodations |
| Patents | Insurance Laws | Assessable Improve-ments |
| Currency | Family Laws | Basic Public Service |
| | Morals Laws | |
| | Public Health & Quarantine Laws | |
| | Education Laws | |
| | General Penal Laws | |
| | Public Works Laws (incl. eminent domain) | |
| | Construction Codes | |
| | Land-use Laws | |
| | Water & Mineral Resources Laws | |
| | Judiciary & Criminal Procedure Laws | |
| | Electoral Laws (incl. Political Parties) | |
| | Local Government Laws | |
| | Civil Service Laws | |
| | Occupations & Profes-sions Laws | |

Brief note might be taken of the shortness of the list of national government policies that are actually to be found in the annual session laws of the U.S. Congress. Not only are they few in number, they are very special in character. They all have to do one way or the other with the husbanding of commerce, and they all use government power to facilitate rather than directly to regulate by imposing limits and obligations directly on citizens. Column two of table 2 confirms what any reading of the original articles and the Tenth Amendment would say with unambiguous clarity—that traditionally the states did virtually all the fundamental governing in this country. The states made more policies, the policies were about things that were a great deal more important to Americans and their society, and the states used primarily regulatory power, directly coercive policies, imposing limits and obligations directly on citizens.

One other thing can be said about the list of state government policies: although many state policies fit comfortably within the liberal theory of regulation, most of them are conservative. To put the matter another way, most of what has been conservative in American government will be found in these state policies. The fundamental aspects of property were deeply part of the American moral code. Trespass laws themselves were intrinsically part of the American concept of the moral obligations inherent in property. The penal code is obviously a dimension on which virtually all citizens are conservatives, because the penal laws and their punishments do not require justification in terms of harmful consequences but only that murder, assault, rape, robbery, fraud, and other such crimes are plain and simply immoral. Conservatism is of course found in the enormous range and variety of laws that deal with sexual conduct, family and divorce, estates, vagrancy, Sunday closing laws and other religious observances, education, children, and all the "crimes without victims."

There is no need to belabor the point. The home of conservatism is the states and the localities, and the tradition of conservatism at that level has been rich and successful. In contrast, as the national government grew, beginning even in the late nineteenth century, it grew along liberal lines. The government grew much larger, and liberalism was transformed from a market variety to a statist variety; but the policies were justified in the liberal terms of concern for regulating conduct deemed to produce harmful consequences—the "external behavior and not the inner life of man." And the debate over the expansion of the national government was between and among liberals, over whether sufficient harm was being done to warrant a particular government intervention. There was little if any joining of debate between a liberal and a genuine conservative concept of what the national government ought to do. Liberalism and conservatism literally coexisted. On matters that went to the core of the moral code shared by the adult white male Protestant leaders and voters, the states had jurisdiction, and the state legislatures acted with firmness to impose, by law, the appropriate moral obligations. On other matters of great national import that went beyond the confines of state boundaries, and where a good theory made a connection between unwanted effects and their causes, the national government ultimately came to be defined as a government of appropriate jurisdiction. And liberalism set the terms of discourse. The terms were normative, in the sense that government had an obligation to intervene; but those terms were as neutral as possible as regards the substantive morality of the conduct. The best case in point has been capitalism. Unlike the left in Europe, liberals have never taken a moral position toward capitalism. Capitalism is composed of various kinds of conduct that may or may not produce harmful consequences; and it is the consequences that are of legitimate concern to government. Liberalism and conservatism were as ships passing in the day.

Once again we find Madison, not Marx, having the last word. "Moral Majorities" so likely to tyrannize over nonbelievers could be permitted to prevail where they were literally the overwhelming majority—in the homogeneous populations of localities or individual states. The virtue of federalism, as articulated in *Federalist* No. 10, was that such majorities were, in the larger, continental context, nothing but minority factions which would find almost overwhelming barriers to becoming real majorities on a nationwide, therefore tyrannical, scale. Factions would essentially regulate themselves, such that the purity of their moral position would be adulterated on their way toward competition in the national electorate and the national legislature. Meanwhile, since only the states had the authority necessary to deal with all those issues of most fundamental concern to moral minorities or moral majorities, it was to the state legislatures and not to Washington that moral leaders and moral interest groups went for their satisfaction. Why go to Washington at all? A march on Washington or the hiring of a lobbyist to send to Washington would have been a waste of time.

All that changed as liberal policies began to intrude on matters within the tradition of state government and the tradition of conservative leadership. People who were accustomed to obeying state laws and local ordinances on such intimate matters as prayer and patriotism or, indeed, state laws declaring as crimes any kind of sex between consenting adults except legally married males and females engaging in sex in the missionary position were not prepared to accept laws imposed on them by governments controlled by distant majorities. Then, beginning in the 1980s, Americans regardless of the state in which they resided found that they now shared common political experiences, emanating from a single source: Washington. And for the first time, every neighborhood preacher and parish priest with a social or political criticism and access to a radio or television outlet suddenly found a regional and then a national audience. These people became movements ready for a leader.

The emergence in the late 1960s of the Catholic bishops as an important national political presence took people by surprise. So did the emergence of Jerry Falwell, the Moral Majority, and other evangelicals to positions of immense influence. So did the emergence of Pat Robertson as a potential presidential candidate. None of this should have been any more surprising than the fact that four of the most important politicians of the last decade, including the two most recent presidents, were second-born Christians. Liberal policies, in fact some of the most high-minded and disinterested policies, had contributed to a national counterconstituency, conservatism.

This was no national moral majority. The Reagan *electoral* majority was made up of much more than the organized conservatives. Genuine conservatives had always constituted the right wing of the Republican party, but they always lost to the liberal wing, except for the Goldwater debacle, which proved the point. Now the two wings were in uneasy concordance, with a genuinely conservative president. Reagan's electoral majority also included populist Protestantism—which had never been a significant part of the Republican party—plus an unexpectedly large segment of the Catholic church. It also included large numbers of libertarians, beyond those who had always been part of the Republican liberal wing. And a surprisingly large number of intellectuals were mobilized or radicalized toward the Reagan majority—indeed, the conservative wing of that majority. They had been deeply disaffected by the social policies of the 1960s, especially affirmative action, by liberal willingness to deal with the Soviet Union, and in general by the absence of priorities and the overall tentativeness of liberal leadership. However, the core and the novelty within the Reagan electoral majority was conservatism—and this conservatism has been an influence far in excess of the proportionate place conservative leaders hold in the leadership around Ronald Reagan and his administration.

## THE CONSERVATIVE APPROACH:
## FROM DEREGULATION TO REGULATION MANAGEMENT

### *Some Real Deregulation—Mainly by Ford and Carter*

Just as the regulatory binge of the early 1970s was bipartisan, the reaction against the binge and its burdens was also bipartisan. President Ford and his Democratic-controlled Congress inaugurated the deregulation movement in 1975, and candidate Carter included a critique against regulation as part of his larger campaign against the very Washington over which he sought to serve as president. As a Brookings Institution study concludes, "most of the changes in government policies that produced [the procompetitive reform] occurred between 1975 and 1980."[9]

Nothing in the five years of the Reagan administration comes anywhere near to matching the deregulation record of the previous five years, which includes, among other actions: the Securities Acts Amendments of 1975, the Railroad Revitalization and Regulatory Reform Act of 1976, the Staggers Rail Act of 1980, the Railroad Revitalization Regulatory Reform Act of 1976, the Airline Deregulation Act of 1978, the Depository Institutions Deregulation in Monetary Control Act of 1980, the Motor Carrier Act of 1980, and the beginnings of community cable deregulation.

President Reagan contributed mightily to the climate of public opinion favoring deregulation. But he did not go to Congress and seek legislation terminating any important regulatory programs. His first such effort may come with the request to terminate the ICC, but this is at the end of his administration, and concerted effort even here had not yet begun in earnest in mid-1987. Instead, the Reagan administration has sought and has taken on significant increases in managerial power. President Reagan has sought to deregulate not by terminating or shrinking any of the authority now held in the executive branch but by retaining the power and using it to control the agencies so as to reduce or delay the output of rules. His approach is quite distinctive. It enables the president to reduce the level of regulatory activity in favor of the private sector, but it also enables him to change the direction of regulation, and to leave the capacity for intervention intact for himself and his successors. The most appropriate characterization of this approach is regulation management.

## Evidence of Regulation Management

**Impoverishing regulatory agencies.** In place of legislative requests for termination of regulatory authority, Reagan from the start proposed budget and staff cuts that would in effect impoverish the agencies. Nearly 15 percent of the FTC budget, 30 percent of the CPSC budget, 22 percent of the OSHA budget, and 25 percent of the toxic substances segment of the EPA budget were the result of supply-side Reaganomics. This of course meant very little actual freeing of supply, because regulatory budgets are small, and even a 25 percent cut in one of the budgets contributes little more than a fly speck to the total budget or the deficit.

The cumulative outcome of actions on staff cuts that were initiated in the first year of the Reagan administration produced 8 percent cuts across the board plus; for example, 20 percent at CPSC, 30 percent at EPA, and 27 percent of inspectors alone at OSHA. Attrition and resignation accounted for 2,500 personnel reductions at EPA. All this suggests a strategy of attrition to weaken the agencies into submission.

**Appointing hostile commissioners.** Because President Carter had already so far advanced deregulation in the older "economic regulation" agencies, President Reagan's appointment pattern was somewhat uneven, with some commissioners hostile to their agency's mission and others not so. For example, his appointment of

Reese Taylor as chairman of the ICC was sponsored and supported by the Teamsters Union, whose interests were definitely favorable to ICC regulation in the traditional sense. However, Reagan's other appointees to the ICC fit the pattern of hostility to the agency's mission. [10]

In most other agencies, but in particular the "new regulation" agencies, the typical appointee was a person who had been an adversary and critic prior to appointment. Significant examples include James Miller III at FTC, Thorne Auchter at OSHA, Raymond Peck at NHSTSA, and Mark Fowler at FCC. The best known example was Ann Burford (Gorsuch), appointed to head the EPA. It is not only that she was a dramatic contrast to the Carter appointments. She was actively antagonistic—directly responsible for reducing EPA's operating budget by nearly 30 percent, reducing the total number of employees by 2,762, and cutting the research budget by 46 percent. Burford-Gorsuch did not even bother to fill an important R & D position on a permanent basis. She sought to derange the enforcement process of EPA by first abolishing the enforcement office, reallocating its duties to other units, then recreating the office as a separate but smaller unit, then reorganizing it four times in a ten-month period in 1981–82. The number of cases referred to the Justice Department for suit dropped from 252 in 1980 to 78 in 1981. And she very dramatically reduced the level of federal supervision of state environmental implementation activity. [11]

The point here is not to criticize President Reagan for appointing commissioners sympathetic to his point of view. The significant point is that this appointment pattern was in preference to efforts to seek clear, legislative reductions of regulatory authority. Appointing hostile commissioners is not a sign of desire to deregulate as such. It is better understood as "discretionary deregulation." The firing of James Watt and the legal actions against Ann Burford-Gorsuch are in no way indicative of a change of heart on Reagan's part but are in fact more a reflection of the extent to which these Reagan commissioners were operating contrary to the legal obligations and momentum of the agencies.

**Strengthening presidential oversight.** One of the first actions taken by President Reagan after his inauguration was Executive Order 12291, issued February 17, 1981, giving the Office of Management and Budget the power to oversee all major regulations issued by the executive branch agencies. Agencies were required to present extensive cost-benefit analyses to justify each new regulation. This was euphemistically called "Regulatory Impact Analysis." Shortly before his second inauguration, on January 4, 1985, President Reagan issued a new executive order extending OMB supervision to "pre-rulemaking actions" by regulatory agencies. This order not only requires notice of intent to initiate rulemaking, but also annual submission of a "Draft Regulatory Program" listing all significant regulatory actions each agency plans to take during the upcoming year. This gives OMB the opportunity to have agencies redo their plans and proposals.

In 1983 the Supreme Court declared unconstitutional the "legislative veto." The legislative veto was a practice of long standing whereby Congress by law required certain regulatory agencies to submit to Congress any rule they proposed to adopt, prior to publication in the *Federal Register*. If during a period of sixty to ninety days (as prescribed by law) Congress took positive action to disapprove of the proposed rule, the rule died. If Congress in both Houses or in one House (as provided variably in different laws) took no action, the rule then became law as though adopted as a statute by Congress. The demise of the legislative veto and the establishment of the regulatory review power of the President lodged in OMB is a significant shift toward the executive and toward regulation management. OMB regulatory review gives the President substantive item veto through the back door even as he is failing to get budgetary item veto through the front door.

**"Regulating the poor."** Since the Reagan administration proposed several important welfare changes to Congress, it is more difficult to separate out management from legislation in welfare policy. However, since Congress failed to act on most of the legislative changes Reagan sought, he was forced to use all the more vigorously the administrative discretion available to him, especially due to changes in legislation made by the previous administration. As one observer put it in regard to the Social Security Disability Insurance (SSDI) program, "In response to growing concern about the 'explosion' in the SSDI roles over the prior decade, Congress mandated tighter review procedures shortly before Reagan took office. However, the new administration implemented these with a zeal that quickly became controversial with Congress, the courts, and the states (who generally administer the procedures)."[12]

Case load investigations and benefit terminations increased fourfold between 1980, Carter's last year, and 1982, the second year of the Reagan administration. There were also administratively determined major cutbacks in the Unemployment Insurance (UI) program to such an extent that at the height of the 1982 recession, an average of only 45 percent of the unemployed received UI benefits compared to 76 percent in the previous recessionary year of 1975.[13]

Reagan had more legislative success in regard to the changes he sought for AFDC, seeking to make it a last resort for any family with children. Some of the changes were to be directly legislatively imposed, but a good deal of discretion was sought for and obtained to enable OMB and the Social Security Administration to make important changes administratively. Similar discretion was obtained for "workfare," to enable state administrators to force more recipients to find jobs to get them off the eligible lists. The impact of both was to clear the eligible lists of a significant number of previously eligible persons. As investigations of eligibility went up, the number of working poor and near-poor dropped. One estimate reports removal of 400,000 to 500,000 AFDC families and nearly a million potential Food Stamp beneficiaries.[14]

Some shrinkage of the eligibility rolls was inevitable, regardless of the outcome of the 1980 election. However, two things are distinctive about the Reagan administration. The first is the extent of the effort and of the success to cut down the welfare rolls. The second difference is that the cutting down was done in a conservative rather than liberal manner, by stigmatizing welfare concomitantly with reducing it from budgetary necessity. Stress on the "truly needy," careful and public distinction between the "deserving" and the "undeserving" poor, emphasis on welfare as a "work disincentive" and as a corrupter of families—all of these are examples of the new rhetoric of a conservative approach to welfare through not merely the regulation of the poor but the moral guidance of the poor. As a number of people have observed, the theory of the Reagan administration has been to encourage the rich to work harder by rewards and to encourage the poor to work harder by punishments.

**Using the deficit as regulation management.** There are at least two different theories toward the deficit. One theory treats the deficit as a fiscal instrument, in the Keynesian tradition. The other defines the deficit as a regulatory instrument, which may become a new tradition of supply-side Reaganism. The Keynesian approach views the deficit as part of a general policy of "counter-cyclical compensatory spending," where it is the economy and not the budget that ought to be in balance. This means that government should in fact treat deficits as a virtue during periods of deflationary tendency and then seek a budgetary surplus to retire part or all of the debt during periods of inflation, where too many dollars are chasing too few goods. The Reagan alternative does not concern itself very much with the fiscal aspects of the deficit, despite the fact that the large and growing deficits in 1981 and 1982 probably contributed significantly to the conversion of that recession into prosperity. But the important thing about this deficit theory is that the deficit can work as an automatic control or ceiling over domestic commitments by the government itself. This can be considered an aspect of regulation management precisely because governments don't merely "have" deficits. Deficits have to be managed. A big deficit on top of a big debt is a sign of big government. Thus, it is not a matter of whether to have a deficit policy, but which one.

### Evidence of Pro-Regulation: Restoring Power to the States

Although President Reagan did not try as hard as his far-right wing demanded, his efforts to restore regulatory power to the states were a strong indication of the attitude of conservatism toward government power. The Reagan administration unqualifiedly endorsed the restoration to the states of such powers taken away from them by a series of federal court decisions beginning in 1954 and accelerating after 1959. It should be emphasized here that none of these efforts amounts to "turning back" to the states powers that were assumed by the national government. They are powers the states traditionally exercised that the federal courts stepped in and terminated or severely restricted. These include: power over persons accused of crimes; power over religious observances in the secondary schools; power over pregnant women and what they do with their bodies and their fetuses; power over

doctors and the rest of the medical profession in regard to pregnant women; power of local and county welfare administrators
over welfare clients in regard to eligibility without entitlement;
and power to deal with environmental impacts without hindrance
from federal courts.

The point here is that there is almost nothing about the Reagan administration at the national, state, or local levels that
indicates any inclination to reverse the fifty-year tendency toward
greater intervention, more discretion for administrative agencies,
and more centralization of management power in the executive
branch. The difference between conservatives and their liberal
predecessors is only in the direction and in the unit of government
to exercise the regulatory power. One not so hypothetical case can
be used to close this argument. This is the case of what can be
directly anticipated by the restoration to the states of power over
pregnant women. If a constitutional amendment or a new Supreme Court majority should reverse the line of cases subsumed
under *Roe v. Wade,* and if with that restored power a state such as
Arizona adopted new laws criminalizing abortion, based upon the
argument that human life begins with conception, then immediately all pregnant women must be registered with state police
authorities the moment their pregnancy is diagnosed. In the
event of a miscarriage, the police would have to investigate, and
some kind of hearing would have to be held in order to determine
whether the miscarriage was a case of criminal negligence, man-
slaughter, or premeditated murder. All doctors and nurses with
any relationship to the pregnant woman with the miscarriage
would also have to be investigated, as would the hospitals with
which they are associated. And such a law would not be nearly as
difficult to implement as the prohibition law, because women
who are registered as pregnant must turn up with a child within
nine months or the absence of such a record would trigger off the
possibility of foul play. Picture, for example, a nice, middle-class
lady having lunch at her club, overheard expressing regrets that
she got herself committed to a fourth child. She then goes out for
a brisk set of tennis, following which she has a miscarriage. An
inquest must be held, and questions must be asked as to whether,
given her comments, the vigorous game of tennis in, say, her
sixth month, amounted to premeditated murder or at least criminal negligence.

It is difficult to imagine a police force conscientiously taking on such a responsibility or a state and local public health agency and judiciary accepting this kind of role and responsibility over all current and potential pregnancies and the vast service forces related to them. To me it looks more like an effort to use government to restore moral hegemony to local authorities by making all individuals much more vulnerable to that authority. One need not express a personal opinion toward when life begins or women's rights or privacy rights in general in order to perceive a very profound difference between the conservative and the liberal approach to regulation—and the difference between them is not pro- versus anti-government. Treating a fetus as a moral obligation of the mother, versus treating it as a problem of practical choice within the power of the mother, involves two very different concepts of government. This of course extends over into welfare. The liberal would look at the consequences of the teenage pregnant girl and the ultimate cost to the community before deciding on the appropriate welfare policy decision. The conservative would tend to view the problem as President Reagan did in a press conference early in 1985:

> Under existing welfare rules, a teen-age girl who becomes pregnant can make herself eligible for welfare benefits that will set her up in an apartment of her own, provide medical care, and feed and clothe her. She has to fulfill only one condition— not marry or identify the father.

The teenage pregnant girl and the middle-class lady with her miscarriage are the kinds of cases that separate liberalism from conservatism in a clear and consistent manner.

## SOME REFLECTIONS ON THE FUTURE OF POLITICAL DISCOURSE

If Ronald Reagan accomplishes nothing else, his place as a strong president is assured alone by his contribution to the establishment of a real liberal/conservative dialogue in the United States. The conditions had been ripe for the mobilization of conservatism and its elevation from the parochial to the national. And I say parochial deliberately, not to discredit by labeling, but to emphasize the conservative base as being both from the parish and of the parish. But conditions don't inevitably produce results; they could have turned from ripe to rotten if there had not been the national focus and sustained leadership provided by Ronald Reagan. Although the most radical members of his constituency may be frustrated, even to the point of accusing him of betrayal, Reagan's unprecedented programmatic persistence and the underlying logic of it not only galvanized conservatism into a true national movement but have provided it with sufficient basis to perpetuate itself.

The question remains as to how large this movement is and how much it can accomplish as a new public philosophy for the nation. The most extreme scenario would be a true *conservative realignment,* in which not just the Republican party but a conservatively dominated Republican party would become an electoral majority for a significant period of time beyond the Reagan presidency and would during that time be able to maintain the conservative program as the national agenda comparable to the liberal realignment that kept the New Deal as the national agenda long after FDR had departed the scene.

There are at least five factors that lead me to put a quite low probability on the conservative realignment scenario. The reasoning here is instructive even if others would put different weights on the factors and conclude with a different probability rating for this scenario.

First, while some national policies continue to cut into local moralities, there are far larger numbers of national policies and issues that do not. On the latter policies, conservatism has nothing in particular to say. In fact, without much concern for consistency, they tend to adopt the libertarian line on these. But the libertarian line has been the mainstream line of the Republican party for a very long time.

Second, morality in public policy develops a politics tending toward violence unless there is a homogeneous mass and elite. Puritan democracy is an oxymoron except where everybody is puritan. The American national arena is far too heterogeneous to accept a puritan democracy, or any other such hyphenated democracy.

Third, and closely related, although a "Reagan coalition" is comparable to the New Deal coalition in being a congeries of religious, sectional, and economic groupings, ideology is a much more important element of the Reagan than the New Deal coalition. Thus, whereas the New Deal coalition could hold itself together with patronage and logrolling, piggybacking some substantial programs on that coalition, the Reagan coalition would have a much harder time holding itself together without Reagan.

This points to factor four, Reagan himself. Charisma is one of those qualities that cannot be passed along to others as a legacy. Already there are signs of strain within the Republican ranks, and these are not likely to become less intense as the several presidential candidates square off in the fight to succeed President Reagan.

Fifth, there is liberalism itself. Liberalism is down but not out. It has returned before, and it is usually stronger after its regeneration. And liberalism will, in one form or another, always be most attractive to most politicians confronting the tremendous range of moral codes in this nation. If liberals can learn about the inherent limits of liberalism and how to cope with them, liberalism could once again become as appealing to an American consensus as it once was.

There are of course other scenarios. Reagan and his successors could go for purity over victory and divide the Republican party into moral minorities. Some radical conservatives have been talking that way, using people like Pat Robertson as their stalking horse. Although I personally do not set a high probability on this scenario, it is not altogether unrealistic. A division of the Republican party would only be one more way of recognizing that both the present major parties are far from majority parties. And insistent conservatism could contribute to fundamental political change in the United States if out of their insistence came a multiparty system.

A third and probably higher-probability scenario would begin on the premise that Reagan is after all a pragmatic fellow who would prefer to be president than right and would prefer to leave practical legacies rather than philosophic ones. But if this turns out to be the case, Reagan will be remembered as simply one more statist president, albeit a strong one. There would be no transformation; there would be nothing worthy of being called a Third Republic. If anything, we would call it interest-group conservatism or, just as well, interest-group liberalism with an opening to the right.

However, there is one certainty in all of this, and that certainty is that a liberal/conservative dialogue is here to stay. There is not likely to be a return to a liberal consensus with the debate exclusively between two varieties of liberalism. In whatever form, American national politics will be a great deal more polarized, more programmatic, and more ideological in the future than it has been in the past. Despite what most Americans believe, theory can be more powerful than practice.

# Notes

1. Revisions and extension of this chapter were made during my tenure as Caroline Werner Gannett Professor of the Humanities at the Rochester Institute of Technology, during the 1986–87 academic year.

2. This and the next paragraph are taken from an earlier piece of mine, "Ronald Reagan—Revolutionary?" in Lester Salamon and Michael Lund, *The Reagan Presidency and the Governing of America* (Washington, D.C.: The Urban Institute, 1984), 32–33. See also Michael Sandel, *Liberalism and the Limits of Justice* (New York: Cambridge University Press, 1982), 1. To Sandel, the "core thesis" of liberalism is that "society . . . is best arranged when it is governed by principles that do not *themselves* presuppose any particular conception of the good" (emphasis in original).

3. Theodore J. Lowi, *The End of Liberalism,* 2d ed. (New York: W.W. Norton, 1979), 115. Revisions provided by Gary Bryner.

4. Charles Noble, "Regulating Politics: Conflict over Working Conditions before and after OSHA" (Paper delivered at the 1983 Meetings of the American Political Science Association, Chicago, Ill., 1–4 September 1983), 18.

5. For a very good argument that the programs were by no means a failure, see John E. Schwarz, *America's Hidden Success* (New York: W.W. Norton, 1983).

6. Compare with Owen Fiss's essay in this volume.

7. George Will, *Statecraft as Soulcraft* (New York: Simon & Schuster, 1983), 12, 20.

8. The Burke passage and the Sabine quote are from George Sabine, *A History of Political Theory,* rev. ed. (New York: Henry Holt & Co., 1951), 615–16.

9. Martha Derthick and Paul Quirk, *The Politics of Deregulation* (Washington: The Brookings Institution, 1985), 5.

10. Ibid., 33–34.

11. Kenneth J. Meier, *Regulation—Politics, Bureaucracy, and Economics* (New York: St. Martin's Press, 1985), 163–65.

12. D. Lee Bawden and John L. Palmer, "Social Policy—Challenging the Welfare State," in John L. Palmer and Isabel V. Sawhill, eds., *The Reagan Record* (Cambridge: Ballinger Publishing Co., 1982), 190.

13. Ibid. For further data and commentary, see Bernadyne Weatherford, "The Disability Insurance Program," in Anthony Champagne and Edward Harpham, *The Attack on the Welfare State* (Prospect Heights, Ill.: Waveland Press, 1984), chap. 3.

14. John L. Palmer and Isabel V. Sawhill, "Overview," in Palmer and Sawhill, eds., *The Reagan Record* (Cambridge, Mass.: Ballinger Publ. Co., 1982), 13–14.

*Discussion*

**Gawthrop:** I finally see your point, Professor Lowi. Any discussion of morality, ethics, or the like, you automatically classify as a conservative, authoritarian type of political action. The definition that you have given to "liberal" seems to preclude automatically any kind of concern or discussion of ethics or morality. This is unfortunate. Frankly, I think one can develop an ethical, moral consciousness without necessarily advocating a conservative, authoritarian public policy. I don't see where every discussion of ethics or morals necessarily leads to the kind of conservative authoritarian type of projection that you posit.

**Lowi:** I agree, but only as to ethics. You make a distinction between ethics and morality. I am not sure what you mean, but as for me, I think of ethics as the proper mode of conduct; and, of course, liberalism, like most any other public philosophy, is ethical. To me, ethics still has to do with the process aspect of things, as with the whole notion of rule of law, of proper procedure, of due process, and of things of that sort. The thing that liberals put off limits or do their best to avoid is morality, that is, morality in public, letting a particular moral code determine the goal of policy. Everybody's morality will come into play. If one prevails, that can be authoritarian. Liberals try to avoid that by letting consequences determine policies. In your context, morality would become authoritarian when bureaucrats are trained in what is right to do and go do it. That to me, while it may sound good, is a counsel of fear. That is frightening.

And that is conservatism. The ideal of a good administrator as one who will have a vision of the public interest and will take the risks for other people's lives (that lovely felicitous phrase of Jeffer-

39

son's you quoted) is a matter of concern. I am not ready to immigrate, but it is to me a signal. You can hear it now among important conservative thinkers, articulate thinkers, in Washington. They find me rather tiresome in talking about oversight of administration, in talking about setting up procedures, and so on. What they would like is to have good administrators and then give them room to operate. Note the public admiration for Lieutenant Colonel North and Admiral Poindexter. Discretion in the hands of good people who have a good sense of the public interest is not in itself a good thing, but it is not off limits to discussion. I would say it puts you in a category apart from what liberals seek, but that is not the same thing as saying, "Let's not discuss it."

What is the place of morality in liberalism? It is something that when it leaks in it is a mistake. It is something to avoid, and, when it does arise it is the sign of some aristocratic or conservative element in the context of the administration. We are all to be encouraged to talk about moral things, because, since we are motivated by those and since they set the agenda, those will be the things on which voting takes place. But liberals would try to avoid letting that be the main provocation.

**Shapiro:** Doesn't that do a lot of damage to our kind of standard usage of the word "liberal?" Don't we have two terms for liberals—process liberals and substantive liberals? I view Owen Fiss as a kind of prototypic modern, substantive liberal. What I mean by that is that he has attached himself to some values that I believe are liberal values, particularly the equality values, and he wants courts to ram those values down our throats. I'm used to calling him a liberal and I don't want to give up calling him that.

**Lowi:** I don't object to having adjectives attached to some kinds of liberals. But it is the same thing with equality; that is, liberals can argue about the need—the urgent need—for equality on the basis of the consequences of not having it. And that's exactly what happens. Not, for example, that there weren't a number of significant factors in the decision rendered in *Brown vs. The Board of Education,* but certainly the compelling factor was what segregation does to black kids. The justices were moved by that even though the psychologists' studies weren't very good ones. They were moved very much by the effect of inequality, the effect of the deprivation of equality. Now, you can then talk about a substantive concept of equality that has to do with the equality of *conditions* as opposed to the equality of *opportunity*. And I would go on to say that what separates some liberals from other liberals is the extent to which they want to put substantive meaning on equality. One of the critical things that led me into writing a book on the welfare state is that in recent years liberals of all kinds (whether Owen Fiss and I are the same kind of liberal or not) have come nearer and nearer to a substantive concept of equality that has to do with conditions that you implement in the welfare state.

Now, that creates enormous tension among the liberals. When you start talking about the right *to* a thing (*I* have a right to something that *you* have), that is something alien to the tradition of liberalism. And as liberalism courts that, it is going to run into serious problems. I'm not saying let's don't do it. I'm saying as soon as you do that you are positing a moral position about a condition, and that is a perilous position for liberals to be in. This is why liberals have tolerated a great deal of inequality in history—because they are not willing to state a substantive outcome of that process. So I repeat that the term "equality" has to have adjectives attached to it. And as you get more toward substantive equality, equality of *conditions* (I prefer that terminology), liberals will separate from each other and a critical moment or a critical epoch in liberalism will have been reached.

**Sorensen:** If I understand Professor Lowi, when he started out he said something like this: Liberals think of a framework of rights within which individuals can seek their private ends. In the history of ethics that would be one kind of ethical or moral theory, that is, one in which right is somehow prior to good. So you start out with a concept of right, right off. When you analyze the concept of right, and when you analyze the required concept of a person in order to have a seat for that right, and, further, when you analyze what sort of person there must be even to have private ends, and, still further, when you analyze what sort of procedures are needed in order for people with private ends to have those ends somehow adjusted to one another or contained (the conflict between them contained, etc.), you get a rather elaborate value system.

**Lowi:** You get a state.

**Sorensen:** You get some very elaborate value system. One might say that morality has to do with the fundamental values of *any* system. (Maybe we have arrived at the point where we should do a little legislating on use of the word.) Or we could say that morality has to do with those fundamental norms that are designed to protect the fundamental values of any system. A system of rights has to include a large package of values for it even to be a sensible possibility in human life. And when we talk about the role of the state in a free society, we have to talk about that role in relationship to those fundamental values that make the person possible and that make it possible for rights to exist and for individual ends to be sought within a framework of rights.

What worries me about the so-called liberal state (with this definition that I have been given) is that it seems as if some of its policies have turned on the very values that make it possible. Some liberals are not seeing some of the implications of this fact. For example, one implication concerns what it takes to raise a new generation in a caring way so that the values, which help make possible persons and the rights they enjoy, can be passed on to human beings who can function within the system they are advocating. A lot of that has gone unnoticed. And I think one reason it has gone unnoticed is because of the way liberals think about values. That is the nature of the debate. I find myself agreeing on a number of points they make until they start talking about values; then I find them to be inconsistent. They want to have their cake and eat it too. I think that the part of the crisis of legitimacy occurring in this country has to do with the fact that this liberal view of things has turned on itself by the way it makes public policy ignorant of and inconsistent with the fundamental values on which the very system is based.

## II

# THE SECRET OF SAFETY
# LIES IN DANGER

★

## *Aaron Wildavsky*

Of the many new things in the Constitution of the United States, perhaps the most important is not directly stated: the belief that mankind might design rather than inherit or have imposed upon them the institutions under which they govern themselves. Self-government is a noble, indeed one might well say a risky enterprise. How were the risks apportioned?

Without free institutions dependent upon public support there could be no self-government. Yet the very existence of central institutions empowered to exert coercive authority over individuals, the crucial difference between the Articles of Confederation and the Constitution, opened up the possibility of abuse. How, then, rate the risks?

Every institutional actor is considered risky, that is, prone to abuse. That is why powers are separated. Powers are not merely shared to prevent abuse, they are also dispersed to encourage innovation in the form of a multiple approach to problems. The Framers felt able to anticipate a few major problems, such as war and debasement of currency. For these they created as strong a central authority as consent of the governed would permit. For

*Aaron Wildavsky is a professor in the Department of Political Science and the Graduate School of Public Policy, and a member of the Survey Research Center at the University of California, Berkeley. This paper is taken from his* Searching for Safety *(Transaction Press, 1988).*

the rest, expecting that life would reveal difficulties of which they and their successors might well remain unaware, they dispersed the capacity to consider the unknown as widely as possible. The residual police power to secure the general welfare was left with the states. The glittering generalities for which the Constitution is famous constitute a rejection of the view that central authority knows best. In that case, a long list of dangers to be avoided would be followed by an even longer list of policy prescriptions for avoiding them. Instead, a House of Representatives based on population, a Senate elected by state legislatures, and a president presumably chosen by local elites with national reputations, are placed in partly cooperative and partly conflicting relationships and then superimposed upon a federal structure so that diverse views of dangers—geographical, social, philosophical—are considered.

The Framers placed the resilience of the system ahead of the safety of its parts. It was in the system as a whole rather than the sanctity of its parts that such safety as is given to human beings was thought to reside. This essay seeks to build strategies for securing safety from technology on the foundations of similar principles.

Contrary to current doctrine, "trial and error" is safer than "trial without error." Opportunity risks are exceeded by opportunity benefits. Highly dangerous low-probability events are overwhelmed in importance by highly probable low-benefit actions. Richer is safer, not sicker. Resilience is superior to anticipation as a strategy for reducing risk. Playing it safe hurts people. Adding to the pool of global (flexible, fungible) resources secures safety for more people than trying to protect any single part of the population against adversity. Since safety has to be discovered, not merely chosen, trial-and-error risk taking (unless strong evidence exists to the contrary) rather than risk aversion is the preferred strategy for securing safety.

## GLOBAL RESOURCES

Safety is a function of the general, global level of resources in a given society at a certain time. By general resources I mean knowledge, education, wealth, and any other resource (energy is a proxy for national product) that can be used for diverse purposes. General resources, like the primary colors, are fungible: they can be converted into other things. They are not just crops but the capacity to grow food and to alter what one grows according to the conditions of the time. The global level stands for overall resource capacity—the ability to convert and to redeploy resources.

Conceivably, there could be a limit on global resources, a limit not only at an instant in time but for all time thereafter. While the materials out of which energy is transformed should last for eons, for instance, it is possible that at some time their cost will increase. Where physical resources may be limited in amount and usability (a topic covered under the elusive subject of entropy), however, the currency of human ingenuity is information and I am not aware that it faces exhaustion.

Improvement in overall capability, that is, a generalized capacity to investigate, to learn, and to act, without knowing in advance what one will be called to act upon, is a vital protection against unexpected hazards. Acquired Immune Deficiency Syndrome (AIDS) is a recent example. An editorial in *Nature* observes that

> The understanding of AIDS that has now been wrung from a seemingly obdurate problem is striking proof of the value of the basic biomedical research on which people have for decades enthusiastically lavished their talents—and governments, less sure of themselves, their resources.
> In these terms, rapid demonstration that AIDS is indeed caused by a virus is a triumph. . . . The triumph is that the research community has been able to respond so quickly to an unexpected development such as the emergence of AIDS. The explanation is again simple, exasperatingly so—the richness and diversity of the biomedical research enterprise in the United States in particular but also throughout the world.[1]

## THE AXIOM OF CONNECTEDNESS

Dangers will arise; everyone agrees on that. Uncertainty about the consequences of present acts and about others as yet unforeseen cannot be reduced to zero. The axiom of ever-present uncertainty is based not only on the self-evident premise that no one knows it all but on the slightly less obvious consideration that as human beings act on their environment they create still more consequences of which they are as yet not fully aware. Although some uncertainties may be reduced under some circumstances, a modicum of uncertainty is a universal condition. Hence Kenneth Boulding writes about "irreducible uncertainties."[2]

To the axiom of ever-present uncertainty I wish to add another: The axiom of connectedness states that the good and the bad (safety and health effects) are intertwined in the same acts and objects. There may be unalloyed goods (though I doubt it; after all, even a perfect safety record may tempt us to lower our guard) but, if so, they are few and far between. Taking the two axioms together—uncertainty cannot be eliminated and risk cannot be avoided—stipulates the conditions under which the question of how to increase safety should be considered.

Suppose the things of this world, the substances in it and the practices people follow, were all good or all bad for securing safety. Then nothing (including differences between local and global effects) would matter, except the injunction to discover and choose the good and discard the bad. The end—secure safety—is given and a decision rule is known for choosing among available means. But life is not so simple or straightforward. For the most part, safety and danger are interwoven into the same objects and practices. Under the right (or wrong) conditions, everything we need for life can maim or kill: water drowns, food poisons, air chokes. Since there are many, many things out there, interacting in innumerable ways, moreover, the axiom of connectedness—the good and the bad are mixed in the same objects—must be generalized to the relationships among them. Everyone is likely to do something or be subject to some elements not good for them. The trick is to get more of the better and less of the worse.

## SAFETY IS A BALANCING ACT

Without trial there can be no new error, but without new error there is also less new learning. Science, its historians say, is more about rejecting than accepting hypotheses. Knowledge grows by criticizing the failure of existing theory to explain or predict events in its domain of applicability. Learning by criticizing implies that existing theory is in error, not necessarily absolutely, but relative to better, though never perfect, knowledge. Rules for democracy say little about what one does in office, but much more about getting officials out of office. "Throwing the rascals out" is the essence of democracy. Similarly, in social life, it is not the ability to avoid error entirely (even Goncharov's *Oblomov,* who spends his life in bed, cannot do that), but learning how to overcome it that is precious.

Even if it were true that following the principle of trial and error would provide for more health than harm, it is possible that people would still be better off by not allowing certain things to be done. Why not, then, follow public policy in the United States by prohibiting new things unless they are proven to be safe? Indeed, why take chances with public health? The assumptions required to make good this proposition—no trials without prior guarantees against error—are hard to meet. The first such assumption is that the safety benefits of trial and error would be maintained while only its harms would be eliminated. While the desire to pick the eyes out of the potato of life is understandable, it is not achievable. For a second assumption requires that society, acting through government, know the difference between actions that will increase or decrease safety in advance, allowing the good to go on and stopping the bad. Otherwise, harm will be done to more people by preventing actions that would have made their lives somewhat safer.

The most persuasive and the most common argument against learning by trial and error is that it should not be used unless the consequences of worst-case errors are sufficiently benign to permit new trials. If errors lead to irreversible damage to large populations, there may be no one around to take on the next trial.

## PLAYING IT SAFE IS DANGEROUS

The most seductive form of playing it safe is prudential conservatism: when in doubt, add margins of safety. Why be half safe? Why allow anything new unless it can be shown to do no harm? Better not to ceaselessly search for novelty but rather to insist that the new do good. In such fields as toxicology and engineering, conservatism has honorable precedents.

But how much conservatism should there be? First, one estimates the dangers of a product or practice according to existing knowledge. At every step there are decisions to be made as to where to bound uncertainties. Caution, presumably, is the by-word. Having arrived at an estimate (or range of estimates), one chooses the upper bound of danger. Then that upper bound is multiplied by a safety factor of, say, ten to a hundred. Observe what has occurred. As uncertainties are repeatedly resolved by exaggeration, then multiplied by others similarly manipulated, estimates of potential damage may be increased thousands of times over. So what? What is wrong with being supercautious?

There is no stopping point. If supercaution is to be the guiding principle, there is no reason why estimates should not again be increased so as to become even safer. Since virtually everything has some harm in it, extending that degree of danger by conservative calculation is bound to show that the activity in question should be disallowed.

In order to comprehend the consequence of rejecting trial and error by counting only costs, without allowing compensating benefits, an example from everyday life is in order. Were no errors permitted, no hospital in the world could stay open. Since people get sick from being in hospitals, a phenomenon called iatrogenic (hospital-related) disease, these organizations would have to be closed, despite the good they do, on the undeniable ground that they also do harm. The same is true for vaccines. By penalizing the small damage done, without offsetting it with the big benefits, society is endangered.

## TRIAL WITHOUT ERROR AS PUBLIC POLICY

The doctrine I have been discussing—no trial without prior guarantees against error—is embodied in practice. Old products and substances are still subject to trial and error in that the burden of proof justifying regulation is on government, but new ones operate under the rule of "no trials without prior guarantees against error" in which producers have the affirmative obligation of proving that their product will do no harm.[3]

The disinclination to consider benefits while focusing largely on costs creates a bias towards technological inaction. Yet there are reasons for society to encourage trial and error risk taking. By reducing old, still-existing dangers, not merely avoiding new ones, risk taking is made socially desirable. There are not merely new gains or losses but old hazards to be eliminated or alleviated in ways that improve human life. I call these "opportunity benefits." The opportunity cost of a given expenditure, following the concept used by economists, is the other valued goods that might have been purchased with the same resources. The opportunity risk of a given act or policy, as defined here, is the additional danger brought about by doing or producing something new. This general concept, if not the particular dangers, is well understood in common parlance about risk. Hardly understood at all, perhaps because not yet formulated, is the concept of opportunity benefit—the loss of opportunity to reduce existing harm that society forgoes as a consequence of decisions to delay or deny the introduction of a new substance or technology. Wise decision making should consider not only the opportunity risks but the opportunity benefits, the chance to diminish existing dangers, inherent in a given act.

An advantage of trial and error is that it renders visible hitherto unforeseen errors. Because it is a discovery process that makes latent errors manifest, so we can learn how to deal with them, trial and error reduces the scope of unforeseen dangers and hence lowers risks.

Rosenberg argues that "many significant characteristics of . . . products are revealed only after intensive or, more significantly, prolonged use."[4] Technological innovation is mostly accomplished by users who modify, not designers who originate, products. The potential of a product depends not only on what is in it but also on how others choose to use it. And what these relevant others do depends on what they learn both about the thing itself and the uses to which it might be put. Users are more numerous and more diverse than producers. Their number and diversity suggest that more tests in use will be made under more varied conditions. The larger the number and the greater the variety of hypotheses tested ("Is this product satisfactory under my conditions?"), the greater the probability of learning about good and bad impacts and the conditions under which they apply. No trials, no users, no learning, no mitigation of existing dangers.

Both doing something and doing nothing can be dangerous. Acts of omission—failing to take advantage of opportunity benefits—as well as acts of commission—damage to health by trying something new—can lead to making life less safe.

Whether and to what extent action or inaction is safer must depend on the balance of circumstances. As political radicals are wont to say in reaction to conservatives, inaction is action in support of the status quo. Yet the existing state of affairs contains hidden harms that might well be mitigated were society to secure opportunity benefits.

The iron law of skiing—you are not learning unless you are falling—exemplifies learning from mistakes while suggesting a condition limiting this process: errors must not be made on purpose. If all you do is fall down, you will not be able to distinguish between better and worse technique. You have to be making an effort to be error free (while realizing you won't succeed) in order for error to tell you what you don't know. You even have to succeed to some extent in order to differentiate error from something better. Thus, real progress arises from mistakes that occur when you are doing everything you can to avoid error. Both trying to avoid error and still experiencing it are essential. These are integral attributes of market processes.

## MARKETS AND SAFETY

Does economic competition increase safety? Why, given the desire for individual advantage in economic markets, does society end up benefitting by better health? For everywhere in the world, within and among nations and groups, the richer are indeed healthier. Economists, so far as I know, have not turned their attention to the relationship between markets and safety.

If income and health are positively related, it stands to reason that the larger the proportion of the population with higher incomes, the better the health of the nation's people on average. And since we know that being surrounded by educated people improves the safety of the entire area, there may be positive contagion effects: the healthier one's neighbors, the healthier one is likely to be.

This is the postulated line of causality: competition increases income, which provides protection for people's health. The direct effects come from public health and medicine. The indirect effects, which are much larger, operate through material advantages, such as food; educational benefits, such as superior safety practices; and technological progress, which teaches us how to do things better, including how to have our cake—higher incomes—and eat it too—while improving our health.

Rather than attempting to anticipate hazards before they occur, unless the risks are compelling, market processes work to increase wealth so as to be able to respond resiliently to dangers as they manifest themselves. In addition to creating wealth, markets also combine decentralized anticipation (numerous independent probes of an uncertain future) with pluralistic resilience (learning how to cope with danger by diverse groups) so as to achieve a greater degree of safety. The ability of market competition to interrogate the unknown at a low cost to society, while simultaneously encouraging individuals to overcome adversity, has been underappreciated. Another way to pose the question that has occupied us is to ask whether, and in what respects and under which conditions, strategies of anticipation are better or worse than strategies based on resilience?

## ANTICIPATION VERSUS RESILIENCE

Anticipation is a mode of control by central cognition; efforts are made to predict and prevent potential dangers before damage is done. Resilience is the capacity to use change so as to cope better with the unexpected. It is learning to bounce back. Are risks better balanced, we may ask, by attempting to anticipate them before they occur or by trying to mitigate their effects after they have manifested themselves? What proportion of anticipation and of resilience is desirable under which conditions?

Resilience is concerned with realized hazards; anticipation attempts to avoid hypothesized hazards. If it were possible (1) to anticipate efficiently—that is, to predict (or guess) right often enough to make up for the costs of guessing wrong—and (2) to react effectively—controlling the expected condition so as to leave life better off—anticipation would be the preferred strategy. Why suffer unnecessary damage? Usually, however, the uncertainties are so substantial that we cannot tell in advance which ones among a multitude of hypothesized dangers, if any, will actually turn out to be the real ones. Consequently, the effort to anticipate all or most dangers is likely to lead to a societal immune reaction: death not through invasion but through exhaustion as resources are used up in a futile effort to anticipate the future.

A strategy of resilience does not mean waiting for a disease to strike before trying to respond to it. Rather, it means preparing for the inevitable, the appearance of a new disease, by expanding general knowledge, technical facility, and command over resources. If this knowledge were to be sought in an effort to anticipate particular diseases, it would be less useful than if it could be directed at a broader range of dangers.

The rationale for reliance on resilience as the major strategy lies in inherent uncertainty; if, try as we may, we are not likely to be successful anticipators, we resort to resilience. For resilience is an inferior strategy only when rather strict conditions—know what, know when, know how, know how much, act as indicated—are met. Resilience is a superior strategy for making use of inherent uncertainty to do better. The evidence from ecological studies is suggestive: anticipation suits organisms that flourish in a narrow niche; resilient organisms that learn how to cope with adversity do much less well in any single niche but better over a number of environmental bands.

Going to extremes—all resilience, no anticipation, or vice versa—would be destructive. If you have no protection against expected and controllable hazards, you would constantly be faced with foreseeable emergencies that will be dealt with too late, too hastily, and too wastefully. Were there dangers with irreversible consequences, we would be overwhelmed before we could act. Followed faithfully, a strategy of anticipation might well use up all resources in a vain effort to guard against unknown (and, perhaps, unknowable) danger. What to do?

Anticipatory actions do have their place in a sensible safety strategy; the difficulty is to know what mix of anticipatory and resilient measures is optimum. Given inherent uncertainties, in my opinion, a little anticipation goes a long way. Instead of attempting to guard against most dangers, only the most likely or most dangerous should be covered, fully expecting that whatever was missed would be countered as and after it occurred, thereby building up resilience for the unknown danger that will surely come.

## INTERROGATING THE UNKNOWN

It is useful to distinguish between certainty—the ability to predict the consequences of actions—and uncertainty—knowing the kind or class of events that will occur but not the probability of their happening. Ignorance involves knowing neither the class nor the probability of events. When we are uncertain, we know about the type of events that will occur but not how likely they are to take place. But when we are ignorant, we know neither how likely the consequences of our actions are nor what class of consequences—hailstorms, burst dams, train wrecks, economic decline—will confront us. Yet we can be still worse off. Ignorance may be exceeded by superignorance—thinking we know and not knowing we don't know. And superignorance itself may give way to astonishment—expecting one class of events and getting another. Surprise, as I shall use the term, is based on ignorance. Astonishment occurs when superignorance results in anticipatory measures that lead to overconfidence.

Now there are at least two kinds of surprise. One might be called quantitative surprise. We know the kind of thing that can happen but are surprised by the fact that it occurs more frequently than we had supposed. I call this expected surprise because we know it is coming but not how often. The other category is qualitative surprise. This is "true" or unexpected surprise.[5] My thesis is that the growth of resilience depends upon learning how to deal with the unexpected, a term that Jerome Bruner identifies as striking "one with wonder and astonishment," that is, with qualitative surprise.[6]

Since it is neither possible nor desirable to anticipate all actual catastrophes, what is wanted is a method for interrogating the unknown. This method should pick out both potential trouble and potential advantage, sample each, give society some experience in warding off or coping with the bad and taking advantage of the good, without requiring a huge expenditure of resources or premature commitment to a single approach. The more people that participate in this strategy, the more widespread the search, the more diverse the probes and the reactions, positive and negative, the better. Evidently, this method should be democratic—decentralized, participatory, based on diverse and repeated probes and responses by various people differently situated.

This method is familiar to us. It belongs to the family of self-organizing systems. It is a form of social spontaneity, not social control. It is called, though it is not just any kind of, trial and error.

Until now I have not asked a crucial question about the strategy of anticipation, namely, anticipation by whom? It is all too easy to assume that governments or other large collective entities must do the anticipating. That is why we are so concerned about resource depletion following upon wrong prediction. Aside from the difficulty of arriving at collective judgments about theory through bureaucratic procedures, we are concerned about conjectures turning out to be false because the implications are so large. Since preventive measures are so expensive, and their consequences so profound, the need to be right is far greater than limited knowledge of cause and effect can support.

Suppose, however, that anticipation is decentralized. There are very large numbers of anticipators (think of them as entrepreneurs trying out new products or users modifying old ones), each of whom pays not all but a substantial part of the cost of error. Should they fail to predict future events, they bear the financial costs. Should their products turn out to harm others, they can be sued. Instead of society guessing about consequences, it can hold producers to account for the actual damage they do.

While spurring innovation, to be sure, the discovery procedure called trial and error is also creating new knowledge of actual consequences, of which some will undoubtedly be bad. How, its critics ask, can anyone be given the right to impose unknown harm on others? Hence they propose the rival doctrine of allowing no trials without prior guarantees against error. Alongside these undoubted costs to society, however, opportunity benefits are being created. And one of these, not previously discussed, is exploration of the unknown. For it is precisely the lack of central control and command that permits a wide variety of hypotheses to be tested so as vigorously to sample the unknown, thus bringing us into contact with events about which we would otherwise have been ignorant and in regard to which one or another of us would not have garnered experience.

If it is experience in coping that is desired, an evident riposte goes, why not institutionalize fire drills or other exercises designed to give practice in responding to emergencies? A strategy of expected surprise has its uses. Practice may well make perfect. Emergency preparedness makes sense so long as one has the right emergency in mind. For qualitative or real surprise, however, there are no ready-made drills. The underlying premise of expected surprise is that the unknown risks must be limited to the same sorts of risks that you deliberately practice to meet through planned failure. Precisely because it fails to interrogate the unknown, a strategy of expected surprise provides only the appearance but not the reality of resilience.

The way to keep society's coping mechanisms well exercised is not through deliberately tolerating known and avoidable sorts of failure, but through progress, since only new development keeps producing unpredictable risk situations. Only managing these presently unknowable hazards keeps coping ability in shape. Even better, because such progress-related risks can be viewed as a statistical sampling from the entire universe of possible unforeseen risks, successfully coping with such risks as arise from progress does provide real information about most possible risks. Hence, our coping mechanisms will, most likely, be strengthened in just the sorts of ways that will be needed against the truly unexpected. This is another reason why a rapidly progressing society will usually be safer than a static one.

## Does Adding Safety Devices Increase Safety?

Against this rather rarified wisdom—rely on resilience—may be posed the urgings of common sense: When you see an opportunity to increase safety, take it. Theorists may talk all they want about roundabout strategies of resilience, but direct strategies of anticipation, the bird in hand, are preferable. A straightforward statement of this proposition would be that adding measures designed to secure safety actually increases safety. But does it? Because adding multiple safety measures has been the practice of the nuclear power industry, under the whiplash of regulation, a study of the inspection of nuclear power plants provides an opportunity to explore the direct, anticipatory hypothesis: Take safety measures to increase safety.

Nuclear welding codes require the reworking of welds in which even tiny voids occur; rework itself, however, can weaken the materials used (e.g., stainless steel pipe). Given differing skills among those who do the rework, it is not always clear that correction of minor defects will produce an increase in safety. Similarly, pipe restraints are often installed to prevent damage to nearby equipment from the whipping motion generated when and if a pipe rupture occurs. These restraints, however, may produce a binding of the system that decreases safety by introducing additional strain.

Testing can also be counterproductive. The availability of electrical power is essential to reactor safety. Control of the plant during normal operation and the ability to keep the plant safely shut down during emergencies depend on maintaining a reliable system of alternate electrical sources. Because off-site power is not sufficiently reliable, diesel generators are required to be installed to provide a backup on-site source. Because these generators themselves may fail to operate on demand, there are usually two or more at a given site. If the probability is relatively high that off-site power will fail, the ability to prevent any series of events that would lead to reactor core damage depends on reliable on-site diesel power. The reliability or unreliability of the emergency diesel generators determines the probability of a serious accident. Given their importance, it might seem reasonable to require that these diesel generators be tested regularly to ensure their operability. Testing, however, may not always be advisable, since the test itself may make the generator less dependable.

As a means of further increasing system reliability, it was at one point suggested by a company that during times when its power distribution grid was on "alert status," nuclear plant personnel should "idle-start the diesel engines and run them for a short period of time" to verify their availability. The NRC staff agreed that this would probably be the simplest way to determine availability but pointed out that idle-starting diesel generators and running them unloaded "could unnecessarily hamper their performance in a real emergency."

Safety devices can themselves be a source of danger as well. Reactor coolant pumps are clearly essential safety features in any reactor; these pumps, however, require lubricating systems, and these lubricating systems are one important cause of fires within reactor containments.

Increasing protection in one area may create difficulties in others. Protecting against low-probability events, for example, may interfere with more everyday threats to system stability. The seismic design requirements for nuclear plant piping, for example, have been continually increased. Even in the most seismically active areas, the probability that a sufficiently large earthquake will occur over the plant's lifetime is relatively low. The anticipated damage from such earthquakes is, however, quite high. Extra precautions therefore have seemed justified. Recently, though, questions have arisen concerning the consequences of adopting extra precautions to guard against such a remote "worst case."

Reinforcement of the piping system against earthquakes has some important negative consequences for the viability of the system as a whole. The parts have their own failure rates and these rates are highly dependent on the way in which they are maintained. Servicing the pipe supports (snubbers) requires procedures which also increase the likelihood of failure. Even where the snubbers are successfully maintained and work properly, tightly bound systems are subject to much greater stress during normal operation than are more flexible systems.

Among the consequences of solving seismic problems by strengthening individual supports and adding more and more of them are (1) limitation of access for routine maintenance of equipment, (2) limitation of access for in-service inspection of equipment and the piping itself, and (3) creation of a relatively rigid system which may be less able to withstand stress in everyday operation.

## A Taxonomy of Risk Errors

The beginnings of a "taxonomy of risk errors" can now be suggested. I propose six categories of such errors.

1. Ignoring opportunity benefits, that is, overlooking those existing risks that will continue unabated by the choice to delay the introduction of new technology that could reduce them.
2. Ignoring the risks associated with a proposed remedy.
3. Ignoring large existing benefits while concentrating on small existing risks.
4. Ignoring the effects of economic costs on safety.
5. Ignoring the inevitable tradeoff between Type I and Type II errors. (A Type I error is falsely raising an alarm when in fact no hazard exists, and a Type II error is falsely ignoring a hazard that is in fact real.)
6. Ignoring the displacement of risks onto other people as a consequence of reducing risks for some.

These categories are not mutually exclusive, and indeed all of them might be viewed as special examples of the same basic error, focusing only on one dimension of the overall risk situation.

## IGNORING "OPPORTUNITY BENEFITS"

Among the experiments delayed by the moratorium on genetic engineering is an interesting effort to make crop plants selectively resistant to certain herbicides. Some of the newer herbicides are effective in very small doses—only a few grams per acre are needed rather than the kilograms per acre required for older herbicides—or else have much lower toxicities for animals and insects. But, being nonselective (in contrast to such herbicides as 2, 4–D or 2, 4, 5–T), they will kill the desired crop as well. Both Calgene (a small genetic engineering company in Davis, California) and DuPont have developed genetic engineering methods for making crops selectively resistant to such herbicides, which would allow existing herbicides to be displaced with these environmentally safer ones. No consideration is given to the opportunity benefits, the health benefits delayed or denied, that result from the moratorium.[7]

## IGNORING LARGE EXISTING BENEFITS WHILE CONCENTRATING ON SMALL EXISTING RISKS

Many times the remedy is worse then the disease. Safety precautions may lower small risks while increasing more major risks.

Two forms of smoke detectors are currently available in the United States. One uses a tiny amount of a radioactive element to detect smoke, and is called an "ionizing unit." The other uses a photoelectric cell. Ionizing units cost as little as one-fourth as much as photoelectric units and so are much more commonly used. Yet, they emit radiation, and there is a move afoot to eliminate them as an unnecessary and unacceptable source of cancer risk. Entirely ignored in this thinking is the demand curve for smoke detectors. Quadrupling the cost of having any smoke detector, which would be the result if only the more expensive photoelectric units were available, will inevitably lead substantial numbers of people at the margin to decide to forgo purchasing smoke detectors entirely. Since current estimates are that 7,500 lives are lost each year that might have been saved had smoke detectors been in use, the risks associated with having no smoke detectors at all are neither insubstantial nor hypothetical. The opponents of the cheaper ionization unit are trading an immeasurably small cancer risk for a quite significantly larger and also much more immediate risk of death and injury from fire.[8] Making smoke detectors more expensive lowers the buying power of consumers; hence, less wealth means less health. Low-income consumers must either do without smoke detectors, or forgo other investments that might also increase safety.

## IGNORING THE INEVITABLE TRADEOFF BETWEEN TYPE I AND TYPE II ERRORS

There is a kind of irreducible statistical uncertainty that limits how safe we can become, namely, the complementary relationship between Type I and Type II errors. Both kinds of error are well exemplified in the fable of the boy who cried wolf. His first alarms, being false, were Type I errors, while the ignoring by the villagers of his final alarm—which was a valid one, since the wolf was indeed there—is a Type II error. The interesting thing about this fable is that it raises in a graphic way the profound question of what sort of decision criteria the boy should have used in order to reduce his Type I error. His constant cries of "wolf" might well have arisen out of conscientiousness rather than mischievousness; they very possibly could have resulted from his having only limited and uncertain information as a basis for deciding whether or not a wolf was present—possibly only a tuft of hair on a bush, or a footprint, or a dropping, any of which could have come from a coyote or dog as well as from a wolf. Given this uncertainty, he might well have opted to be "prudent," reasoning that no one would be seriously hurt if his alarm turned out to be false, but that the village would be grievously injured if he failed to raise the alarm when a wolf truly was there. In this situation he might have decided to "err on the side of safety," by calling out a warning every time an ambiguous bit of evidence came to his attention. As the fable illustrates, there was an unforeseen catch to this decision strategy: The inability to distinguish true alarms from false alarms became so great that *all* alarms came to be ignored, with the perverse outcome that a decision strategy chosen purposefully so as to reduce to a minimum the chance of missing a true hazard led instead to an increase in that very risk.

Roughly half of all chemicals tested in animals under the conservative rules of conducting and interpreting animal tests have turned out positive, i.e., have been judged to be "wolves." Hence, regulatory agencies are swamped with chemicals needing to be regulated. So much so, indeed, that there is a huge backlog of chemicals awaiting regulatory consideration. The core problem is that no one can know which among this vast backlog are the chemicals that pose a truly significant risk of cancer to humans, if any, and therefore deserve to be regulated first. Once again, as with the boy crying wolf, valid cancer "signals" are getting lost among the swarm of signals from trivial or falsely identified risk; that is, there is a tremendous loss of *discriminatory power* inevitably associated with erring "on the side of safety." The result is that substantial regulatory resources are being expended to reduce risks that are already trivial, while the public's exposure to the carcinogens that matter is being prolonged.

Exactly this same principle can be seen in a case involving naval security. Deciding to "err on the side of safety," that is, on the side of overclassifying documents, made it necessary to grant security clearances to so many people that it became impossible to investigate them adequately, and, especially, to do follow-up checks to see that they stayed loyal. In this way, a breach of security now admitted to be of enormous impact went undetected for some twenty years. Once again, the effort to be "all-safe" led not merely to being "half-safe" but to not being safe at all.

Ultimately, the debate over risk comes down to how best respond to dangers that cannot be fully comprehended in advance. My vote goes to the resilience that comes from passing many trials and learning from many errors so that the defects of society's limited current imagination are made up by larger amounts of global resources that can be converted into meeting the dangers that its members never thought would arise.

Suppose the United States of America sets up a superfund costing $10 billion to clean up chemical carcinogens. Suppose the dangers from such chemicals are modest. Why not spend the money to improve health? My answer is that this good deed is likely to harm health as well as wasting money.

For one thing, there is danger in safety measures as there is in anything else. Just calling an act a safety measure does not make it so. For another, the money thus diverted from private uses— vacations, enjoyments, labor-saving devices—detracts from the health of users. If money were bad for you, richer people wouldn't be healthier than poorer people and reformers wouldn't be trying so hard to improve the financial position of poor people.

Amidst all the talk about threats to human safety, the overwhelming fact is one of continuous improvement. Any theory of risk prevention, therefore, must simultaneously be able to explain why things have gotten better. The coexistence of technological progress and increases in life expectancy cannot be wished away. We must be doing something right. Ignoring and rejecting what is right—trial and error, resilience, markets—in favor of their opposites—trial without error, anticipation, and regulation—is likely to leave us less safe than we have been.

# Notes

1. "Attrition, Not Conquest, of Disease," *Nature* 309 (May 1984): 1–2.

2. Kenneth Boulding, "Irreducible Uncertainties," *Society* 20 (Nov/Dec 1982): 1:15–17.

3. Peter Huber, "Exorcists vs. Gatekeepers in Risk Regulation," *Regulation* (Nov/Dec 1983): 23–32.

4. Nathan Rosenberg, "Learning by Using," *Inside the Black Box: Technology and Economics* (Cambridge, England: Cambridge University Press, 1982), chap. 6, 121–40.

5. Qualitative surprise might more simply be called "ignorance." But I prefer to reserve that term for situations where neither the class nor the probability of consequences are known but the ignorant do not know that they don't know. A beginning taxonomy of ignorance is provided by Robert Wolfson and Thomas Carroll:

> By ignorance we mean that state of knowledge wherein the decision maker lacks awareness of some objectively possible states of the world which he faces. We can detail three types of ignorance.
>
> 1. *Ignorance of actions*. There are some actions which are objective alternatives but about which the individual is unaware. We take this to mean that he is in ignorance of all outcomes attributable solely to these unknown alternatives.
>
> 2. *Ignorance of outcomes*. There exist some outcomes of which the decision maker is completely unaware. He believes that the *n* outcomes he has in mind constitute the full set of consequences attributable to a particular set of actions; but in fact there are *m* others.
>
> 3. *Ignorance of values*. There are some outcomes of which he is aware, but whose nature is a complete mystery to him. That is there are *n* possible outcomes which he knows well enough to say that if the *i*th occurs, it will benefit or disadvantage him in some imaginable manner and/or amount. There are *m* others which he knows might occur, but which he cannot describe in any such fashion. (Robert J. Wolfson and Thomas M. Carroll, "Ignorance, Error, and Information in the Classic Theory of Decision," *Behavioral Science* 21 [1976]: 107–15.)

6. Jerome S. Bruner, "The Conditions of Creativity," in Howard E. Gruber et al., eds., *Contemporary Approaches to Creative Thinking* (New York: Prentice Hall, 1962).

7. "How Safe Are Engineered Organisms?" *Science* 229 (July 1985): 34–35.

8. Milton Copoulos, "It's Effective—But Is It Safe?" *Reason* (March 1985): 29–30.

# Discussion

**Wolin:** It seemed to me that in your discussion, particularly at the outset of your essay about risks, what I thought was notably absent (except at one small point) was the question of distribution of risks. For example, I suppose it's probably incontestable that, in terms of the impact of early industrialization in this country and elsewhere, the incidence of risk was different for some classes than for others. And that, as you said yourself (in fact it is one of the basic themes of your essay), was the hypothesis that as one gets richer, richer is better, and better means healthier. I presume the same would hold that in terms of being poorer the risks are greater and that being poor is always a possibility even in a society as economically successful as ours. The first question comes down to the class nature of risk distribution.

The second one is much shorter and much briefer and perhaps not much of a problem for you. At one point you declared that the present generation is healthier than any previous generation. But if the present generation is healthier than any previous generation, the present generation has lived during a period in which manufacturing processes have been more closely regulated than in the past and public policies have been concerned with reducing the risks to health. Isn't there some correlation between greater regulation and greater health?

**Wildavsky:** Let's start with the second question. In a very general way the kinds of regulations that have had large effects on health are almost entirely public health measures. Sometimes the big changes come from things nobody anticipates—the change from smokestacks and processes of coal-burning plants with large particulates to small ones.

Nobody is against all regulations, and the benefits of some are immense. So I will substitute a question of my own, one that I have researched. It became clear to me that if the argument was that wealth led to better medical devices and care it would not carry the weight that I wanted it to, mainly that the diffusion of wealth (better clothing, houses, food, etc.) is what leads to the great increases in health. I used to take my kids to a little place called Pescadero, down by Half Moon Bay, where there was not only a super restaurant but a little cemetery, turn of the century. Whole families died in their late twenties and early thirties—nine, ten of them. That very seldom happens today. The evidence I have is that it wasn't until the 1910s to 1920s that doctors started to do more good than harm.

Plumbing is at the heart of everything. That is, it was the technological improvements and the general quality of life far more than medicine that improved health. Medicine, if you have a specific illness, is a good thing; but in general, health depends on how people live. I can give you good health advice: Don't worry; worrying is very bad for you. Eat regularly: three meals a day is fine; eating episodically is bad. Sleep six or eight hours a day; four or fourteen is bad for you. That is, develop regular habits. Being married is of immense significance. People who are single, and especially who never marry, are among the sickest people in the world.

The improvements, decade by decade before we had the post-1960s—the Clean Air Act and the rest—have been substantial. They are either as large as those afterwards or larger. What I have only to show is that, as far as anybody knows, to state it directly, the health benefits of the current regulations are very small, whereas the expenditures are very large. To put it another way, if we regulated only a small portion of what we do now, we would have almost as many health benefits and much lower costs. These resources would go into peoples' pockets and be used for other purposes and the health benefits of those trial-and-error opportunity benefits would be much larger.

Now to the first question. As a political scientist, I would always and without exception take it as my obligation to look at the distribution of costs and political benefits. I must ask who gains and who loses, whether by class or by some other mode. And in the expanded work of which this is a part, I do.

In a chapter on "richer is safer," I show that richer people are healthier everywhere. Health benefits do not depend, as far as can be ascertained, on a more equal distribution of income. They do depend on absolute increases in command over resources. Another comparison that could be made, and it is one that historians have been looking into, is whether before the Industrial Revolution, or in rural communities, or in countries without the modern apparatus of technology, the people were safer. That is to say, as an old Yiddish joke goes, "Harry, how is your wife?" And he says, "Compared to who?" In the same way, we can ask whether a person who has less income than other people—we could call this, if it wasn't so un-American, a working-class person—would have been better off without this technology. Now, there might have been ways to industrialize other than the way we did; if so, there might have been a fairer distribution.

As far as anybody knows, and I have looked at a fair amount of the material, the transition from pre– to post–Industrial Revolution left most people better off. Take the situation of black people now. What we can say is that their health rates are considerably below those of whites, but they are considerably above where they were fifty, forty, thirty, twenty, or ten years ago. What is one to make of this? I am willing to concede that there is some other mode of social organization that might have distributed the dangers more fairly. But, we have such rapid improvements in life span and in general healthiness that the length of time that our actions are vigorous and independent has greatly increased. That is not only true for the richer people or even middle-class people; it is true for people at all ranges of income. That this might have been improved is doubtful.

# III

# FREEDOM AND REGULATION IN A FREE SOCIETY

★

## *A. Don Sorensen*

The primary role of government in a free society is something to which every generation in that society must give some thought. The occasion of the bicentennial of the United States Constitution makes reconsideration of this role appropriate in our own society. I focus on certain very fundamental concepts that help provide a framework for understanding the basic design of a free life and the primary regulatory role of government in such a life.

I begin by examining the source of human value itself. The basic assumption I make is that persons and social life are constituted by theory—some theory about themselves called here a "theory of human life." And a basic thesis is that conceptions of a certain kind in any such theory are responsible for the very existence of intrinsic human value. My first task will be to consider the value-creating conceptions and the direction they provide human life.

Let me mention that comparable theses are found in major works in the history of political and moral philosophy. For example, in Plato's *Republic,* human society and the very soul of man

*Don Sorensen is a professor in the Department of Political Science at Brigham Young University.*

come into existence and are ordered by ethical forms such as justice and temperance. According to the New Testament, man puts off his old nature and puts on a new one by embodying the word of life, which is perfectly incarnate in Jesus, who accordingly is called the Word. Thomas Hobbes, in the *Leviathan,* thought that without speech and language (which makes speech possible), there could not be human society any more than among lions and wolves.[1]

After considering the source of human value, I bring out the general moral norms whose object is to realize and preserve value in human life. I call these norms the morality of human society. It is in relation to these norms that the primary role of government in a free society can be worked out. My discussion then turns to the Constitution and the general viewpoint from which it must ultimately be understood. Finally, I conclude the essay with brief applications of the norms of freedom to certain problems of public policy.

## INTRINSIC HUMAN VALUE

Some things came into existence through theory; others have natures separate from theory. For instance, copper and other physical substances have existences independent of theory. This is true even though our perceptions of or perceptual judgments about copper and other physical substances are laden with theory. Call these brute facts. But other things, such as games and the practice of voting, literally come to be by reason of a theory. These facts are theory-constituted.[2] Persons and the values they pursue are not brute facts but constituted facts. They come into being when persons learn or develop a theory about themselves which I here call a theory of human life.

It is apparent that many things in human life may have intrinsic value for persons—including status, power, sports, artistic expression, love, and knowledge. It is also obvious that various conceptions—conceptions that help form what I just referred to as theory of human life—are involved in making possible this variety of human values. For example, the conceptions that must be learned successfully to use political power differ from those that must be learned to do physical science well. Still, it may be that intrinsic human values in their variety have something in common as values, and consequently that underlying or running through them are certain conceptions which are in a fundamental way constitutive of them. If this is so—if there are conceptions that are value-creative in a fundamental way—then if these conceptions were somehow subtracted from the person's life, that life could not have intrinsic value in it; and if added again, one's life once more would contain intrinsic value.

This suggests a test for separating conceptions in a theory of human life that, if such exist, are fundamentally value-creative from those that are not. I refer to this test simply as the value test. Roughly speaking, for any kind of conception C in a theory of human life, given that the conditions exist necessary and sufficient for the operation of C in the person's life as it is designed to do, then C is fundamentally creative of intrinsic human value if and only if it is logically inconsistent (a) to assert that C operates in the person's life as it is designed to do and to deny that intrinsic value exists in his life by virtue of the operation of C, or (b) to affirm that intrinsic value exists in the person's life and to deny that C operates in his life as it is designed to do as the source of that value.

If a certain kind of conception passes the value test by satisfying either (a) or (b), then it is constitutive of intrinsic human value, and fundamentally so. If such a conception passes both parts of the test, then it is, in the sense indicated by the test, both necessary and sufficient for the existence of intrinsic human value.

Since space is very limited, I want to take up immediately with no preliminary discussion a feature of a theory of human life that appears to be constitutive of intrinsic human value and fundamentally so. The feature I have in mind is nothing less than the basic design of a typical theory of human life and of the society it brings into existence. That design is twofold. One part of it is to perpetuate human life. By that I mean that persons in human society, by reason of learning a typical theory of human life, desire to create new life and are organized to nurture it and otherwise provide for it. The second part of human society's basic design is to realize human life. What I mean here is that, again by virtue of being taught a typical theory of life, persons desire to pursue and are organized to pursue life so that as a whole it will turn out well rather than badly in some sense. This, then, is the basic design of a theory of human life: to perpetuate human life (create and provide for new life) and to realize human life (life turning out well rather than badly). I will refer to it, for obvious reasons, as a caring-for-life conception. A theory of human life is, in its basic design, a complex caring-for-life conception that manifests itself through every major institution of human society brought into existence by such a theory.

When the value test formulated earlier is applied to a theory of human life as a caring-for-life conception, we get positive results. The basic caring-for-life feature of such a theory is value-creative and fundamentally so. The person comes to value life, both its realization and perpetuation, by virtue of assimilating a theory having that feature. In other words, it is not possible to imagine a theory of human life, considered as a caring-for-life conception, organizing a person's life as it is designed to do and the life thus organized containing no intrinsic value. This caring-for-life feature of a theory of life is a sufficient condition for the existence of intrinsic human value. It satisfies the value test in one of the two ways. To clarify things, let me consider two prominent examples of caring-for-life conceptions and then contrast them with other conceptions that are sometimes constitutive of intrinsic value but not in a fundamental way. The two examples are justice and benevolence. Distributive justice, or at least one important view of it, concerns equal treatment of persons as ends in themselves in the distribution of good and evil. In a just society, persons are treated in ways that contribute equally to the goodness of their lives, and things are required of them so as to keep their chances of a good life equal.[3] Benevolence, too, concerns bringing about good and the absence of evil in the lives of persons for their sakes.

It seems clear that benevolence is a value-creating conception, and fundamentally so. The benevolent person necessarily has intrinsic value in his life by virtue of having become a benevolent person. If the conception of benevolence operates in a person's life as it is designed to do, that person cannot but have intrinsic value in his life. The same is true of justice, as defined above. That conception of justice, which requires the equal treatment of others for their own sake in the distribution of good and evil, is value-creative in a fundamental way. Some intrinsic value—for instance, the intrinsic value of others—enters into a person's life by reason of his becoming a just person. What is true of benevolence and justice is true of the complex family of caring-for-life conceptions that characterize this or that theory of human life, for example, human rights, love, friendship. They are fundamentally value-creative. That is, when the conditions exist that make it possible for such conceptions to operate in the person's life, they constitute a sufficient condition for the existence of intrinsic value in his life.

Let me contrast conceptions like benevolence and justice with other conceptions that are constitutive, but not fundamentally, of activities that may have intrinsic value for some people. Consider such activities as building things, painting pictures, solving mathematical problems, exercising power, skiing, and the like. For example, for some persons, building houses is an activity having intrinsic value. So in a sense, the activity of building is constitutive of intrinsic value for some persons. For them, the intrinsic value of building and the activity of building are inseparably connected. The value is in the activity of building itself.

But even in cases where, say, building houses is literally constitutive of intrinsic value, the complex know-how conceptions that make possible building a house do not by themselves entail or imply the existence of value. It would not be inconsistent to claim that the person possesses the expert's know-how for building a house and to deny that he thereby possesses something which he finds has, or which he might discover to have, intrinsic value for him. It is possible to imagine, contrary to fact, all persons who are in possession of such know-how finding that for them building houses has no intrinsic value at all. In short, the conceptions that make possible the activity of building houses do not pass the value test. By themselves they are not fundamentally creative of value even though they help institute activities that have intrinsic value for some people.

What is true of building houses is true of many human activities that, as a matter of fact, have intrinsic value for various persons—gaining knowledge, exercising power, having status, earning money, painting pictures, fishing, or whatever. The conceptions that make such activities humanly possible are simply not value-creative in a basic way. This is so even though many persons find some of these activities intrinsically valuable.

So it appears that a theory of human life is constitutive of intrinsic human value by reason of being a caring-for-life conception. But must a theory of human life (in bringing persons into existence and organizing them into a way of life) be a caring-for-life conception in order to be creative of intrinsic human value? In other words, are caring-for-life conceptions necessary as well as sufficient for the existence of intrinsic value? If the answer is yes, then that means intrinsic human value consists in caring-for-life states of personal being. If that is so, then life is what ultimately has intrinsic value for the person, and *caring for* is what his valuing something consists of. Are there reasons for accepting this? I think there are, and I will indicate where they can be found.

Consider the term "life." It refers here to life that is distinctive of being a person. A person is a particular self-conscious being (one who is aware and aware that he is aware) who, as agent, has the power of decision and action and, as subject, the capacity for positive and negative experience. Accordingly, life distinctive of being a person consists of the person having and realizing his possibilities as agent and subject. Now, what analysis reveals about typical intrinsic human values is that they ultimately consist in life in this sense, that is, in the person having and realizing his possibilities as agent (e.g., in the form of meaningful work) and as subject (e.g., in the form of enjoying beautiful music). So it may be plausibly claimed that intrinsic human value involves life that is characteristic of being a person. It is a mode of life or being alive. One might describe life in this sense as "significant vitality," or life that consists in possessing and realizing intrinsic value.

This does not mean that the activities and undergoings that constitute intrinsic value for the person are only his own activities and undergoings. That this is not the case can be simply illustrated. Suppose one friend wants the other to enjoy a piece of beautiful music he just heard simply because he loves her. This means he wants that for her because he thinks she will enjoy it. Her enjoyment of the new music is of intrinsic value for him. His wanting her to hear the music depends on his belief that she will enjoy listening to the music for its own sake. If it turns out that she does enjoy the music, this will be satisfying to him—again because he loves her. Both her enjoying the music and his seeing that she enjoys it have intrinsic value and consist of doings or undergoings of the person.

Shortly I will examine the term "life" further to better reveal its nature as intrinsic value. But before I can do that, I need to consider what it is for the person to value something. Analysis reveals that to value something consists of taking one or more attitudes like the following: having respect for, taking an interest in, having a fondness for, being concerned about, having regard for, and the like. In other words, valuing something is a caring-for state of personal being. Caring for involves a complex family of such attitudes, one or more of which describes what it is for a person to value something.

These states of caring for are brought into being by caring-for conceptions that are part of a theory of life which brings persons into existence. Caring-for conceptions create what they are about—caring-for states of the person. Without such conceptions, caring-for states of personal being could not exist. Human life would be without intrinsic value.

Having treated, separately, valuing as a caring-for intentional mode and intrinsic value as life distinctive of being a person, let me consider the relation between the two—between life and caring for. Think of what the person's life would be like in the absence of caring-for-life states of personal being as I have now described them. In the absence of all such states, the person would be "dead" as a person. By death I do not mean biological extinction, but death in the sense of human life drained or empty of its distinctive vitality—of that vitality that consists in possessing and realizing intrinsic value. Conversely, the presence of caring-for-life states of personal being constitutes the "life" distinctive of being a person. Again, "life" in this sense is not primarily a biological property, but a condition of human animation that may be described by the term "significant vitality."

Let me put the point being made in another way. Life distinctive of the person, as noted earlier, involves his activities as agent and undergoings as subject. These activities and undergoings are infused with significant vitality by virtue of being the object of caring-for conceptions operating in the person's life according to design. This is analogous to looking at an ashen world with an unusual pair of splendidly colored glasses. The glasses transform the experience of the world into a place of color and beauty. Similarly, the person's possibilities as agent and subject are transformed from deadness to life by caring-for conceptions. By removing all such conceptions, those possibilities would be drained of life.

So if my analysis is correct, intrinsic human value consists in caring-for-life states of personal being constituted by caring-for-life conceptions. This identity between caring-for-life conceptions and caring-for-life states of personal being explains why these conceptions pass the value test given earlier and why other conceptions—that make possible, for example, being a skilled builder or wielder of power—by themselves do not. That identity makes it inconsistent to say either (a) that such conceptions organize the person's life as they are meant to do, and to deny that intrinsic value exists in his life by virtue of that fact, or (b) that intrinsic value exists in someone's life and to deny that caring-for-life conceptions are at work in his life according to design as a source of that value; whereas, logically, know-how conceptions could be present in a person's life without creating value or could be removed without destroying value, since all value might already be absent.

We may say, then, that intrinsic human value consists of a distinctive mode of human experience—of significant vitality or life. There is precedence in the history of moral philosophy for equating human value and life in this sense. The Greek term that came to signify this equivalency is *Zōē*. In New Testament morality, *zōē* typically means everlasting fullness of life, which is the ultimate good of man. Fullness of life occurs when the person incorporates into his nature through spiritual rebirth divine *agapē*—a very rich, caring-for-life conception that is the fundamental precept of biblical morality. In what follows, I will use the term life *(zōē),* and put *zōē* in parentheses, when I speak of the person's aim of realizing intrinsic value. I might have used with some modifications Plato's term for living well or well-being. In Plato, living well as the distinctive function of the person is ultimately rooted, in the language of the *Phaedrus,* in "care for all that is soulless" and ultimately in care for "that being which truly is."[4] For him, caring for *(erōs)* is the motive force in everything that the person does whether or not he lives well. It constitutes his vitality as a living being.[5]

So far, life *(zōē)* and death in the sense of the presence and absence of significant vitality have been treated dichotomously. But they may vary inversely to one another in degree, ranging from fullness of life to "fullness" of death. Fullness of death, as already indicated, refers not to biological extinction primarily but to human existence devoid of all value—of all life *(zōē)*. Both life and death are real possibilities and together constitute the overall possibilities of human existence. The person faces these grand alternatives as the caretaker (more or less) of his own life. I call this situation the person's fundamental position in the world. In this situation the person's natural aim is to realize his life (significant vitality) and avoid death, and his rational end is that his life be as full and lasting as possible.

The person's rational end being what it is does not mean that his final aim is to realize his own life exclusively. It turns out that fullness of life as an ideal possibility is constituted by a rich set of caring-for-life conceptions that include wanting others to enjoy the full life. The person's own life is full because he cares very much for other life and for a great variety of things that enter into life, such as nature, art, and music. Death, considered in relation to life *(zōē)*, represents the possibility of value degeneration. It occurs when the person lives by caring-for-life conceptions that are self-denying or self-defeating. Such conceptions are self-denying for the individual if his rational aim of realizing the fullest and most lasting life possible for himself is worse achieved because he tries to achieve that aim by living in accord with those conceptions. And caring-for-life conceptions are self-defeating for the individual if the possibility of life *(zōē)* constituted by those conceptions is undermined because the person successfully realizes that possibility.[6]

As an example of a caring-for-life conception that is both self-denying and self-defeating, consider the principle of rational egotism. That principle tells a person to make his own fullness of life his ultimate and exclusive aim. The egotistic life is self-denying because when the person tries to realize the full life *(zōē)* by living in accord with the principle of egotism, that aim is worse achieved. The explanation is in part that egotism as a caring-for-life conception is impoverished compared to nonegotistic conceptions in which the person has deep and wide regard for other persons as ends. Take, for instance, the carnal life as one mode of egotism. Carnality as a caring-for-life conception directs the person to realize fully his own material and physical desires. That conception as the governing principle of the person's existence impoverishes his life because it turns him away from caring for others toward caring only for self, so that others are treated as means and not as ends; and it reduces the intrinsic value in his life still further by limiting the dominant concern of his existence to satisfying material and physical desire. Consequently, his noncarnal possibilities as a person, including those that might be otherwise awakened by intrinsic concern and respect for others, remain dead.

The egotistic life is also self-defeating because the possibility of life *(zōē)* constituted by the egotism principle is undermined when the person successfully achieves the particular ends of his life as an egotist. For the egotist, the power of such ends to satisfy, to give significant vitality, declines with the success of satisfying them. For example, the more the carnal person possesses and consumes, the less the possessing and consuming by themselves fulfill. Only within a framework made up of rich (nonegotistic) caring-for-life conceptions can the power of material and physical ends to fulfill be preserved and fully realized. Without such a framework, physical and material satisfactions, impoverished to begin with, decline over time in significance.

It is time to tie together by way of summary the general features of my very brief account of intrinsic human value in preparation for what follows. According to this account, intrinsic human value consists in caring-for-life states of personal being brought into existence by caring-for-life conceptions. These conceptions are constitutive of society's basic design, which is to realize and perpetuate human life. They also are core conceptions in the formation of personal being inasmuch as they create the life *(zōē),* or significant vitality, distinctive of being a person. What emerges from this account is a picture of the person facing the grand alternatives of life *(zōē)* and death as the caretaker of his own life. I call this the person's "fundamental position" in the world. In this position, the person's rational aim—the ultimate point of human existence—is away from death toward the fullest and most lasting life possible. Though the person has a natural disposition to seek life *(zōē)* and avoid death, he also has a disposition to do so through ways that diminish and even destroy life *(zōē).* In other words, he has a disposition to realize significant vitality through ways (e.g., through carnal ways) that impoverish and eventually lead to death—to human existence devoid of value.

For this reason, a theory of human life is normative in nature—

it directs persons to avoid the ways of death and realize the ways of life *(zōē),* and it works to protect the ability to do so. The basic norms that provide this direction and protection make up the morality of human society. I turn now to a general account of that morality.

## THE MORALITY OF HUMAN SOCIETY

The features of a theory of human life just summarized can be expressed by a single formulation that describes the basic design of that theory and of the society of persons it makes possible. Accordingly, a theory of human life's basic design is to realize and perpetuate the possibility of human life and its fullness against the possibility of degeneration. Put differently, the design of human society is to enlarge and preserve human value. This formulation indicates the life-promoting nature of a theory of human life and provides the content of a general norm. That norm reads: It ought to be the case that the basic design of human society be fulfilled.

This norm expresses in an abstract way the morality of human society and the normative nature of the theory that makes possible such a society. Needless to say, the general moral norm of human society just described is very complex. In the space that remains, I will begin to unravel some of that complexity by examining the nature of and relations between three types of moral norms which are implicit in the general norm just presented. The second type that will be considered are norms of freedom which play a critical role in determining the place of regulation in a free society.

The place to begin my examination is with the person's fundamental position in the world that I arrived at in the first part of the paper. There the person was portrayed as the caretaker of his own life, facing the grand alternatives of fullness of life and death. It is within this picture of the human situation that the three types of moral norms in a theory of human life appear.

The first type of norm addresses the person as caretaker of his own existence and directs him to realize life that is full and lasting. We may say that this norm works to preserve and enlarge the existence of intrinsic human value itself. In other words, its design is to move persons away from death toward life *(zōē)* in its fullness. The underlying conditionals are, roughly, that a person can enjoy a full life *(zōē)* only if he realizes rich, life-enlarging conceptions; but the more he lives in life-opposing ways, the more impoverished his life will become until he suffers death. Let us refer to this first type of moral norm as the general norm of *agapē,* a Greek term that is in contemporary society somewhat misleadingly translated into English as "love." In effect, the norm of *agapē* tells each person that he ought to live daily according to the richest set of life-enlarging conceptions of which he is capable and to avoid living in life-opposing ways.

The norm of *agapē* concerns the person's fundamental direction in the world, or his rational aim as a person, which is to realize life *(zōē)* and avoid death. The second type of moral norm in a theory of human life involves the person's fundamental position in the world. It has to do with the fact that the grand alternatives of life *(zōē)* and death that define that position are alternatives of freedom. The movement away from death toward life *(zōē)* by the person is necessarily a matter of self-direction. This means that he cannot be compelled to abide by the norm of *agapē.* We should call this freedom fundamental freedom, since it characterizes the person's fundamental position in the world. Accordingly, the second type of norms implicit in the morality of human society are norms whose subject is fundamental freedom. These norms can be represented by a general norm which reads: It ought to be the case that fundamental freedom be established for all persons.

A little reflection reveals that the norm of *agapē* and norm of fundamental freedom are inseparable, because being a person in pursuit of life *(zōē)* and being a self-directed person are inseparable. We may say, then, that the norm of fundamental freedom protects the very possibility of living in accord with the norm of *agapē* and therefore of avoiding death and realizing life *(zōē).*

The third type of norm in the morality of human society is a second-level norm. It indicates what ought to be done when the norm of freedom is violated in certain ways. I call this norm the norm of fundamental justice, for reasons that will become clear as we proceed. A metaphor I find useful, though somewhat inelegant, for simplifying and clarifying the nature of fundamental justice is that of open and closed human possibilities. Moral norms and the human values they secure typically close off and open up human possibilities that a person in fact has the ability to realize. For example, moral proscriptions close off certain possibilities, such as murder and robbery. The moral proscription to prevent unnecessary human suffering allows (opens up) certain actions that reduce harm and forbids (closes off) others that cause harm. To be more general, the capacity of a theory of human life to organize persons into a society rests on the fact that it is a normative system which closes and opens in certain ways the actual possibilities of the person as agent.

Fundamental freedom itself entails open and closed human possibilities. For example, freedom of religion opens up normatively the option of worshiping God or not doing so as one pleases and closes off interference by others. This is true of fundamental freedom in general: it normatively closes off interference by others in the pursuit of life *(zōē)* and avoidance of death. Now, the open and closed possibilities of fundamental freedom make possible the person's fundamental position in the world. It is in that position, it will be recalled, that the person faces the grand alternatives of life *(zōē)* and death as the caretaker of his own life. So logically these normatively open and closed possibilities constitute the first step in organizing persons into human society. They are the basic open and closed possibilities in a theory of human life as a normative system. They make that system a system of self-direction—one that enables persons to live the free life.

The important thing to notice here is how the open and closed possibilities of fundamental freedom must themselves be connected in order for persons to live in a self-directed way. They must be connected so as to serve the person as premises of self-direction. Simply put, to serve as premises of self-direction, those open and closed possibilities must take the form of action conditionals. Roughly, those conditionals indicate that if a person avoids the free life's closed possibilities, then he can enjoy its open possibilities; but if he does not avoid the closed ones, then he cannot enjoy the open ones. These two conditionals underpin the person's fundamental position in the world and his ability to pursue his ultimate aim of realizing life *(zōē)* and avoiding death. Indeed, these conditionals are the basic premises on which human society and the free life are erected. The person can live the life offered by human society only if it is true, and he believes it is true, that the two conditionals hold.

But the basic action conditionals are not laws of nature. It is possible for some persons, but of course not all, to violate the conditionals of (a person's) freedom—to realize the closed possibilities while enjoying the open ones. So it is also possible for other persons to avoid freedom's closed possibilities and yet not enjoy the ones that are open, because others interfere in their lives. In an imperfect world, if the two conditionals are to hold, then they must be made to hold. In other words, society must see to it that they obtain. The justification for doing so is fundamental freedom itself. Fundamental freedom itself forbids the possibility of enjoying its open possibilities while not avoiding its closed ones. This implies that if a person fails to avoid freedom's closed possibilities, then he ought not fully enjoy freedom's open possibilities. His doing so is forbidden. I call this principle the principle of fundamental justice.

The principle of fundamental justice as stated needs, of course, much refinement. Two modifications are conspicuously wanting. One is that the loss of the opportunities to enjoy fully the free life due to violations of freedom should be a matter of degree, depending on the nature of the encroachment. Another refinement involves a theory of exonerating excuse. For example, some serious infringements of freedom may be partially or wholly excused if the person committing the infringement was insane at the time. However, now is not the time to enter into a lengthy discussion of a theory of punishment. Enough has been said to indicate that a principle of retributive justice is required by the norm of fundamental freedom.

## REGULATION IN A FREE SOCIETY

Having considered three types of moral norms implicit in the basic design of human society, I turn now to the question of regulation. In taking up this question I will confine myself to examining the primary role of coercive orders that have legal status and impose duties on persons. I will assume what seems to be a truism, that the general regulatory role of government in a free society is to help preserve and fulfill the basic design of that society in ways consistent with its design. If the regulatory role of government is not related in consistent ways to the basic design of the society of which it is an indigenous part, then it is not easy to imagine what that role could be. Of course, in actual practice the government in a free society could develop and enforce policy inconsistent with the basic design of that society.

The basic design of human society is, as I have tried to show, to realize and perpetuate the possibility of human life *(zōē)* and its fullness against the possibility of degeneration. This design is normative in nature and was presented earlier in summary form as the general moral norm of human society. Briefly, that norm requires that human society's basic design be fulfilled. This norm is a first-level prescription. The primary role of government itself may also be formulated as a prescription telling it to use coercive regulation only to help realize that general moral norm and to do so in ways consistent with it. This second-level prescription represents the general rule of regulation in human society. The question of regulation, then, can be raised as one concerning the relation between law and the morality of human society.

To work out the nature of this relation, let us consider as a possible subject of regulation each type of norm implicit in the morality of human society. The first type is represented by the general norm of *agapē,* which directs the person to realize life-enlarging conceptions and avoid realizing life-opposing conceptions. There are several reasons why this norm should not and cannot be the subject of coercive regulation. First, such regulation would violate the norm of fundamental freedom. Second, in any case the person cannot be compelled by threat of sanctions to be a life-promoting person, to live the life of *agapē.* This is ultimately a matter of self-direction, of free choice, something the person does for its own sake. Finally, the use of governmental regulation to compel the person to behave in a manner that could result in his discovering that some ways of living constitute life *(zōē)* and that others produce death is much more likely to obstruct that discovery than to facilitate it.

If government does have a coercive role to play in human society, as I will assume it does, then that role consists primarily of helping to establish fundamental freedom—of interpreting and enforcing the second type of moral norm. The nature of fundamental freedom is such that the enforcement of it must be done in ways consistent with it. Accordingly, the primary role of government may be more specifically described as a requirement to help establish a life of self-direction in ways consistent with fundamental freedom.

To clarify this general rule of regulation, let me examine briefly its basic parts and their relations. First, "helping establish a life of self-direction" may involve four things. Two concern (a) the development of persons capable of self-direction and (b) the exercise of that self-direction. Together the development and exercise of self-direction constitute the realization of fundamental freedom. So one part of the primary role of government is to help realize fundamental freedom. The second part of that role, and the third thing government is designed to help do, is to perpetuate the free life for future generations. Finally, government in a free society should be concerned with the value of freedom and the vulnerability of that value to degeneration. The degeneration of the value of freedom is logically distinct from not realizing freedom and not perpetuating it.

The question arises concerning what the relationship should be between the realization of the free life and its perpetuation. Clearly, one way the free life may degenerate is for the realization (enjoyment) of that life by the members of society to undermine its perpetuation. But whatever the cause of this form of degeneration, if government plays a contributory role, or fails to use its limited powers to prevent it, it violates the general rule of regulation and the norm of fundamental freedom itself. In my opinion, the general guideline that government should follow in helping to establish the balance between the realization and perpetuation of the free life is that regulation (or the absence of it) should not leave near future generations worse off in their opportunity to enjoy the free life than present persons. I will not try to justify this guideline here.

The role of government in helping to realize and perpetuate the free life must be done, according to the general rule of regulation, "in ways consistent with fundamental freedom." So we see that fundamental freedom sets limits on its own realization and perpetuation. Some might argue that these limits are absolute, that society is never justified in violating fundamental freedom in order to better realize or perpetuate the free life. In my opinion, a more defensible position is that the limits set by freedom on furthering the free life should be given great weight but should not be made absolute. This means that under certain circumstances the benefits to be gained or harms to be avoided in realizing or perpetuating freedom reach a point where they outweigh the limits set by freedom itself. I cannot go into this further here.

The requirement that government help establish fundamental freedom in ways consistent with freedom means that it necessarily becomes involved in interpreting and enforcing the norm of fundamental justice. According to this norm, if the person does not avoid certain of fundamental freedom's closed possibilities, and is without legitimate excuse, then he ought not enjoy fully the free life. We saw earlier that this conditional is among the basic premises of self-direction in human society. So part of the regulatory role of government is to enforce fundamental justice and help secure those basic premises of self-direction. Government carries out this role by determining by law what violations of fundamental freedom are legally prohibited and what the punishments will be for such violations, as well as by creating the institutional means for enforcing and adjudicating that law.

The general relation between government and the basic design of human society has now been indicated. Society's basic design is to realize and perpetuate the possibility of human life *(zōē)* against the possibility of that life's degeneration. Government's primary role in realizing this design is limited, consisting of the task of helping to establish (realize and perpetuate) the free life in ways consistent with freedom. Since moral degeneration is a real possibility, and government's role in helping realize human society's basic design is quite limited, the primary means for preventing or reversing life's degeneration is self-regulation, not regulation by law. However, it may happen that the power of self-regulation itself degenerates, thereby inevitably enlarging as a matter of fact the role played by legal regulation and greatly restricting human freedom. Let me briefly explain.

The free life is an experiment in life *(zōē)* and death. That is, it is a process of discovery and rediscovery, made possible by fundamental freedom, of what is life *(zōē)* or value enlarging and what is life *(zōē)* or value diminishing. The thought is that when moral decline sets in, the experience of living by conceptions that produce death will provide reasons for turning toward conceptions that enlarge life *(zōē)*. Coercive regulation that moves much beyond the establishment of fundamental freedom will very likely interfere with that experience of discovery, seriously hamper the process of self-regulation, and thereby prevent the renewal and enlargement of life *(zōē)*.

However, self-regulation itself is vulnerable to moral decay. As a person's life becomes more and more life-opposing, his capacity to experience good and turn away from evil is increasingly lost. When the loss of the capacity for self-regulation becomes serious and widespread among a people, a great increase in coercive regulation becomes necessary to preserve social order. Then the combination of moral corruption and regulation makes the free life impossible, and social order becomes authoritarian or totalitarian.

## THE GENERAL ROLE OF THE CONSTITUTION

The framework is now in place for understanding the general role of the Constitution in our free society. In doing so, I will not repeat many of the particulars of this framework already covered. To begin with, it seems obvious that the Constitution is part of some larger theoretical context or other. Separating the Constitution from any such context in interpreting and understanding it makes no sense and, in fact, cannot be done. That context, according to my analysis, is formed by the basic values and norms discussed in this essay that enable a theory of human life to bring into existence and preserve the free society. These are the principles that underlie the Constitution and on which it depends for its meaning and significance.

According to these values and norms, the primary role of government is to help establish (realize and perpetuate) the free life in ways consistent with fundamental freedom. Given this description of government's primary role, the basic purpose of the Constitution, put simply, is to help establish a government that can and will carry out that primary role. In doing this, the Constitution both confers power and secures human freedom. The object of the power conferred and freedom secured is to help realize and perpetuate the free life in ways consistent with human freedom. Establishing government for this purpose—creating the primary relation between government and the free society's basic design—is what makes the Constitution significant and provides the viewpoint from which to interpret its meaning.

That the Constitution as a legal conception is an integral part of a larger theoretical context provided by a theory of human life means that it shares the general aim of that theory. That aim is to move persons away from death toward life *(zōē)*. So with respect to the person's ultimate possibilities—fullness of life and death—the Constitution is not neutral. Like the larger theory of which it is a part, the Constitution itself is a life-promoting conception and as such is constitutive of value in a fundamental way when it operates according to design. That the Constitution is a life-promoting conception is apparent in its general purpose, which is to establish a government that is capable of helping to realize and perpetuate the free life in ways consistent with fundamental freedom—to secure the blessings of liberty to existing and future persons. Furthermore, the language of freedom in the Constitution—for example, due process, equal protection, the Bill of Rights—indicates a deep commitment to the high intrinsic value of persons and their ends. Finally, the structure of power created by the Constitution—with its separation of powers, checks and balances, and provisions for political representation—is designed to protect freedom while requiring that the varied interests of society be taken into account in helping to establish the free life, ultimately because that is the right thing to do in a society of free people. The features of the Constitution that create power and secure freedom stand, by design, as a partial barrier against the real possibility that the free life can degenerate in its power to organize human life and give it significant vitality.

So, again, the basic aim of the Constitution as a fundamental legal conception is to assure that political power exists to help realize and perpetuate the free life against the possibility of degeneration. This represents the general intention of the Framers. I do not mean the Framers' intentions in the psychological sense. I mean the intentionality implicit in the theory of human life, embedded in the language of their day, in terms of which they understood their world and formulated the Constitution. In their day, as in ours, that theory was not perfectly understood nor fully articulated. Then as now there was much room for elaboration and improvement in what constitutes freedom and life *(zōē)* and what opposes them. Our understanding of the Constitution differs from theirs due to subsequent modifications, not all for the better, in the underlying theory of human life. Nevertheless, the general aim of that theory and its basic moral norms and values remain essentially the same, if my account of them is correct. For this reason and in this sense, the general intention of the Framers remains a relevant and authoritative criterion for understanding the Constitution today. This general intention is the starting point for working out more specific intentions.

But as noted earlier, the free life is an ongoing experiment in life *(zōē)* and death. It is a process of discovery and rediscovery of what is life *(zōē)* creating and what is life *(zōē)* destroying. This ongoing experiment gives rise to opposing views of what constitutes life *(zōē)* that inevitably get expressed in the debates and adjudications which characterize the politics of the free society. Inevitably, as a result the Constitution is continually reinterpreted, and the relation between regulation and freedom changes. Hopefully, the process of discovery and the constitutional reinterpretations it gives rise to will in the long run enrich life and strengthen freedom. But of course the free life might also be impoverished and weakened by false discoveries and their accompanying misinterpretations of fundamental law. When this happens, the future of the free life and its constitution depends primarily on the people's capacity for self-discovery and self-correction and on the responsiveness of government to the results.

## FAILURE AND ABUSE OF TRUST

The primary role of government in a free society is to help establish the basic design of that society—in other words, to help realize and perpetuate the free life in ways consistent with fundamental freedom. This is government's basic trust. But government may fail in or abuse its trust. It fails in its trust if it does not employ its constitutional powers, when the occasion requires, to establish the free society's basic design. And government abuses its trust when it uses power to weaken or undermine the basic design of the free society. Limited by space, I will provide several illustrations of what I think are abuses and failures of trust. These illustrations will also serve to indicate how the norms of freedom and regulation I have set forth in an abstract way might be interpreted and applied to familiar problems of public policy.

The basic design of a free society contains three norms of freedom. Government may abuse or fail in its trust in helping to establish any or all of these norms. Consider first the norm which reads that it ought to be the case that, within the limits of the norms of freedom as a consistent set, persons enjoy the most extensive systems of equal freedom in determining the outcome of their own lives. The free society, much like any society, provides a structure of opportunities from which the person can determine the outcome of his own life. Examples are opportunities for an education, to buy and sell, to seek employment, to worship, and to vote. What freedom is primarily about in a free society is the person being free from restraint by others both to develop the ability to pursue and then actually to pursue these opportunities, thereby realizing his own life in a self-directed way. The primary role of government includes protecting in an equal way the enjoyment of freedom in this sense.

One way government may fail in its trust would be in its unwillingness to exercise its constitutional powers to protect persons from discrimination involving state action on the basis of race, sex, or national origin in the enjoyment of basic freedoms, such as owning property, voting, and attaining an education and employment. Government would abuse its trust by using its power to establish such discriminations.

Consider one more example of governmental abuse of trust in protecting the norm of freedom that is before us. Recall that fundamental freedom entails both open and closed human possibilities. For example, freedom of speech and religion entail noninterference by others in speaking one's mind and worshiping as one pleases. This means that parasitic ways of living—ways in which persons enjoy freedom's open possibilities but fail to avoid its closed possibilities—are not among the options of fundamental freedom. To permit them is to allow the violation of fundamental freedom in the name of that freedom. So fundamental freedom does not protect persons who seriously advocate or otherwise attempt to realize social orders or public policies formulated in terms of freedom's closed possibilities and therefore aimed at the infringement of other persons' fundamental freedom.

Consequently, government abuses its trust when it protects the public speech or acts of groups or individuals that seriously intend the violation of fundamental freedom. For instance, speech or actions that advocate or intend the physical destruction or suppression of Jews or blacks, placing them under duress or fear for themselves, violates their fundamental freedom. The protection by law of such speech or actions would be a violation of trust.

A second norm of freedom requires that human life in general and the free life in particular be perpetuated for future generations. Both the perpetuation of the free life and its realization are basic intrinsic values created by a theory of the free society as a caring-for-life conception. Typically, these two basic values are intimately and positively related. The deeper that people experience human life's significance as something freely to be enjoyed, the deeper their sense of human life as something that must go on being. When this is so, the perpetuation of the free life is an integral part of the fulfillment of the free life in human society. But the two parts of a free society's basic design—to realize and perpetuate the free life—may come into conflict with one another. The resources needed, including the person's life span (which is short at best), both to enjoy the free life and to perpetuate it are scarce, and so it may be tempting to sacrifice the perpetuation of the free life to its enjoyment. In this situation, the imperative to perpetuate the free life stands as a moral barrier to prevent the pursuit of the free life from undermining its perpetuation. It prohibits, for example, the accumulation of a huge national debt, the misuse of natural resources, and the destructive pollution of the environment. Insofar as government policy contributes to the serious weakening of the critical balance between perpetuating and realizing the free life, it abuses its trust.

Now the core value in the complex social process of perpetuating the free life, the one to which all others are referenced, is the creation of new human life itself and the nurturing of it to full personhood. The caring-for-life conception that defines human life as something to be lovingly created and nurtured is deep-seated in the basic design of a free society. Accordingly, the norm that requires the perpetuation of the free life is aimed at preserving and even enhancing the profound value of creating and nurturing new life against practices inconsistent with it. If government policy encourages or materially supports such practices, then it abuses and fails in its trust.

Consider two ways this abuse or failure might occur. The first concerns the family, which is the primary institution in a free society in which human life is lovingly created and nurtured to full personhood. In the family is housed the rich morality of the home needed to awaken in new life the full value of personal being. This abundant morality stands in contrast to the much thinner morality of the marketplace and political arena, where even minimally decent Samaritans sometimes absent themselves without guilt or shame. In contrast to the economic or political world, the family is viewed morally as persons related by primary ties of kinship rather than as a collection of isolated individuals. These ties are necessary to the morality of the home and the caring-for-life conception, deeply seated in a free society's basic design, that present human life as something to be lovingly created and nurtured there.

Because government's primary role includes helping to perpetuate the free life, and because the family is the primary institution for creating and nurturing new life, the formal family should continue to have privileged status in the law. The aim of the law should be to preserve and strengthen the family in ways consistent with its autonomy. So the government should not legally sanctify current claims that the relations and functions of the family should be wholly private and not a legal concern or claims that would legally redefine the family as a collection of isolated individuals rather than persons related by primary ties of kinship.

Consider the second way government might abuse its trust to help establish the norm of freedom that requires the perpetuation of the free life. It has to do with the moral status of new human life itself. In a society in which the perpetuation of human life and therefore the creation and nurturing of it have high intrinsic value, new life itself will have high moral status. It is simply inconsistent to claim that the perpetuation of human life is a primary value and also to claim that no new human life has any status until it reaches sentience, viability, personhood, or some state of being beyond conception. That this is so is especially clear when we consider the rich caring-for-life conception that forms the heart of the morality of the home and defines human life as something to be affectionately created and nurtured. From this conception spring those powerful sentiments concerning the creation and nurturing of new human life so essential to motherhood and fatherhood. Unless it becomes impoverished or is misunderstood, that conception confers high intrinsic value on human life from the moment of conception and makes bringing it into existence a sacred undertaking not to be entered into lightly. It would be a serious abuse of governmental power if it were used to protect or foster large-scale, indiscriminate destruction of unborn human life or to impoverish the deep-seated caring-for-life conception on which procreation is grounded.

The last norm of freedom I want to consider protects the intrinsic value of freedom itself. Even though protecting the value of freedom and protecting the perpetuation and realization of freedom are usually inseparably intertwined, as a matter of fact, the three norms are nevertheless distinguishable. It is possible for the value of freedom to decline apart from violations of the norm to realize or perpetuate freedom. In any case, to understanding the role of government to help establish the free life, it is essential to recognize that the intrinsic value of freedom is itself vulnerable to decline and is protected by the morality of freedom.

Earlier I tried to make the case that the free life is an experiment in life *(zōē)* and death. That is, it is a process of discovery and rediscovery, made possible by fundamental freedom, of what is life *(zōē)* or value enlarging and what is life *(zōē)* or value diminishing. I said then that the movement between life *(zōē)* and death is a matter of self-direction and that government regulation would greatly hamper it. The point to be made here is that within a free society the pursuit of life *(zōē)* in a self-directed way must nevertheless take place within the limits set by the three norms of freedom. This means that certain practices which imply the negation of the intrinsic value of freedom are morally out of bounds in a free society. What these bounds are is not easy to specify exactly. The best that can be done here is to mention a few illustrative cases.

The examples I have chosen involve what I think is a misconception concerning human rights. In each case, a conception of human rights operates to protect or foster the impoverishment of the free life's basic design as a value-creating (caring-for-life) conception. In other words, human rights are interpreted so that they become a moral and legal mechanism in diminishing the intrinsic value of freedom itself.

Each of my earlier illustrations may be used again without further elaboration. Each involves a conception of human rights that serves to reduce the intrinsic value of free life as something to be enjoyed and perpetuated. One such misconception enables members of groups who advocate genocide and hatred of other human beings, in violation of fundamental freedom, to stand proud during flag-raising ceremonies. Another is a view of rights which justifies excluding women and racial minorities from full citizenship. Still another is a view of rights that desensitizes large numbers of medical personnel, their patients, and the large public to the wholesale destruction of unborn human life on an unprecedented scale.

Let me add to these examples two others. It is a misconception of human rights that dignifies the production and sale of hard-core pornography depicting the sexual abuse of children and the use of women for violent pleasures. The conceptions in terms of which these obscene themes are formulated are deeply at odds with the basic design of a free society as a caring-for-life conception on which the intrinsic value of freedom itself depends. In other words, when the conceptions that form hard-core pornography are compared to the caring-for-life conceptions that constitute the intrinsic value of freedom itself the two are seen to be at loggerheads. Thus, hard-core pornography violates a basic norm of freedom—the one which requires the protection of the intrinsic value of freedom itself. Because hard-core pornography violates that norm in such a blatant manner, it is without redeeming social value and is inconsistent with community standards in any free society. My final example is a view of rights that enables the haves to ignore the poverty and suffering of the have-nots, especially when the have-nots are old, widowed, or disabled.

Government that produces law that is based on a view of human rights which seriously weakens or undermines the intrinsic value of freedom in ways just described abuses and/or fails in its trust.

# Notes

1. One of the best recent books that discusses the person's coming to be by virtue of learning a theory about himself is written by Rom Harre, *Personal Being: A Theory for Individual Psychology* (Oxford, England: B. Blackwell, 1983).

2. The term "brute fact" and the distinction between it and constituted fact are discussed by John R. Searle in *Speech Acts: An Essay in the Philosophy of Language* (London: Cambridge University Press, 1970), 50-53. Cf. G. E. M. Anscombe, "On Brute Facts," *Analysis* 18, no. 3 (1958).

3. Cf. William K. Frankena, *Ethics* (Englewood Cliffs, N.J.: Prentice-Hall, 1973), 45-52.

4. See, in particular, Socrates' second speech, especially his presentation of the myth, beginning with 246a.

5. This interpretation of Plato is not a settled matter. For authors who seem to support this interpretation, see, for example, Irving Singer, *The Nature of Love,* 2d ed. (Chicago: University of Chicago Press, 1984), vol. 1, chap. 4, and Herman L. Sinailso, *Love, Knowledge and Discourse in Plato* (Chicago: University of Chicago Press, 1965), chap. 2.

6. Derek Parfit, *Reasons and Persons* (Oxford, England: Clarendon Press, 1984), chap. 1.

# IV

# COLLECTIVE IDENTITY AND CONSTITUTIONAL POWER

★

*Sheldon S. Wolin*

*Constitutionalism by dividing power, provides a
system of effective restraints upon governmental action.*
—Carl Friedrich

*The fabric of American Empire ought to rest on the
solid basis of* THE CONSENT OF THE PEOPLE.
*The streams of national power ought to flow immediately
from that pure original fountain of all legitimate authority.*
—Alexander Hamilton

These two statements, one from a twentieth-century authority on constitutional government[1] and the other from the most authoritative treatise ever written on the American Constitution,[2] set forward two principles that form the main paradox at the

---

*Sheldon Wolin, formerly a professor in the department of Politics at Princeton University, is currently Clark Professor at the University of California at Los Angeles, and will be joining the faculty of Cornell University in January 1989 as professor of Political Theory.*

center of the American Constitution and perhaps of modern constitutionalism generally. One principle emphasizes restrained and divided power, the other an ultimate power, theoretically unified and unconstrained, the sovereign power of "the people."

This paradoxical conception of power is as old as the Constitution itself. On the one side, the Constitution provides for numerous arrangements, such as the separation of powers, and prohibitions, such as those embodied in the first ten amendments to the original document, designed to restrain and limit the exercise of power by public officials. On the other side, the Constitution provides for the positive exercise of power. In the form of taxing and spending powers, it makes possible the generation of power on a regular and assured basis. In the form of broad powers to regulate commerce and currency and to wage war, the Constitution encourages the use of power without specifying the ends of its use, provisions Hamilton seized upon in order to establish a high doctrine of state power early in the history of the republic.

## COLLECTIVE IDENTITY: CONSTITUTED AND DISPUTED

But there were stakes other than state power involved in establishing and operating a constitution and these were suppressed by Hamilton's rhetoric. A constitution not only constitutes a structure of power and authority, it constitutes a people in a certain way. It proposes a distinctive identity and envisions a form of politicalness for individuals in their new collective capacity. The Preamble to the American Constitution, while it has no judicial standing, is a striking example of the assertion of a new collective identity to replace the one expressed in the Articles of Confederation: "WE THE PEOPLE of the United States, in Order to form a more perfect Union . . ." The Preamble also specified the values by which the new collectivity aspired to be known: justice, domestic peace, common defense, the general welfare, and liberty. Finally, the Preamble also suggests that a constitution is the result of a collective action, that a people can act collectively: "WE THE PEOPLE . . . do ordain and establish this CONSTITUTION for the United States of America."

In large measure, collective identity is created by and perpetuated through public discourse. Public discourse consists of the vocabulary, ideologies, symbols, images, memories, and myths which have come to form the ways we think and talk about our political life.[3] How that discourse has come to be what it is is the history of American political and legal thinking and practices. Beginning with the controversy over the ratification of the Constitution itself, the basic terms of the discourse have been vigorously and repeatedly contested. The ratification controversy exposed a considerable body of opinion, loosely identified with the Antifederalists, opinion that wanted to prevent political identity from becoming identified with centralized national power and a nationalized people. Identity, they argued, was in fact pluralistic and diffusive, centered primarily in the state and local governments, with only a minimal national loyalty and that owed to some loose confederational authority. In effect, the Antifederalists denied the existence of "We the People" and rejected the mode of collective existence required for effecting the vision of an "American Empire."[4] With irritation but good reason, the British had described the colonists as a "fractious people."

This suggests that a certain problematic quality attaches to collective identity, that it is not just an inheritance but, perforce, an acquisition that is being remade as it is being transmitted. It is natural to assume that, with the ratification of the Constitution in 1789, America's collective identity was settled. It is easy to forget, particularly on celebratory occasions, that in the 1790s, the first decade of the new Constitution, a fierce dispute raged over the constitutionality of the Alien and Sedition Laws. It culminated in the Virginia-Kentucky Resolutions that asserted the right of the states to declare federal laws unconstitutional. During the next half-century preceding the Civil War, a number of equally intense debates erupted: the embargo controversy, the constitutionality of the national bank, the Hartford Convention, the nullification controversy, and "internal improvements." Each of these involved crucial questions about the meaning of such basic terms as power, authority, rights, consent, and federalism. The answers helped to define America's political identity and to legitimate certain ways of talking about it. Yet it is no exaggeration to claim that throughout much of American history the very idea of American collective identity has been a contested notion, contested not only by words but by force as well.

It may be, then, that American political identity lies essentially in its contested character, in the practical denial of metaphysical notions of "the people" or of "national Unity." *E pluribus unum* has been more of an expression of faith, the political equivalent of trinitarianism, than a political fact. For the disputes over collective identity did not end with the Civil War. The dominant beliefs about it were challenged, in the name of anti-imperialism and American exceptionalism, at the time of the Spanish-American War and World Wars I and II. The most significant challenge since the Civil War came, however, during the 1960s when there was widespread resistance to the imperial image being cast for the society by its dominant groups.

Twentieth-century challenges have a surprising element of continuity with their historical antecedents. Antifederalists, nullificationists and secessionists, and Vietnam war resisters have been depicted as antiprogressive, literally reactionary, yearning for a pastoral America—Luddites resisting the march of industrialization and the responsibilities of power. Today there is a special piquancy to the controversy over collective identity. The champions of technological progress and the global expansion of American power are led by a president whose talent is to evoke the same anachronistic values cherished by the "reactionary" critics of unlimited technological innovation and global hegemony. For their part, the contemporary inheritors of the antifederalist tradition see themselves as radicals fighting against the centralization of power and the overproduction of it.

The question of what kind of collective identity is at stake in current debates can be clarified by reconsidering Hamilton's attempted resolution of the paradox of constitutional restraint and the theoretical claim of an unlimited power in the sovereign people. With typical panache, he would resolve the paradox by arguing for a dramatically expanded state power that was made possible because of the paradox rather than in spite of it.

## PRODUCING POWER AND REDUCING POLITICALNESS

No one appreciated more acutely than Hamilton that, while restraint on power was an important element of constitutionalism, it was not its "essence." Rather, insofar as there was a constitutional essence, it was power itself. In Hamilton's expansive view, a constitution represented a way of organizing and generating power for the pursuit of great national objectives. The

Constitution was to be the means of assuring a continuous generation of power. This would require a bold theoretical move that
would transform the meaning of the power of the people while
retaining the traditional meaning associated with contract theory.
In contract theory, the power of the people was identified with a
primal act of consent that legitimated the subsequent exercise of
authority by officeholders. Thus it stood for a formal principle
rather than a material one. Hamilton transformed the power of
the people to mean the substance of power, not simply its authori-
zation. The sense in which the power of the people was sovereign
or unlimited now assumed a different meaning: it referred to the
material power of the entire collectivity the aggregate of its social
resources that consent now made potentially available to the state.

## HAMILTON: THE CONSTITUTION OF POWER AND PEOPLE

According to Hamilton's formula, the "streams of power"
ought to flow from the "fountain of legitimate authority," represented by the consent of the people, to those who govern. But
precisely what kind of power is it that "streams" from the people
and how do they come to have it? Do they "have" power or would
it be more accurate to say that they "compose" it? What does the
introduction of a constitution do to that power—is it a way of
composing consent to assure the flow of power and concurrently
its legitimation and, if so, what are the implications for the
political status of the people? Are they being constituted so as to
be watchers of how their powers are being used rather than participants in those uses?

Hamilton's account seems so formulaic to the contemporary
reader, so similar to the pseudopopulist rhetoric packaged for
today's political candidates, that the temptation is to see in
Hamilton's metaphor only a ritualistic expression devised by a
notorious antidemocrat who was compelled by political circumstances to give lip service to the noxious principle of popular
sovereignty. Read differently it is a formula for the constitution of
power. The formula unlocks access to power, making it available
to the state. Under its terms, consent does more than sanction or
sanctify power. It opens up the possibility of an uninterrupted
transfer of substance from "the fountain." Hamilton's imagery of
a "stream" of power that flows to government suggests that, by

97

consenting, the people concede access to their power—power which the governors collect, as it were, and regularize/channel. The power released by consent consists of resources such as money, skills, and bodily strength which, in the form of taxation and conscription, government can draw upon because, ideally, its claims are recognized as legitimate. By the alchemy of authority, power is transmuted; it is embodied in public agents (e.g., bureaucratic and military personnel) and public policies and decisions. In this respect, Hamilton's imagery was a perfectly accurate representation of his intentions—and of most of the original Framers as well—of reducing popular influence and enhancing the power of the state.

One need not rehearse the familiar story of the numerous devices for restraining and reducing the power and participatory activity of the citizenry. Indirect elections of senators and the president; staggered terms of office for senators and a long incumbency of six years; the reduction of the powers of local authorities. Thus state power begins in the materialization of the activity of the people, that is, in what is produced by their labor and skill. What their consent signifies is their willingness to make over, in whole or in part, their powers and products to be used by the state. While their power is being made available to government, the loss is experienced by them as political passivity.

What is at stake here is an interpretation of the meaning of collective identity as expressed through the constitutionalization of power. Hamilton's interpretation was a theme on which there would be many later variations: it identified the collectivity with the exercise of power by state officials who would define, in policy terms, the meaning of national values or purposes, and who would be held accountable for their policies either by judicial decisions or by popular elections. At the same time, a constitution is an experiment in the forging of a collective identity. The identity of the collectivity, who it is and what it stands for politically, is made known through the constitutionally sanctioned actions of public officials and the response, or lack thereof, of the collectivity to those actions. Thus, a constitution has a circular nature: it is constituted by the collectivity ("We the People . . . do ordain and establish this Constitution . . .") and the actions performed under it, in turn, constitute the collectivity. The inherent danger is that the identity given to the collectivity by those who exercise power will reflect the needs of power rather than the political possibilities of a complex collectivity; it will be a collectivity devoted to consolidating *unum* rather than to encouraging *plures*.

The power-generating nature of the American Constitution tends to be overlooked because so many constitutional controversies have been dramatized in terms of alleged violations of constitutional limits. Important as these questions are, they should not obscure the various ways in which the Constitution has been used to legitimate the enormous structure of power created by later scientific and industrial changes. The peculiarity of the American way of legitimating power is that it tends, simultaneously, to disguise the actual expansion of state power under the category of pragmatic programs, from "internal improvements" in the nineteenth century to Chrysler bailouts in the twentieth, while welcoming the increasing power of "private" economic institutions and interpreting that increase as located "outside" the proper "sphere of government." These tendencies have their source in the narrow conception of a constitution which marked off the political thinking of the Framers from that of contemporaries such as Montesquieu and Hume.[5] Stated simply, American thinkers conceived a constitution primarily in terms of legal limits and procedural requirements for a selected set of institutions which were then identified as "government" and declared to be formally separated from social institutions of class, status, religion, and economy. Ideologically, the formal separation was justified on liberal grounds; that is, it promoted political equality, toleration, and private rights, especially those of property. In contrast, Montesquieu and Hume were constantly seeking to expose the interconnections between social and political practices and authorities. Indifference to these interconnections would later figure importantly in the Reagan administration's program for "returning" governmental power to local authorities and inviting corporate institutions to assume some of the functions of government.

In what follows I shall be inquiring into the two themes of collective identity and power. My thesis is that a crisis in collective identity began to crystallize in the 1980s and that it was interconnected with important changes in the form and substance of state power.

## COLLECTIVE IDENTITY AND DIFFERENCE

Political rhetoric, even when artfully packaged, may yield important clues about changing understandings of collective identity and of its relationship to political reality. Political rhetoric is public speech fashioned for public occasions. Typically, such moments are highly ritualized (e.g., the presidential State of the Union message) and marked by the recital of collective myths (e.g., the sovereignty of "the people"). The rhetoric of public occasions is often revealing for the promises that it makes, the political vision it unfurls, the metaphors it lingers over, the folk memories it appeals to. Public rhetoric is also concerned with "educating" the citizenry to perform a collective role in ways that will support and strengthen the powers of those who govern. Rulers are continually making judgments about what the "real" world "is," and these judgments often run counter to the understandings and expectations which past rhetoric had encouraged. Recall in this connection President Carter's unsuccessful attempt to revise public perceptions of the Soviet Union. Political rhetoric is not synonymous with mere oratory. It is enveloped by a structure of expectations that limits what a political rhetorician may do and even dictate what he must do.

Presidential campaigns are particularly restricting precisely because of their ritualistic character. The efficacy of ritual depends upon its adherence to the formulas that govern the particular kind of ritual in question. Presidential campaigns serve as rituals of renewal. They prepare society for the reconfirmation of authority which will follow upon the ritual of combat reenacted by the two claimants. What the society expects from the two rivals is not only a demonstration of prowess but, equally important, a restatement of collective identity. The people want to be reassured of who they are, where they have come from historically, what they now stand for, and what is to be done about the perils and possibilities that lie ahead of them as a people.

Although presidential elections are often described as though they were military engagements in which "campaigns" are waged, "strategies" devised, and supporters "mobilized," the struggle rarely pits sharply opposing conceptions of collective identity against each other. Rather, what is offered are nuances daubed over the same collective images. The apparent unanimity about common identity contrasts strikingly with the actuality of difference in American society. While the sharpness of the lines may be disputed, there is no arguing that Americans are importantly marked off from each other by distinctions of class, region, race, ethnicity, religion, gender, and by deep contrasts in education, wealth, literacy, health, and life prospects generally. In this context, collective identity appears as a superimposition, as a way of suppressing or containing difference. Differences can be especially painful among social groups in areas threatened by dislocative changes. It produces anxieties that are frequently expressed as a dogmatic demand that difference yield to unity. Groups whose identities are most threatened are often the most insistent champions of collective unity. During the 1960s, bumper stickers demanded "America: love it or leave it"; while the stickers could commonly be seen on pickups, they were rarely observed on sports cars or limousines.

The past two decades have seen the proliferation of varieties of differentiated consciousness. Blacks, feminists, Hispanics, Native Americans, homosexuals, and many others have challenged the images of homogeneity that have accompanied the dominant conceptions of collective identity. The images of homogeneity have been strained further by the global dislocation occasioned in part by American political and economic policies. These have caused thousands of human beings, many of them Asians and Hispanics, to flee their homelands for the United States, thereby helping to produce new differences and to accentuate existing ones.

In the course of American history, some differences have been celebrated, others suppressed; in some eras a difference that had previously been suspect, as in the case of the Nisei during World War II, is later accepted, even admired. Acceptance into the collectivity or "mainstream" is predicated upon acceptance by aliens and immigrants of the mainstream institutions and their prerequisites. This results in a paradoxical situation in which the newly arrived groups unintentionally connive at their own repression—and by repression here I mean no more than the inability to express difference freely. The mere fact of their presence signifies that they expect to find a freer life and a materially better one. Since the vast majority have come from countries which are poor and ruled oppressively, their condition in the new land is bound to be experienced as an improvement. For them, the contrast is not between the promise of American democracy and the realities of corporate America, but between a life lived in fear and repression and a life in which one is left alone to compete furiously for economic survival and, occasionally, large fortunes. In short, they become a force for conservatism, concerned mainly with economic opportunities and nondiscrimination.

## THE NARROWING OF COLLECTIVE IDENTITY

From another perspective, however, the influx of potential citizens and resident aliens represents a population for which most of the symbols, myths, and memories that compose the meaning of collective identity are meaningless. There is, at the same time, not much confidence that the public schools will be able to initiate the varied groups into the common store of collective symbols, a task made all the more problematic by the pressures for increasing the number and variety of private schools and for promoting bilingualism. The implication is that collective identity will survive in a sharply attenuated form, unable either to give generous expression to differences or to assume a significant fund of shared symbols and representations.

The development toward a minimal collective identity is reflected in the way that both of the major political parties have settled upon ideologies that oscillate no farther than from right-center to center. The "center" symbolizes a collective identity in which the only meaningful differences are represented by taboos, that is, "the extremes of Left and Right." Immigrant groups eager to learn the recipe of material success in America thus complement a political system that finds it easy to reward difference when it is sublimated into entrepreneurship (e.g., "black capitalists") but difficult to represent political differences when they challenge the status quo, even modestly (e.g., the isolation of Jesse Jackson by the Democratic party).

There are pressures from a different source that work toward the same result. American business, in its efforts to compete successfully with its counterparts in Japan, Taiwan, and South Korea, has placed special emphasis on the importance of a "stable political base" and of "supportive" state policies. By a "stable political base," business spokesmen mean the absence of domestic unrest, that is, a politically passive population that is not likely to demand sharp departures in governmental policies or to take to the streets in the event of austerity measures. By "supportive" state policies they mean nothing less than an active state that will intervene to offset the advantages perceived to be enjoyed by business in rival societies. The one thrust reinforces the tendency toward constricting the expression and representation of difference, while the other presupposes an enlargement of state power and thus produces a situation where, as state power enlarges, its base becomes narrower.

The disparity between state power and its grounding in collective identity is inherent in the dilemma confronting advanced capitalist societies generally. Compelled by the fierce demands of international competition to innovate ceaselessly, capitalism resorts to measures that prove socially unsettling and that hasten the very instability that capitalists fear. Plants are closed or relocated; workers find themselves forced to pull up roots and follow the dictates of the labor market; and social spending for programs to lessen the harm wrought by economic "forces" is reduced so as not to imperil capital accumulation. Thus the exigencies of competition undercut the settled identities of job, skill, place, and the traditional values of family and neighborhood which are normally the vital elements of the culture that sustains collective identity and, ultimately, state power itself.

## COMPETING MYTHS: ARCHAISM AND FUTURISM

These developments are reflected in the opposing myths at the center of American self-understanding. One myth looks to the past for reassurance, the other to the future for hope. The first is a myth of fundamentalism. It wants to restore the system of free enterprise, recover the intentions of the Founding Fathers and the original Constitution of limited governmental powers, and revive religious faith. Fundamentalism wants schools "to go back to basics" and to teach the elements of morality; it wants to restore the traditional family and to keep sexual relations firmly within it.

If the one myth is archaic and restorationist, the other is futurist and innovative, caught up in the excitement of recurrent technological revolutions and convinced that only a rapidly changing, adaptive society, committed to superiority in the sciences, can preserve American hegemony. The futurist myth was expressed recently by the secretary of state on the occasion of the celebration of the 350th anniversary of the nation's oldest academic institution. "The advanced nations," he declared, "are already in the throes of a new scientific and technological revolution . . . an Informational Revolution [that] promises to transform the structure of our economies and the political life of the planet as thoroughly as did the Industrial Revolution of the 18th and 19th centuries."[6]

In keeping with his postmodern temper, the futurist is inclined toward agnosticism, preferring to emphasize national power rather than its constitutional limits, scientific inquiry rather than religious values, and schools that will prepare students for a high-tech economy rather than unduly worrying about their moral character. If he is like Secretary Shultz, the futurist will even warn against the "dangers" posed by the very values of the fundamentalist. The absorption in the American past and pride in America's uniqueness, he warned, lie close to a "thoughtless escapism" and "isolationist throwback" that ignores America's global responsibilities and its interdependence and produces evils such as protectionism. He also attacked "self-righteous moralism" because it distorts political realities. He singled out "the fervor for punitive sanctions against South Africa" as an example. The image of collectivity which the futurist Shultz summoned up was far removed from the images evoked by the archaist Reagan in his appeals to the Declaration of Independence, the Constitution, and the morality of plain folks. It was, instead, an image whose basic elements were not political or moral, but economic and scientific.

> So it is no coincidence that the free nations have once again been the source of technological innovation. Once again an economic system congenial to free scientific inquiry, entrepreneurial risk taking and consumer freedom has been the fount of creativity and the mechanism for spreading innovation far and wide.[7]

One of the striking features of Ronald Reagan's rhetoric in the past two presidential campaigns was his skill in combining the two myths of archaism and futurism. Sometimes he would identify American collective identity with the remote past, recalling the nation's founding myths, its favored self-images of freedom, progress, moral superiority, piety, chosenness, and free enterprise. He warned that collective identity had become blurred and compromised by the growth of governmental power, by the erosion of freedom and economic initiative, by the neglect of national security, and by the laxity which had come to characterize sexual conduct.

But he also spoke enthusiastically of new technology and of the importance of reshaping society and government to accord with the demands of the new age, and all the while insisting that conservatism did not necessarily mean clinging to the past. His campaign speeches created a mood of expectancy that fundamental changes were in the offing, that regulatory power would be diminished while state power (foreign affairs, military, and police) would be increased, symbols of authority would be restored, and that, collectively, the society would be encouraged to think of itself in more assertive, hopeful terms. The ultimate reassurance was that the society could have it both ways: early modern fundamentalism and postmodern agnosticism.

The election of Ronald Reagan signaled a change that went beyond the simple transference of office from one political party to another or the replacement of a liberal centrist program by a self-proclaimed conservative ideology. The fact of the election should be interpreted in the context of national myth and ritual. For it was not only the fact of Reagan's victory that matters in the ritual of renewal, but also what was signified by the defeat after only one term of the incumbent, an event that had not occurred for almost half a century. It is far more traumatic, and because of that far more redefining of collective identity, when the highest symbol of authority is ritually sacrificed than when that authority fulfills his appointed term and hands over the regalia of office. Carter was dramatically stripped of office. It may be too strong to say that a ritual murder was being performed, but it would not be to say that a ritual of rejection was being acted out and that the decisiveness of the election had to do with the dissatisfactions felt by voters over the kind of collective political identity they had come to embody. The rejection of Carter was the expression of collective fear inspired by the hostage crisis, with its attendant feelings of frustration and anxiety about American "weakness," and by the gathering economic recession, with the doubts it inspired about the strength of the economy in the new era of international economic competition. Reagan's campaign first focused then exploited a widespread wish for an altered collective identity. As we shall see, that wish reflected deep-running changes in the nature of state power in America that raise the question of what kind of state or political order requires, or is congenial with, the newly emerging collective self-conception.

## FINDING A VOCABULARY FOR THE REDEFINITION OF COLLECTIVITY

At the time of Reagan's striking electoral victory in 1980, numerous commentators sensed that a deep change in national orientation and consciousness had occurred. The notion they felt best expressed it was "revolution." Even before the inauguration it was seized upon by defenders of Reaganism as well as by critics. There were some, for example, who contended that the actions of the Reagan administration were an attempt to reverse nearly five decades of enlightened social change by launching a counterrevolution against both civil rights and the doctrines of social equality associated with the welfare state founded by FDR's New Deal and completed by LBJ's Great Society. There were others who saw the Reagan record as a revolution manqué because, instead of restoring public piety and private morality, their leaders surrendered to the temptations of "pragmatism." And there were still others who were convinced that the campaign rhetoric about "a new beginning" was being realized in important ways and that everything would turn on whether the revolution would be consolidated and perpetuated. Despite these opposing views, it is clear, I think, that "revolution" was a surrogate for talking about a fundamental change, real and imagined, in collective identity.

We can make a start on the task of sorting out these interpretive efforts by posing the question: What kind of a revolution is it that seems bent upon breaking, not with the distant past, but with the recent present?

A plausible response to that question might be to say that it is a revolution of a limited sort: it has brought a measure of efficiency and fiscal prudence into the operation of state and local governments while reducing the scope of some federal operations. It can, therefore, be described as a progressive change, perhaps even a modernizing one. It suggests further that the society may have reached a point in its history when administrative reform constitutes the meaning of progress/modernization and indicates their limits. In so doing, of course, this line of inquiry provokes the question of what all of this has to do with the self-proclaimed conservative character of the Reagan regime. That question presupposes, mistakenly, that Reagan conservatism can be reduced to nostalgia for the past. Perhaps, however, there are more complex, even contradictory tendencies reflected in Reaganism and perhaps these reflect a larger change in American political identity.

## THE CONTRIBUTION OF THE NEW DEAL

Analysts who argue that Reaganism is a counterrevolution directed against the legacy of the New Deal tend to focus primarily on the administration's animus toward government-sponsored social programs. While many of today's historians discount the revolutionary nature of the changes introduced by the New Deal, a strong case can be made that the New Deal did produce profound changes in collective identity and it did legitimate an enlarged conception of state power. The New Deal attempted to resolve a domestic economic emergency occurring within the international economy of capitalism by a variety of measures that signaled an unprecedented degree of state intervention into a peacetime economy and the beginnings of national social policy.

There was, of course, ample precedent for government action of a nonwelfare kind. Government intervention and regulation of the economy is as old as the republic itself. Alexander Hamilton, the first secretary of the treasury, devised a program of state action that would simultaneously lay the foundations for national economic power by subsidizing domestic producers and financiers and attaching the "affection" of the "propertied classes" to the new national government.[8] The difference between Hamilton's conceptions and those of later politicians was that, while he never faltered in his conviction that the economy was an instrument of state power, his successors tended to view the state as an instrument of private economic purposes.[9]

Although the period from roughly 1850 to 1880 was notable for regulatory legislation enacted by state governments,[10] federal regulation can be conveniently dated from the Interstate Commerce Act of 1887 and the Sherman Antitrust Act of 1890. The half-century following the Sherman Act saw a number of so-called independent regulatory commissions established to regulate various sectors of the economy, but with very few exceptions and rarely for very long. That experience has testified less to the growth of independent state power than to the growth of a form of state authority that legitimated the economic strategies of powerful business corporations.[11] Thus, the New Deal inherited a tradition of what we might call the strong but heteronomous state. The one exception was the wartime state. During World War I the first experiment in government control over the economy as a whole was undertaken. Although the experience was too brief to be conclusive, it did plant the notion of a fully planned and regulated economy serving ends that were the projection of national power abroad, rather than of domestic policies, and were, at the same time, largely beyond the control of a mass electorate.[12]

## THE REGULATORY/WELFARE/WARFARE STATE

As is well known, the New Deal evolved into a warfare state, bringing with it not only the regulatory traditions from the turn of the century but the newer welfare functions of the thirties. The evolution of the New Deal signified that a new synthesis of power was being consolidated, one that conjoined three distinct elements: regulation, welfare, and empire. The first can be regarded as attempts to enlarge the meaning of rationality for a capitalistic society by tempering the pursuit of self-interest by more genial notions of the common good, social justice, and a socially guaranteed economic minimum for all. The third element, empire, was not new; but its previous forms—the practical implementation of the Monroe Doctrine in Central and Latin America, the Mexican War, the Indian wars, the Spanish-American War and the pacification of the Philippines, and World War I—were inhibited by the relatively undeveloped quality of America's economic and military power.

World War II, however, marked the beginning of the American bid for supremacy among world powers and within the international economy. Henceforth the society would be encouraged to think of itself as having a special mission of defending the free world and combating communism and, therefore, of having to incorporate into its identity the economic and technological imperatives demanded by world hegemony. Thus, a new collectivity was being forged around the powers of the state as regulator, welfare dispenser, and a global suzerainty that depended less on the occupation or seizure of territories than on the penetrative power of American capital, productivity, technology, and a contagious culture of affluence.

To sum up: the New Deal falls into the typically American pattern of revolution; it was less a social than a political revolution. Its achievement was the extension and consolidation of state power and what might be called "the social legitimation of state power."[13] By means of programs such as social security, agricultural subsidies and marketing schemes, the Tennessee Valley Authority, the National Industrial Recovery Act, the National Labor Relations Act, and many others, vast numbers of Americans were tied into the system of state power both by benefits and by new participatory devices. Social legitimation, we might say, was the American way of avoiding radical social change and serious challenge to a system of state power, a system based on bureaucratic, military, and corporate institutions and operated by elites equally at home in any one of the components.

The New Deal State defined the American collective identity for roughly four decades. The pattern would be repeated later among its lineal descendants—the Truman Fair Deal which ended in the Korean War, and the Johnson Great Society which ended in the Vietnam War. These mimetic repetitions culminated in Lyndon Johnson's hubristic attempt to combine the vast social programs of the Great Society with the vast military expedition into Southeast Asia. That identity was profoundly shaken during the sixties by ghetto riots, military defeat, and the crisis of the presidency, which had first been intimated by Johnson's decision not to seek another term and was then intensified by the Watergate revelations of the early seventies. It was further undermined by a series of developments which signified the end of American world hegemony: OPEC's threat to deny access to petroleum supplies; the hostage crisis in Iran; and, above all, the successful challenge to American economic dominance, especially from Asian countries. "The decline of American power" became a standard topic in the mass media, while the sense of a "loss of control" in the face of a suddenly threatening environment became a familiar subject of discussion. And scholars composed disquisitions on "the vanishing presidency."[14]

## REGRESSIVISM AND THE BACKLASH THAT FAILED

That changes in the world were presented so as to persuade Americans of a threat to their autonomy, even to their national existence, was a measure of how deeply the collective identity had come to depend on power for its gratification. The elements were present for a strong, xenophobic reaction: foreign competition was beating America at its own game; multinational corporations were challenging the power of the state to control the national economy; foreign investors were becoming increasingly visible, in politics as well as in the economic life of the society; and, most threatening of all to a society whose history was marked by violent nativist reactions, huge waves of immigrants entered the country with different skins and cultures. The fact that many entered illegally seemed further evidence of weakness; the country was not even master of its own borders. That in some well-publicized instances some of the new immigrants displayed remarkable adaptability to American entrepreneurial ways, while others were willing to work for substandard wages, seemed merely to accentuate their un-American qualities. Suddenly there was a question of whether, in the face of this invasion by seemingly alien cultures and of the disappearance of boundaries, there was anything "American," any distinctive collective identity, at all.

Ronald Reagan's election could easily have been the catalyst for a strong nativist backlash. This would have been in keeping with the regressivist tendencies in Reaganism noted earlier. During the campaign and the subsequent years of office his public speeches continually appealed to the stuff of nativism: to patriotism, to national superiority, to the American past, to colonial and frontier myths, to traditional morality, to fundamentalist conceptions of religion, and to the parochial images of rural and small-town America. Even more ominous, as candidate and as president Ronald Reagan played to deep-seated resentments, especially among blue-collar citizens, by his coded references to "welfare cheats" and by his refusal even to acknowledge the existence of racial problems. Some of his cabinet officials made it clear that they were eager to discard many of the legal devices employed by previous administrations to combat discriminatory practices.

## REGRESSIVISM AND MODERNIZATION

This move to reinstate American identity around traditional symbols and myths could have led to a politics of *ressentiment*. It did not, however, and that fact reveals much about the political function of regressivism. The appeal to the past and its values was not meant to point the way back to the past. Such a notion is totally incongruous in an administration so completely beholden to corporate interests, the great modernizers of our age. Rather, it was meant to ease the path toward the future. Pseudotradition-alism mediates between the average citizen and the harsh reality that modernization imposes on even the most highly techno-logized societies. Pseudotraditionalism helps to mask the costs of adaptation to the intensely competitive political economy being ushered in by high technology, a political economy whose global boundaries are already being effaced by the outline of an interstel-lar economy. The dilemmas in protectionism, declining indus-tries versus sunset industries, industrial relocation versus the de-struction of established communities, the priority of inflation over unemployment, the rationalization of agriculture, and a host of others all point to the hardships involved.

By describing this ideological element as a "pseudotradition-alism" I am not suggesting that it was insincerely held, only that it is inherently contradictory to the outlook and aims of the corporate interests, whose spokesman Ronald Reagan has been from the beginning. George Bush, Donald Regan, James Baker, George Shultz, and Caspar Weinberger are not symbols of nineteenth-century rural America. This contradiction is not hid-den but is embodied in the dualism located at the ideological center of Reaganism. Regressivism is paired with an explicit progressivism that distinguishes Reaganism's conservatism from most other conservative orientations. It is a progressivism that not only places itself squarely behind the drive for technological supremacy—Star Wars is merely the latest example of this thrust—that is, behind the modernizing forces which are daily eroding the remnants of an older America celebrated in the regressive side of Reaganism, but it also places itself against another fundamental principle of Reaganism, the principle of reducing governmental power. "Government growing beyond our consent had become a lumbering giant," the president claimed, "slamming shut the gates of opportunity, threatening to crush the very roots of our freedom."[15]

Contrary to the impressions created by presidential rhetoric, however, the historical importance of the Reagan administration will not be the return of power to the people or the scaling down of centralized, bureaucratic power, but the continued modernization and strengthening of state power. Its vision is managerialist, not Jeffersonian. It is of "a leaner, more careful focused Federal role" and "a leaner and more efficient Federal structure."[16]

The increase in state power is registered most spectacularly in the rise in military expenditures and in the strong efforts toward tightening centralized management within the government. But it is also being bolstered by the strengthening of the agencies of law enforcement; the relative indifference to the rights of the accused; the steady development of surveillance techniques, especially those relying on centralized data collections; federal drug-testing programs; and tightened security procedures for federal employees. The Reagan administration is not, then, committed to the dismantling of state power but to its enhancement. Looked at in this way, the administration's efforts to prune social programs appear as an effort to strengthen the state by making it less unwieldy, more susceptible to managerial control. This does not mean hypocrisy but rather something far more important that was prefigured in the avowed aim of Reaganism to change radically the boundaries between the so-called "public" and "private sectors." Here I am referring to the well-publicized commitment of the Reagan administration to reducing state power by encouraging the "voluntary" assumption of governmental functions and responsibilities by the "private sector." On the face of it, that aim would seem to violate an elementary axiom of politics, that no state voluntarily surrenders its powers. Why, then, is this regime apparently unlike any other? Why does it, as the guardian of state power and of public order, look so confidently to the private sector?

## THE PUBLIC/PRIVATE INVERSION

President Reagan has said that "private values must be at the heart of public policies."[17] The distinction between "public" and "private" had traditionally occupied an important place in our political and legal notions. In the president's words cited above, however, the express aim is to challenge a traditional distinction older than the republic itself. Among eighteenth-century liberals and progressives the public and private stood for two different realms, each with different ends and controlling ideals. The public denoted the "realm" or "domain" of proper government action. War, diplomacy, taxation, regulation of commerce, law enforcement, protection of life and property, education, and, more recently, welfare have been recognized as functions that are peculiarly a matter of public "interest" in which the generality of citizens, regardless of class interest, has a stake. The notion of public functions publicly discharged also implied that there was a greater chance that these functions would be impartially performed if they were in the hands of accountable public officials sworn to serve the public than if they were controlled by entrepreneurs responding to the dictates of self-interest and the pressures of the marketplace. The underlying assumption was that public purposes and public officials were to be judged by different criteria. The public should be the realm of the common good while public service should be conducted in a spirit of disinterestedness.

The private realm, in contrast, was conceived as the domain where individuals were free to exercise the various rights guaranteed by the Constitution such as property and religious rights. It was the realm of discretionary behavior where individuals were expected to pursue their own ends, to follow their self-interest. Historically, the dominant belief has been that the private "sphere" is frequently threatened by the invasion of the "public," that public authority tends to impose regulations on private behavior and reduce freedom of action. In the 1980s, however, there are signs that these metaphorical boundaries are being reshuffled and one of the main impetuses has been the Reagan ideology of "voluntarism," which encourages the "private sector" to undertake a variety of social services hitherto regarded as a public monopoly or as predominantly a public function.[18] For a long time, private non-profit or charitable organizations have existed alongside and have supplemented public services, especially at the state and local levels. But now, in the words of a champion of this development, there is a concerted attempt to make "a profitable business out of social problems" previously thought to be in the public domain.[19] Hospitals, prisons, detention centers, welfare services, and education are among the objects of voluntarism. The privatization of public safety has proceeded rapidly. The number of private security guards is estimated to be 1.1 million, of which 36,000 are employed by governmental agencies. There has also been a concerted effort to increase private or corporate responsibility/control in the domain of high culture; it already exists, of course, in the popular culture disseminated by the mass media. The same impulse is at work in the proposals by the Reagan administration to sell public power projects, railroad systems, and the assets of the FHA. It has been reported that the Reagan administration has slated some 11,000 commercial activities of government to be taken over by private contractors whenever feasible.[20]

Thus a radical inversion appears to be in the making: the private realm is invading the public. Consider an especially striking example of privatization. It involves the projection of private initiatives into the domain of warfare and foreign policy, supposedly the classic preserve where state action has been accepted as an unchallengeable monopoly. Since the Bay of Pigs invasion, where private armies of anti-Castro Cubans were assisted by American intelligence and military advisors, that monopoly has been challenged. At the present time there are conservative foundations and individual donors who have recruited soldiers and furnished material to support anti-Marxist movements aimed at overthrowing governments with which the United States government has formal diplomatic relations. In Nicaragua these "private" efforts are coordinated with official American policy aimed at toppling the government of that country. In El Salvador, on the other hand, American Protestant evangelical movements, which make no secret of their anti-Marxism and of their determination to assist American policy in defeating the leftist enemies of the government, have made striking inroads into the traditionally Catholic population. According to a *New York Times* reporter, "The dramatic growth of the [evangelical] sects [in El Salvador] and elsewhere in Latin America is a result of an intense multimillion-dollar evangelical campaign by American-based churches and religious agencies."[21]

Clearly, these developments blur and confound the distinctions between public and private. Public and private power are intermingled and the result is not a net reduction of state power but its articulation through different forms. The appropriation of public goals by private enterprise means that state power is being decentered without being decentralized. State power is being expanded but it does not necessarily flow from a common center as pictured in modern theories of state sovereignty. It includes private agencies that work in an adjunctive relationship with state power. Contrary to the official interpretation, these tendencies do not signal a decrease in state power or in the state's apparatus but rather their literal transformation. What is "private" about these new forms of power is principally their location in a privatized rather than a public/political context. The new location helps to obscure their coerciveness by transferring formal accountability from traditional political processes, such as legislative oversight and elections, to the allegedly impersonal forces of the market.

## THE REVOLUTIONARY TRANSFORMATION OF CIVIL SOCIETY

At this point, a crucial question arises and the answer takes us to the heart of the Reagan revolution. What is happening in the private realm such that its institutions are deemed capable not only of taking over functions previously thought to be the unique preserve of the state but of appearing to favor functions—such as schools, prisons, and hospitals—that are particularly coercive/disciplinary?

The question points toward a change as fundamental as the changes taking place in the power of the state and is, in fact, its complement. It involves the transformation of the private domain, of that system of private relations and associations which the eighteenth and nineteenth centuries called "civil society." In most theoretical formulations, civil society comprised the family, various social relationships (e.g., friends and neighbors), churches, schools, professions and crafts, and economic organizations. These were perceived as "private" bodies and relationships and they were thought to be importantly different from political institutions:

they were freer, more spontaneous, less coercive, and more voluntaristic.

Whatever historical truth there may have been to this conception of civil society, it was radically changed by the rationalization of society effected by late modern capitalism. Civil society now presents itself as a structure of control and discipline rather than as a paradigm of freedom and spontaneity. The contemporary business organization is not only a mechanism for economic decisions; it is also a carefully cultivated life-form which is deliberately imposed, with varying degrees of severity, on its employees. In the same vein, recent demands for reschooling society have placed great emphasis upon restoring "discipline in the classroom" and modeling students for life in the era of high technology. These same trends are evident in the rigors of Protestant fundamentalism and in the reactionary pronouncements of the Vatican. In short, now civil society represents structures of power which self-consciously exercise disciplinary functions that erase the differences between state and society, public and private. How far the evolution has gone may be gauged by the parallel efforts by private and public employers to impose drug tests and lie-detector tests on their employees and to insist on security clearances for numerous employees in both sectors. As a consequence, it becomes increasingly more difficult to discern where the public sector begins and the private leaves off. From this vantage point, "deregulation," with its faith in market "discipline" and "free economic forces," appears less as a policy than a Freudian slip.

The transformation of civil society is strikingly registered in the messages which are now regularly inscribed in television commercials. Many of the most powerful advertisers no longer are content simply to promote their products; they promote an ideology. One of the most persistent themes invites the viewer to become dependent on a particular economic institution which is typically described in images that emphasize its hugeness and its great power. The relationship is conveyed in language and imagery that is strikingly paternalistic and condescending. Thus, a couple is reduced to pygmy size and plucked up by the huge hand of a bank while a friendly voice assures them that the giant wants no more than to serve them. Or there is the assurance tendered by All-State [*sic*] insurance that its customers will be in "good hands"—and huge hands are then opened invitingly. Then there is General Motors inviting its truck buyers to "lean" on that corporation in the sure knowledge that it can be counted on.

The long-run implications of the double transformation, of state and civil society, can be roughly summarized. But to do that we need to locate them in the proper context of certain twentieth-century tendencies regarding power.

Modernizing societies of this century have displayed two inter-related responses to the rapidly changing environments produced by their policies. One is severe social dislocation. It is described by such common terms as "anomie," "fragmentation," "class conflict," and "social disintegration." Power tends to be centrifugal. The other response is to employ the technology of modernity to amass and centralize power in magnitudes unavailable to previous ruling groups—then to use power to penetrate and change the social relationships, economy, and belief systems of civil society. The twentieth century is the century of totalizing power, of the concerted attempt to unify state and civil society.

Until now that attempt has taken the form of the state dominating civil society, as in Nazi Germany, Fascist Italy, the USSR, and the People's Republic of China. What might be emerging in the United States is a new form of totalizing power that blurs the domination of the state by contracting its functions to representation of civil society while at the same time the disciplinary procedures of society are being tightened. The new form is represented not as "the state" or "the dictatorship of the proletariat" but as "the system." In order to call attention to its tendencies toward totality, I call it the system of the economic polity.[22]

## COLLECTIVE IDENTITY AND THE LOSS OF COLLECTIVE POWER

In light of the close integration of public and corporate policies and the cooperation that exists today between state officials and corporate representatives, the old dichotomies between the political state and the private economy are anachronistic. We live in an economic polity in which the state is merely the symbol of legitimate public authority, not the autonomous power suggested by early modern political theory. In the context of the economic polity voluntarism, or the acquisition of public functions by private power, does not point toward the reduction of power but toward its decentering. Most contracts regulating private operators of hospitals or prisons, for example, enable public authorities to set standards and to enforce compliance. Thus, voluntarism does not presage a freer society but, on the contrary, a more controlled one in which the centers of control will appear "decentralized" and "local" but in an administrative rather than a democratic or participatory sense. The confusion of privatization with voluntarism and of voluntarism with participation, which has been such a conspicuous feature of the Reagan rhetoric, reflects a turn toward different means of increasing social control at a time of diminishing confidence in the traditional state as the most reliable agency for supplying social control and coordinated direction. Let me consider this point by briefly describing the American response to its own centrifugal tendencies.

There are present in our public discourse, I want to suggest, profoundly contradictory notions/emotions about power. Some forms of power are, with only slight exaggeration, perceived and welcomed because they promise power without limits. Among these are the powers associated with "the economy," the military, science, and technology, Yet there is also another, more uneasy, feeling that as these forms of power become enlarged they render the society more rather than less vulnerable. Thus, industrial processes based on advanced technologies turn out to have seriously contaminated whole areas, rendering them unfit for human habitation. Or those processes may, by a mere human error, prove deadly to a whole region and harmful to a whole continent. These doubts have become so commonplace in discussions of nuclear arms that there is no need to cite the obvious fact that as nuclear power has grown so have nuclear fears. The suspicion is that the new forms of power have grown beyond the ability of traditional political institutions to manage them. One result is to seek solutions that seem to be able to dispense with forms of power that have become suspect.

Consider, for example, deregulation. Deregulation is widely regarded as a policy prompted by an ideological conviction that if economic actors were allowed freer rein, a more rational allocation of resources would result and more efficient practices would be introduced by producers and suppliers. But deregulation can also be interpreted as expressive of a loss of confidence in the power of the state to deal rationally and effectively with economic activities. In order to compensate for the weakness of purposive action, as symbolized by the state, magical powers are attributed to the market: the market is said to reflect "forces" and to impose a "discipline." Thus, there has to be faith in the workings of the market because there has been a loss of faith in the ordinary processes of government and politics. Meanwhile, very real forms of power, such as represented by large corporations, expand and evolve ever more complex ways of amassing power by playing the politics of markets—for example, in takeover strategies and arbitrage.

Deregulation is merely one of several signs of a pervasive belief that, as a collectivity, we lack the power to control our social environment. The national deficit seems beyond control. The Gramm-Rudman Act, which arbitrarily set dates for the reduction of deficits and then abdicated legislative power to allow the executive to allocate the cuts, was a desperate effort to assert control by decreeing what could not be accomplished by deliberative action. The same fears are reflected in the proposed constitutional amendment mandating a balanced budget. The distrust of the capability of normal processes of politics to achieve a desired goal produces an attempt to impose it upon the process. The rigidity of the solutions stands as a substitute for power.

The sense of powerlessness seems most acute when terrorism irrupts. It is the perfect symbol of frustrated will: the vast majority of Americans want nothing more than to muster all of our vaunted power and use it to annihilate terrorists and the third-rate powers which subsidize them. And yet it seems beyond our capability or to involve prohibitive costs. And no matter how deadly our arsenal of weapons, or how sophisticated our strike forces, we know that at bottom we are helpless. This was strikingly illustrated recently in the outburst of the secretary of state that was directed at a Yugoslav official who tried to suggest that some terrorist "causes" were justified. In his anger, Mr. Shultz pounded the table and declared that a terrorist act has "no connection with any [genuine] cause. It's wrong! (pounds the table twice)."[23]

These feelings of impotence often provoke an extreme demand for security. So the administration proposes a shield to defend the society from any nuclear attack and, until recently, it resisted virtually all Soviet overtures for reducing nuclear buildups. The highly publicized "window of vulnerability" is another perfect symbol: even the smallest opening is enough to justify escalation of the arms race in the hope that we can eventually spend the Soviet Union into exhaustion and thereby finally find security. Or the administration engages in supporting any regime which looks as though it might be anti-Marxist because while the administration is highly cautious towards large Marxist states, such as the USSR and China, and even helps to stabilize the economies of East European communist states, it seems deeply threatened by the emergence of small Marxist states and responds by sponsoring another version of terrorism.

Thus the condition which we have reached as a collectivity can best be described as a near-totality in which public and private distinctions are being steadily blurred. That a conservative administration should push for the extension of state power into the most private areas imaginable (e.g., abortion, sexual conduct, and religion) and should secretly wish to submit the whole society to urinalysis suggests that we are entering a moment in our history when it will become extremely difficult to find the terms for limiting power, or for holding it politically accountable, much less for sharing it. The diffusion of power accompanying the emergence of our new constitution, the Economic Polity, portends a collective identity in which the collectivity—"We the People," in the brave words of the Constitution—becomes the passive object of power rather than the active political subject.

# Notes

1. Carl J. Friedrich, *Constitutional Government and Democracy: Theory and Practice in Europe and America* (Boston: Little, Brown & Co., 1941), 21.

2. Jacob E. Cooke, ed., *The Federalist,* no. 22 (Middletown, Conn.: Wesleyan University Press, 1961), 146.

3. For a further discussion of myth, see my "Postmodern Politics and the Absence of Myth," *Social Research* 52 (Summer 1985): 217–39.

4. On the Antifederalists generally, see Jackson Turner Main, *The Anti-Federalists: Critics of the Constitution* (Chapel Hill: University of North Carolina Press, 1961), and more recently Herbert J. Storing, *What the Anti-Federalists Were For* (Chicago: University of Chicago Press, 1981); Sheldon S. Wolin, "The People's Two Bodies," *Democracy* 1 (January 1981): 9–24.

5. For Montesquieu's views, see *De l'Esprit des lois,* especially bks. 11–12. Hume's position is most accessible in his *Essays Moral and Political* (various editions). See, in particular, "Of the Original Contract," "Of Civil Liberty," and "Of the Origin of Justice and Property." Recent discussions of Hume include Duncan Forbes, *Hume's Philosophical Politics* (Cambridge, England: Cambridge University Press, 1975); David Miller, *Philosophy and Ideology in Hume's Political Thought* (Oxford, England: Clarendon Press, 1981); and earlier, Sheldon S. Wolin, "Hume and Conservatism," in D. W. Livingston and J. T. King, eds., *Hume: A Re-Evaluation* (New York: Fordham University Press, 1976).

6. *New York Times,* 6 Sept. 1986.

7. Ibid.

8. See E. James Ferguson, *The Power of the Purse* (Chapel Hill: University of North Carolina Press, 1961), esp. pt. 4; Forrest McDonald, *Alexander Hamilton* (New York: Norton, 1979), chaps. 6-10.

9. See Robert Harrison, "The Weakened Spring Government Revisited: The Growth of Federal Power in the Late Nineteenth Century," Rhodri Jeffreys-Jones and Bruce Collins, eds., *The Growth of Federal Power in American History* (DeKalb: Northern Illinois University Press, 1983), 62–67; Morton Keller, *Affairs of State: Public Life in Late Nineteenth Century America* (Cambridge, Mass.: Belknap Press, 1977).

10. Harry N. Scheiber, "American Federalism and the Diffusion of Power," *University of Toledo Law Review* 9 (1978): 619.

11. See Harrison, "Weakened Spring of Government Revisited," 63.

12. Paul A. C. Koistinen, "The Industrial-Military Complex in Historical Perspective: World War I," *Business History Review* 41 (Winter 1967): 378–403.

13. See, generally, Jürgen Habermas, *Legitimation Crisis,* trans. Thomas McCarthy (Boston: Beacon Press, 1975).

14. James Sundquist, "The Crisis of Competence in Government," in Joseph A. Pechman, ed., *Setting National Priorities for the 1980s* (Washington, D.C.: The Brookings Institution, 1980), 531.

15. Speech to Joint Session of Congress, *New York Times,* 5 Feb. 1986, A-20.

16. President's Budget Message, *New York Times,* 6 Feb. 1986, B-12.

17. Speech to Joint Session of Congress, *New York Times,* 5 Feb. 1986, A-20.

18. See Lester M. Salamon, "Nonprofit Organizations: The Lost Opportunity," *The Reagan Record,* ed. John L. Palmer and Isabel V. Sawhill (Cambridge, Mass.: Ballinger, 1984), 261–85.

19. For various statements championing private takeovers of public functions, see Harvey Brooks, Lance Liebman, and Corinne S. Schelling, eds., *Public-Private Partnership: New Opportunities for Meeting Social Needs* (Cambridge, Mass.: Ballinger, 1984).

20. On the widespread use of private security police, see the article on the subject in the *New York Times,* 29 Nov. 1985, A-1. For the sale of governmental services and installations, see Martin Tolchin, "New Momentum in the Selling of Government," *New York Times,* 18 Dec. 1985.

21. "El Salvador is Fertile Ground for Protestant Sects," *New York Times,* 20 Jan. 1986, A-2.

22. The concept of the "Economic Polity" is developed at some length in my article "Democracy and the Welfare State," *Political Theory* 15 (November 1987): 4:467–500.

*Discussion*

**Wildavsky:** I agree entirely with Professor Wolin that Reagan is far more radical in what he is attempting to do than is commonly conceived; and Professor Wolin's essay has the virtue of putting forth an interpretation greatly at odds with the existing norm, which is good. Reagan's discrepancies on facts and his apparently bumbling style have blinded almost everyone to the fact that he is a significant figure. However, I would like to start a little dialogue here on what exactly the president stands for. From before the time that Reagan ran for the presidency, through his first term, and now, endless allegations about coerciveness have come. Somehow, American liberties are being restricted everywhere; Somehow Reagan is a menace. I fail to see any significant way liberties are curtailed. One could argue that some secretiveness about research tends in that direction, but you would have to reach very far. It would be difficult to argue, in my opinion, that this country is not as free to dissent on matters as almost any country or any place in the world has been at any time in history. But I will give just a couple of examples to show some avenues opening up. It is not that I want to claim that Reagan is the great advocate of political participation; that is not incumbent on me.

Take the question of federalism. Sheldon Wolin has Richard Nathan as a colleague who has done a great deal of work that illuminates what has happened. There are two ways to organize federalism in this country. I argue to the Reagan people that they initially chose the wrong way, that is, the synoptic cognitive mode of central direction wherein they proposed to get a bunch of academics together and ask what spatial, temporal theories there are for realigning the responsibilities of the central and state governments. Fortunately for Reagan, that was a failure because he wasn't

*123*

willing to put up the money. And it was his fault of course. But what has actually happened is not a failure from his point of view because the other alternative is to place downward force on revenue and expenditure, thus putting pressure on states to differentiate themselves; as Nathan's detailed fieldwork shows, that's exactly what has happened. Now, this is not to everyone's taste. And I don't expect everyone to like it. But in fact some states have picked up quite a bit of what the federal government has let go. Others have picked up less. Some have picked up in this area; others have picked up in that. If one's vision of federalism is not one of uniformity but one in which states differentiate themselves (i.e., one of variety), then there ought to be some high-tax, high-service states and some low-tax, low-service states, and people ought over time to be able to sort themselves out as to where they want to go. Reagan has, by indirection, done more to achieve this end than any president in recent history.

Take events that are never recorded. When somebody storms the Bastille we know it occurred on July 14th. But I will repeat to you overheard conversations in Berkeley, no less, that indicate a certain type of change in participation. "Let's do this and that." "Yeah, terrific idea." "That bastard that lives in the White House, he won't let us." "I guess we will have to get together with other people and see if we can do it ourselves." What Reagan is in part trying to achieve by policy, and in part he achieves indirectly by bumbling, is to persuade people that they ought to rely on themselves and not on the central government. Now again, this is not to everyone's taste; but it certainly is happening. It happens throughout the country; a great deal of organization is going on locally where the feds won't do something that local interests want done.

Moreover, I think that there has been a long-time disagreement over whether (what Hayek calls) spontaneous market processes are indeed forms of participation. So I think what we have is not a diminution of liberty at all, but a fundamental, philosophical, and political disagreement over who should have power and, therefore, over what constitutes participation. If you have incessant bidding and bargaining, if organizations are forming and reforming, being born and dying; if people are trying out all sorts of things through processes of trial and error, in my view those are also forms of participation. One might prefer that these forms took place in public forums—that they were organized differently. But that doesn't make spontaneous organizations any less of a type of participation.

Overall, I think it would be quite difficult to show that private and public participation together have lessened. After all, if you talk about privatization, which has not gone nearly as far in this country as, say, in Britain, most of the functions we are talking about were long performed by private entities—sometimes, of course, very badly. Private prisons, private armies—we have had throughout history an enormous number of institutions that were, for good or ill, done privately. It hardly seems to me revolutionary to talk about some things that are being done publicly to be done privately. Are they more coercive and hidden because they are done privately? I tend, perhaps because I live in the wrong place, to see a lot of expression in American life and not much inhibition. It would hardly seem appropriate to me to characterize America as a rigid and retentive society as opposed to a permissive and expressive one. So I think we are talking about differences in philosophy, not about any empirical assessment of whether there has been a diminution in participation.

Ronald Reagan is not an economist, he's a political philosopher. He wishes to reduce severely the role of the domestic government. He wishes to exert downward pressure on spending. Basically, democratic liberals are people who want to use other people's money to do good deeds. I could put it more positively. They wish to use the collective public weal to improve the lot of disadvantaged people. Reagan wants to leave the money in taxpayers' hands so they can do good as they see it. Is it more participative to do good as the collective sees it or to do good as individuals see it? When you answer that question, you've decided, not only whether there is more or less participation, but whether you like it or not.

**Lowi:** I would hate to see Professor Wolin's argument ride on the analysis of the radicalism of Reagan on a participatory question. It doesn't loom all that large in my understanding of his essay. It is a true issue and I think Professor Wildavsky aggrandized it by picking up on that. I simply want to say, rather than to answer him directly on whether Reagan has narrowed or expanded participation because he is correct, it's a matter of what you define as participation and what its forms are. They could both be right, in a sense. But I'd like to suggest something more important in Wolin's argument than that which I pick up on in my own essay. What is important here is what Reagan has done in contributing to state power. It is not only a quantum increase in the amount of public power, whether it's the power of the states or the power of the state, but also in what form and in whose hands it occurs. I think, first of all, the case can be very clearly made that Reagan has contributed to a net increase in the total amount of public power rather than to a decrease. (This has nothing to do with whether there has been an increase or decrease in participation. Having been in Korea last October, I was terribly impressed by the tremendous increase there is in economic participation. You've never seen anything in the United States to equal the amount of vigor and free enterprise. But you don't have to talk to the Koreans very long to know that participation is very different within a political context. There isn't everyday oppression, but everybody knows what the limits are. But that still leaves us with high economic participation.) Now let me give a couple of examples. Let's look at the nature of the regime itself. Not only is the addition to Defense Department spending a grievous amount in my opinion, but a great increase, objectively speaking, in state power. Another example is the deficit. You don't just have a deficit—you *manage* a deficit. That ever-increasing deficit has to be managed by somebody in the Treasury Department. If that's not an increase in state power, I don't know what is. And it's invisible. I don't know if Professor Wildavsky, who watches these things more closely than the rest of us do, can tell us just how they are doing it, how different it is, which banks are getting it, or whatever, but I know somebody has to do it somehow.

Another example is the question of abortion and the other sort of privacy values, which for some, as indicated in Professor Sorensen's essay, would require an increase in freedom while others feel it is a great infringement. Either way I can tell you that it amounts to a reassertion of moral hegemony of public authority over individuals. It is true we had abortion and statutes before; but, one, they were obsolescent, and two, they were highly inconsistently administered, which resulted in much known abuse and many violations. What if a constitutional amendment is passed reempowering the states to do what they had the power to do before *Roe v. Wade*? Assume then that some states would pass an abortion statute that would give us the kind of moral basis for freedom that Professor Sorensen talks about. Imagine the requirements of implementing that. As Professor Gawthrop says, policy doesn't mean too much until it starts to be implemented. Just imagine the implementation. First and foremost it means that every pregnant woman is in jeopardy to the state. And every pregnant woman who has a miscarriage must be the subject of interrogation, because it's quite possible, quite probable, that she's guilty of criminal negligence. Take the pregnant middle-class lady in her tennis outfit sitting at lunch at the country club complaining "I needed this fourth kid like I need a hole in the head." She's just making a comment that somebody hears. She goes out on the tennis court and later has a miscarriage. Don't tell me that you can let her go without an interrogation as to whether she is guilty of murder. All I'm trying to say is, that's participation. That may be her right to have or not to have. If that's a decrease in state power I'd like to know what an increase is.

**Fiss:** I'm very sympathetic with Professor Wolin's perspective. No one would defend the reenactment of abortion laws as a reduction of state power. It would be acknowledged as an enhancement of state power for certain moral purposes. The interesting claim in Professor Wolin's essay has to do not so much with examples like that, or even the Defense Department or the budget or the deficit. The interesting claim relates to the *relocation* of power, as in the case of privatizing hospitals or prisons. I agree with him that the relocation of power doesn't necessarily result in the reduction of power, but I don't see any basis so far in what Professor Wolin has given us to believe that the relocation is necessarily an enhancement of power. His sentence reads, "Most contracts regulating private operators of hospitals or prisons, for example, enable public authorities to set standards and to enforce compliance. Thus, voluntarism does not presage a freer society but, on the contrary, a more controlled one." I don't think that that case has been made convincingly. It may be that the relocation or the reorganization of the forms of state power doesn't reduce power; but, on the other hand, I don't think it necessarily enhances power. I'm not quite sure whether the enhancement of effectiveness is the same thing as the enhancement of the repressiveness that you're talking about. I think we should be a little more careful there.

**Wolin:** I think you've put a finger on a problem in my essay, but, I guess, like anyone caught short I have an answer. The answer is contained in an essay on the welfare state which will be published soon. There I have developed the notion that the central political category now is not the state; rather, it is the political economy. The political economy stands for a structure of power that includes the state but is not exhausted by the state; it includes state corporate relationships primarily. Enforcement of contracts and the takeover of public functions by private agencies shouldn't be looked at within the context of the old public-private distinction. What we're dealing with here is a network of new relationships that have been emerging, relationships that the old terms cannot adequately describe.

# V

# THE NEW PROCEDURE

★

## *Owen M. Fiss*

R ights are not premises, but conclusions. They emerge through a process of trying to give concrete meaning and expression to the values embodied in an authoritative legal text. The Constitution is the great public text of modern America, and adjudication is the preeminent—though perhaps not the exclusive—process by which the values embodied in that text are given meaning. Adjudication is an interpretive process through which rights are created and enforced.

In my judgment, this has always been the function of adjudication clearly embraced and legitimated by Article III of the Constitution and continuous with the role of courts under the common law, but within recent decades a new form of constitutional adjudication has emerged. It is largely defined by two characteristics: first, an awareness that the basic threat to our constitutional values is posed not by individuals but by the operation of large-scale organizations, the bureaucracies of the modern state; and second, the realization that only the restructuring of these institutions will eliminate the threats to constitutional values. For this complex task the traditional legal remedies—the damage judgment and the criminal prosecution—are inadequate. The injunction is the favored remedy, though it is used not as a device for stopping some discrete act, as it might have been in other times, but as the formal medium through which the judge directs the reconstruction of an ongoing bureaucratic organization.

*Owen Fiss is the Alexander M. Bickel Professor of Public Law at Yale University.*

This new procedure, which I call "structural reform," emerged as a distinctive form of constitutional litigation largely in response to *Brown v. Board of Education*[1] and the special imperatives of school desegregation. Its scope was broadened in the late 1960s and early 1970s; it was then used to test the practices of a wide variety of state agencies—the police, prisons, mental hospitals, institutions for the mentally retarded, prosecutors, public housing authorities, and public employers. The scope of structural reform became as broad as the modern state itself. By the late 1970s, however, history took a different turn. In cases such as *Rizzo v. Goode*,[2] structural reform came under attack, and today its legitimacy is being questioned with an energy and an urgency that are indeed remarkable.[3] This questioning is not confined to structural reform, or for that matter, any particular mode of adjudication, but extends to the 1960s in general and the conception of state power implied by those times.

## DISPUTE RESOLUTION AND STRUCTURAL REFORM

The distinctive features of structural reform can best be understood by contrasting it with a model of adjudication that has long dominated the literature and is often used as the standard for judging the legitimacy of all forms of adjudication. This model, called "dispute resolution," is associated with a story of two people in the state of nature who each claim a single piece of property. They discuss the problem, reach an impasse, and then turn to a third party, the stranger, to resolve their dispute. Courts are viewed as the institutionalization of this stranger and adjudication as the process through which he exercises his judicial power.[4] Although this story is used not as an argument for the primacy of dispute resolution but only as an illustration, it does in fact reflect the various premises that inform that model and that are challenged by structural reform.[5]

### The Absence of a Sociology

Dispute resolution is sociologically impoverished. There is no room in the story for the social entities, such as the inmates of a prison or patients in a hospital have, that are so familiar to contemporary litigation and are a part of our reality. Nor is there any recognition of the existence of groups, like racial minorities or the handicapped, whose interests and identity transcend any particular institution. And no account is taken of the bureaucratic organizations such as the public school system, the prison, the mental hospital, or the housing authority that play such a prominent part in contemporary litigation. The world of dispute resolution is composed exclusively of individuals.

The party structure of the dispute resolution lawsuit reflects this individualistic bias; one neighbor is pitted against another while the judge stands between them as a passive umpire. The structural lawsuit defies this triadic form. What we find in structural litigation is an array of competing interests and perspectives organized around a single decisional agency, the judge. This complex configuration can be traced to two facts. First, the social groups or organizations denominated parties are likely to be internally divided over the issues being adjudicated. It is unlikely that all the members of a group or organization will view in the same way the issue at stake in the litigation. Second, the court must often create auxiliary structures to correct the representational imperfections that naturally arise in such situations. Special masters and litigating amici are typically appointed by the court in structural suits and one of their duties is representational:[6] They are to present views that otherwise might be slighted by those who purport to speak on behalf of the groups or organizations that are officially denominated as the parties.

In addition to altering party structure, the introduction of sociological entities complicates the remedial process. In dispute resolution, an individual is both the victim and spokesperson and also the beneficiary of a court decree; but in the structural suit, the victim and beneficiary are social groups. The judge must determine whether the victim and beneficiary groups should be coextensive and what criteria should be used for determining which individuals are to be included within those groups. Similarly, the bureaucratic character of the defendant forces the judge to move beyond the traditional universe of remedies. A remedy such as the issuance of a narrow injunction addressed to some identifiable individuals and aimed at prohibiting some specific act is unlikely to be efficacious, precisely because bureaucracies tend to diffuse responsibility and acquire a life or momentum of their own. Only restructuring those organizations will remove the threat they pose to our values. Restructuring an organization is a complex and difficult task; it requires a measure of activity on the part of the judge that is at odds with the picture of him as a passive umpire, simply choosing between the two neighbors. In the structural suit the judge becomes the manager of a reconstructive enterprise.

## Private Ends

In the hypothetical state of nature, where the dispute resolution takes place, there are no public values, only the private desires of individuals—in this instance, the desire for property. Peace is a public value, but only insofar as it is a precondition of satisfying private ends. The story postulates that the judge (the stranger) settles a property dispute between neighbors, but it does not tell us how he resolves it, only that it is resolved. The judge may resolve the dispute according to any procedure that will minimize disputes or, more generally, maximize the satisfaction of private ends.

Structural litigation does not begin with an indifference toward public values or ignorance of them. It insists that there is more to our public life than peace. Structural reform proceeds within the framework of a constitution; and the constitution that stands vindicated by a case like *Brown v. Board of Education* is one that does far more than simply establish a form of government. It identifies a set of values—equality, liberty, no cruel and unusual punishment, due process, property, security of the person, freedom to speak, to mention just a few—that inform and limit the activities of the state. As a national charter, the Constitution constitutes the morality that gives our society its inner coherence or identity and serves as the substantive foundation of structural litigation. The very point of the structural suit is to protect our public values from the threats of the bureaucratic state.

In the dispute resolution story, the judge stands neutral between what are seen to be the private ends of the feuding neighbors. He is to be fair and impartial in enforcing the established rules, much as an umpire must be, but that is the limit of his commitment. In a structural suit, on the other hand, the judge is confronted with a claim that public values are being threatened, and the judge's commitment to those values supplements his commitment to procedural fairness. The judge is devoted to serving public values and thus is unwilling to rely wholly on the initiatives and strategies of the various parties, which invariably reflect their private motives and limitations. The judge is asked to abandon the posture of passivity and to take an active role in the proceedings, to make certain that the facts and the law are fully presented and that the defendant complies with whatever decree may be entered.

## Natural Harmony

A third supposition of the dispute resolution story, reflecting either its individualism or its indifference to public values, is that without the intervention of courts or other government agencies, society is in a state of natural harmony. As suggested by the concept of a "dispute" itself, the story assumes that the subject of adjudication—the feud between the neighbors—is an abnormal event that disrupts an otherwise satisfactory world. The story also suggests that the function of adjudication is to restore the status quo; it is to end the feud and to allow the neighbors to go on living as they had in the past. On the other hand, because it is committed to public values and recognizes the imbalances of social power possessed by various groups and organizations, structural reform does not assume a natural harmony. It is premised on a certain skepticism about the justness of the status quo; perhaps neither neighbor is entitled to the property.

This skepticism helps to explain two features of the structural model. One concerns the requirements for initiating a lawsuit, which have become less exacting: In a structural suit, it is unnecessary for the plaintiff to be fully informed of the facts before filing the suit; and once the suit is filed, far-reaching discovery mechanisms become available, not simply to facilitate an exchange of information, but to allow the plaintiff to investigate and substantiate his claim. Discovery is seen as the poor man's FBI. Doctrines concerning standing have also become more permissive and objections based on mootness less decisive. The need for judicial intervention is no longer seen as an aberration, and procedural rules that require the plaintiff to be personally aggrieved and to present an actual controversy have been adjusted to facilitate that intervention. In this way, the foundation for the private attorney general concept has been laid and it too can be seen as an integral part of the structural model.

Second, doubts about the justness of the status quo explain the ambitious nature of the remedial process. The goal of dispute resolution is to set things back to "normal"; the imagined remedy is short and discrete, because it seeks to repair or reestablish the world that existed before the dispute. This is not, however, the aim of the structural suit. It seeks to create a new status quo. Restructuring a prison or a school system cannot be understood as an attempt to return to a world that existed before some dispute arose; it must instead be seen as an attempt to construct a new social reality, one that will be more nearly in accord with our constitutional ideals. This reconstructive process is long and arduous, often proceeding through a series of orders that become more and more specific, and the court's jurisdictions will last as long as is necessary to bring this process to completion—sometimes indefinitely.

### Isolation of the Judiciary

The dispute resolution story depicts the judiciary as an isolated institution. The courts are not viewed as an integral part of government. The quarreling neighbors ask a stranger—any stranger—to resolve their dispute. This mythical account of the process by which courts are created thus implies that courts can be understood apart from the larger system of government. It also suggests that the legitimacy of the judiciary derives from the consent of the citizenry and that this consent is institution-specific. The neighbors agree to take the dispute to the stranger and to abide by his decision.

In modern society, this method of conferring authority on the judiciary is impossible to imagine, but the consensual foundation of judicial power is nevertheless preserved through more subtle forms. Professor Lon Fuller, for example, tries to found the authority of adjudication on the individual's right to participate in that process. Participation supplants agreement but the thrust is still individualistic and consensual. According to Fuller, the right of the individual to participate in adjudication is the source of judicial authority, just as the right to vote legitimates legislation and the right to bargain legitimates contracts.[7] Other scholars, reflecting the *Carolene Products* tradition, have attempted to found the judicial authority on the ability of courts to protect the disenfranchised and powerless in their political struggles.[8] These scholars see the judiciary as an institution dedicated to perfecting those processes through which American society collectively consents to the action of its government.

In my view, courts should be viewed not in isolation but as a coordinate source of government power and as a part of the larger political system. Democracy does in fact commit us to see popular consent as the foundation of government, but that consent is not granted separately to individual institutions. It extends to the system of governance as a whole. Although the legitimacy of the American political system depends on the people's consent, the legitimacy of a particular institution within the system does not depend on popular consent, either in the individualized sense suggested by Fuller or in the more collective sense suggested by the *Carolene Products* tradition. Rather, the legitimacy of a particular institution stems from its capacity to perform a distinctive social function within the larger political system. The power that judges exercise in structural reform, or, for that matter, in any type of litigation, is not founded on consent, but on their competence to perform a distinctive social function, which is, as I have suggested, to give concrete meaning and expression to the public values embodied in authoritative legal texts.

It is not at all necessary, when speaking of this special competence of the judiciary, to ascribe to judges the wisdom of philosopher-kings. The capacity of judges to understand and interpret public values turns not on some personal moral expertise, of which they have none, but upon the process that limits their exercise of power and constitutes the authoritative method for construing a public morality. One feature of that process is dialogue: Judges must listen to all grievances, hear a wide range of interests, speak back, and assume individual responsibility for what they say. Another feature of the judicial process is independence: Judges must remain independent of the desires or preferences both of the body politic and of the particular contestants before the bench. Other agencies may engage in dialogue and also may achieve a measure of political independence, and thus claim a right to construe the public morality, but these processes—dialogue and independence—preeminently and traditionally have been identified with the judiciary. They are the source of the judiciary's claim to a special competence and the foundation of its authority.

In this scheme, the need for popular consent to the existence of a specific institution or its action is minimized. The people's consent is required to legitimate the larger political system, and thus the people must be able to respond to judicial decisions—for example, through constitutional amendments or through new appointments—in order to preserve the consensual character of the system as a whole. But a tighter, more particularized dependence of the judiciary on popular consent would destroy its independence and thus its competence to speak the law.

## THE CRISIS OF LEGITIMACY

The dispute resolution model is at odds with the social and political reality of modern society, and yet it has rebounded from relative invisibility in the 1960s to enjoy a renewed popularity in the late 1970s and 1980s. Structural reform is under attack. This development cannot be attributed to the rather banal poetry of the dispute resolution story or even to some nostalgic longing it may evoke for an oversimplified world. Nor can it be attributed to the fortuities of politics or the character of judicial appointments over the past decade. The causes of the crisis are, I fear, much deeper.

### Instrumental Failures

Many are disappointed in the results of structural reform: It had promised to desegregate the schools, to civilize the prisons, and to curb police brutality, yet many of these promises have gone unfulfilled.[9] And this disappointment has led some to question the legitimacy of structural reform, just as the failure of the Great Society to achieve all it promised has led to a decade of national politics in which both parties dedicated themselves to dismantling "big government."

Disappointment is a function of expectations and the expectations that fuel this particular reaction to structural reform strike me as unrealistic. Success is not perfection, surely not within the relatively short period of time within which structural reform has had to work. The dual school system is the product of a deeply entrenched political and social tradition—almost one century of Jim Crow and another of slavery—and it would be close to a miracle if the legacy of racism could be fully eradicated within a decade or two. The brutality of prisons has an even deeper history—and so on: The problems posed by the bureaucracies of the modern state are almost intractable. In evaluating the performance of institutions—particularly nongovernmental ones—we have learned to adjust our expectations to account for the difficulty of the task they undertake. The judiciary is entitled to this same indulgence.

Of course, even after our expectations have been adjusted, a question might still arise as to whether the achievements of structural reform have been sufficient. I believe they have been; "disaster by decree"[10] has occurred, but in my judgment it has been the exception rather than the rule. I also believe that no other institution would have been more successful in protecting our public values from the threats of the bureaucratic state. The empirical evidence upon which these beliefs depend cannot fairly be presented in this setting, much less analyzed.[11] But some perspectives on these issues can be gained simply by asking whether there is any reason for assuming that the judiciary will be less successful in these reform measures than some other institution might have been. I think there is not.

Admittedly, the judiciary is disabled in the remedial enterprise, because it does not have control over the purse, and because it is constrained by professional norms requiring it to remain independent of politics; desegregating an urban school system will require millions and million of dollars and the goodwill and cooperation of the citizenry that can only come from "playing politics." But what appears, from a purely remedial perspective, as a disability is, from a rights perspective, a special source of strength. Independence may disable the judiciary in its remedial efforts, but it is the reason why we trust the judiciary to interpret the values embodied in authoritative legal texts and to turn them into rights. Maybe a "sensitive" and "deft" politician can get more people to do what he wants than a judge could, but the politician is also likely to want less.

For these reasons, I find the instrumental critique of structural reform to be unpersuasive; success rather than failure is the term I would tend to use to characterize the record, especially when compared to what other institutions might have accomplished and when proper account is taken of the magnitude of the task and the relatively short time within which the courts have been at work. Some may disagree with this assessment, or with my general perspective on these issues, but even then, I wonder whether the postulated disappointments about outcomes can throw the legitimacy of this model of adjudication into doubt. Legitimacy has more to do with authority than with success. Legitimacy is a matter of integrity. People might be disappointed in the outcomes of litigation, but that does not necessarily mean they believe the judges betrayed their trust and acted illegitimately. The authority of the judiciary to do what it is doing in schools or prisons does not turn on the success of its intervention, but rather on the quality of the process upon which the interaction is based, on the willingness of the judiciary both to engage in a dialogue on the meaning of public values and to remain independent from the parties and the body politic.

Indeed, I would go one step further—not only am I reluctant to turn disappointments about outcomes into doubts about legitimacy, but even more, it seems to me that the relationship between remedial efficacy and institutional legitimacy might be just the opposite of that assumed by the instrumental critique. A blind commitment to remedial efficacy—a preoccupation with the how questions and disregard for the limitations of the judicial office—might jeopardize rather than enhance judicial authority. To make a desegregation plan work, for example, the judge most certainly needs the cooperation of parents, teachers, administrators, and legislators, and as a consequence there is also a danger that the judge may begin to bargain, negotiate, or play "politics" with these parties in order to win their cooperation. He may temper his idealism. He may insist on less so as to get something, and when he does, he will undermine his authority. A judge should be admired for his effort to narrow the gap between constitutional ideals and social reality, but he must at the same time recognize the limits of his office and the tools at his disposal.

## The Bureaucratization of the Judiciary

The history of the twentieth century is one of increasing bureaucratization. All forms of power, both public and private, have become bureaucratized, and the judiciary is no exception. When the charge of bureaucratization is levelled at the judiciary, however, the complaint is not the familiar one of excessive rigidity—that an official has become a slave to general rules—for the rule of law requires judges to adhere to general rules. The complaint is instead about the fragmentation of the judicial power and the delegation of judicial duties, both of which tend to diffuse responsibility and insulate the judge from critical educational experiences. The danger is that adjudication will become rule by nobody.[12]

The bureaucratization of the judiciary is not especially tied to structural reform. It is a function of the growing size and complexity of American life, which increases caseloads and makes information, both of a legal and factual nature, more and more difficult to process. Judges would have turned to auxiliary personnel, such as law clerks, and brought them into the decisional process even if they had never heard of structural reform and were simply resolving disputes. Bureaucratization is caused by modernization, not structural reform. There are, however, several aspects of structural reform that aggravate the tendencies toward bureaucratization and that might be seen to constitute a further reason for turning away from it as a model of adjudication. These tendencies can be seen more clearly by examining the practice of many judges to appoint special masters in structural cases—a practice that exemplifies both the achievements of the new procedure and another of its dangers.

As I noted earlier, sometimes a special master is appointed to perfect the representational structure. The judge treats the special master as a party, something like an amicus, though not tied to any identifiable set of interests. The dysfunctions associated with bureaucratization do not arise from this limited practice, but only when the judge goes one step further and delegates to the special master some of his, the judge's, duties. Such delegation occurs, for example, when the judge appoints a special master to conduct an evidentiary hearing, or to dispose of some particular substantive issue; or when the special master is asked to formulate a remedy and convince the parties to accept it; or when the special master is charged with the duty of monitoring the defendant's performance and determining whether there is compliance with the decree.

Delegation of this kind is attributable to a number of factors.

One is the sheer complexity of the case. All modern cases are complex, but a structural one is especially so. It requires the judge to inquire into the operation of a large-scale bureaucratic organization and, if need be, to reorganize it. The volume of detail in such an undertaking is staggering, and the judge may well not have either the patience or the time for it. Second, there may be an unusual need for specialized knowledge; for example, knowledge about how the bureaucratic organization in question works and interacts with its environment. The judge might hope to satisfy this need by appointing as special masters persons with some special background or experience in these matters. Third, the judge might also see the special master as someone who might engage in certain kinds of activities that he, the judge, is denied. An example of such an activity would be meeting the parties one at a time, and off the record, in an effort to convince them to accept the proposed remedy.[13] Such discrete emissaries might always be desired, but they are especially so in the structural context, since the remedy is so ambitious and so dependent on the good will and cooperation of innumerable persons. Finally, the judge might use the special master as a "lightning rod," that is, as a way of deflecting responsibility from himself for the controversy likely to be engendered by the comprehensive and far-reaching quality of the proposed reform.

Obviously, some of the above reasons for delegating power are more appropriate and more acceptable than others, but whatever the reasons, the danger is the same: The judge is dividing his responsibility and insulating himself (to varying degrees) from the presentation of the facts and the law. Such delegation will not compromise judicial independence (in fact, it might have the opposite effect, since it gives the judge the organizational resources necessary to free himself from a dependency on the political branches), but it may well interfere with the quality of the judicial dialogue. It creates the risk that the judge's signature is but a sham. He may not have listened to the grievances, nor decided the issue, nor chosen the remedy, nor even given the reasons for his decision. In such delegation, the judge may well be violating that elemental principle of judicial authority that requires, as Chief Justice Hughes put it, "The one who decides must hear."[14]

Bureaucratization in contrast to the instrumental failures

might thus be a genuine source of the crisis of legitimacy of structural reform. It would be a mistake, however, to assume that it requires a rejection of the structural model or even that judges can never call upon special masters or other auxiliary personnel to assist in the discharge of their duties. Some of the needs that led to these appointments are quite genuine. What is called for instead is a measure of caution and, even more to the point, a rule that would make the appointment of auxiliary personnel, such as a special master, a matter of last recourse. The judge should be required to explore alternatives before turning to special masters. The appointment of amici, for example, might meet the unusual representational needs of structural litigation, and yet avoid the bureaucratic dangers entailed in using a special master. In a similar fashion, expert witnesses might be used to meet the special informational needs of structural litigation. Neither the amici nor the expert witness will shield the judge from responsibility for his decision, or allow him to get rid of unwanted tasks, but that is how it should be and that is exactly why these organizational forms should be preferred.

Moreover, even when the judge must appoint a special master, and exercise this power of last resort, care must be taken to avoid delegation. These auxiliary personnel must be seen as part of the judge's staff, to assist him in the discharge of his duties, not as a means of ridding the judge of certain unwanted and difficult duties. Auxiliary personnel must not be given the power to decide; and in reviewing their work, the judge must avoid the "rubber stamp." He must keep auxiliary personnel under his immediate and direct supervision. Such a rule is, of course, almost impossible to police: It can only be understood by the judge as an ideal of his calling, and even then, it might not altogether avoid the diffusion of responsibility and bureaucratic insularity that threaten the legitimacy of the judicial enterprise. But such a rule does make clear that the principal source of the problem is not the new procedure, not the structural model itself, but the unwillingness of the judge to do all that his job requires.

## The Privatization of Ends

The instrumental critique can be answered by adjusting our expectations; the bureaucratic critique can be answered by making changes in organizational format. Structural reform confronts another challenge, however, and it is, I am afraid, less amenable to such easy prescription. It arises from the fact that we no longer believe that there exists a body of public values that are to be interpreted and protected by the judiciary. All values are privatized. Individual preferences and interests seem to exhaust our sense of values. In such a setting there is little point to structural reform, since its mission is to give expression to public values and to protect those values from bureaucratic threats.

My account of adjudication is premised on the view that courts are a coordinate branch of government, and, thus, it is no surprise that the crisis of legitimacy affecting the judiciary is affecting all forms of government power. We saw this in analyzing the instrumental and bureaucratic critiques and it appears once again here. Just as the privatization of ends has left structural adjudication without much of a purpose, it has also affected our general conception of state power. We live in an age in which all forms of government power are experiencing a crisis of legitimacy, and to a large extent this crisis can be traced to the privatization of ends.

I find it significant that the story of the two neighbors struggling over a piece of property takes place in the state of nature, because it was there that the classical liberals founded the state. It was there that the social contract was formed. Like dispute resolution, social contract theory lacks a sociology; it assumes ends are private, in that power is legitimated through individualized consent, and postulates, at least in Locke's version, that natural harmony generally prevails. The chief end of the state in the social contract tradition is security: to develop those conditions that will allow private persons to engage in commerce and to satisfy their own desires. The conception of government enshrined in social contract theory and preeminent in America through much of the nineteenth century—the so-called night-watchman state[15]—is the analogue to the limited conception of judicial power implied by the dispute resolution model. It too is aimed at keeping the peace.

In the twentieth century, particularly in the decades since the New Deal and World War II, America saw the emergence of a different kind of state altogether. The state was no longer a night watchman but became an active participant in social life, supplying essential services and structuring the very terms of our existence. To legitimate this conception of government power, we had to develop a theory of consent radically different from the individualistic, unanimous consent exalted by the social contract tradition. We also had to develop a conception of social life sufficiently rich and purposive to render intelligible the pervasive and continuous interventions of the state. This was the achievement of the 1960s.

The emergence of the activist state during the sixties parallels the emergence of the new form of litigation that I have called structural reform. Indeed, one can go further and identify a common theoretical foundation for both the activist state and structural reform in much the same way that we identified a common theoretical foundation for dispute resolution and the limited state of classical liberalism. Both structural reform and the activist state take account of sociological realities, both reflect a skepticism about the justness of the status quo, and both contemplate a pervasive and continuous use of government power. Both are grounded in a belief in the existence and importance of public values and a recognition of the need to translate those values into social reality through the use of public power.

Equality was the centerpiece of the litigation of the sixties and the guiding ideal of the legislative and executive programs of that era. It also had a representative significance: It stood for an entire way of looking at social life. Equality denoted a sphere of values that are truly public—values that define our society and give it an inner coherence and are not reducible to an aggregation of private ends. Rights were not seen as entitlements that devolved on us simply by virtue of our status as "persons," but as the concrete embodiment of these public values. Rights were seen as an expression of our communality rather than our individuality.

Today, we feel increasing doubts about that entire way of looking at our social life, and we are witnessing the resurgence of dispute resolution and the night-watchman state as an expression of those doubts. When all ends are private, only dispute resolution and the night watchman make much sense. Structural reform and the activist state become suspect. They contemplate an affirmative use of government power to explicate and protect public values and are experiencing a crisis of legitimacy precisely because we doubt the very existence of those values. We have lost that vision of American social life that appreciates the importance of the public in our individual lives, and as a consequence we tend to deny or distrust all those forms of power that seek to pursue public ends.

I do not know how the public vision can be recovered, or even why we lost it. An understanding of the linkage that I have drawn between the two models of adjudication and broader conceptions of state power will not end the crisis. It does reveal, however, the urgency of the intellectual task we confront. It suggests that what is at issue when we speak of the crisis of structural reform is not simply the validity of a new model of adjudication, which might seem to some to be an arcane and highly technical subject; what is at issue is instead a general conception of government power. An account of the new procedure that links it to the activist state also suggests that the solution to the crisis of legitimacy is not to be found in the law itself, but rather in our capacity to generate a new social vision. The struggle between dispute resolution and structural reform is ultimately a struggle between the private and the public; and the outcome of that struggle will turn on our capacity to understand, as we did not too long ago, that our individual identity and well-being are vitally dependent on all that we have in common.

# Notes

1. 347 U.S. 483 (1954); 349 U.S. 294 (1955).

2. 423 U.S. 362 (1976).

3. See, for example, *Los Angeles v. Lyons,* 461 U.S. 95 (1983).

4. See, for example, Martin M. Shapiro, *The Courts: A Comparative and Political Analysis* (Chicago: University of Chicago Press, 1981).

5. For the presentation of a structural case in all its detail, and for a listing of the literature this model has generated over the past decade, see Owen M. Fiss and Doug Rendleman, *Injunctions,* 2d ed. (Mineola, N.Y.: Foundation Press, 1984), 528–830.

6. Geoffry F. Aronow, "The Special Master in School Desegregation Cases," *Hastings Constitutional Law Quarterly* 7 (Spring 1980): 739–75.

7. Lon L. Fuller, "The Forms and Limits of Adjudication," *Harvard Law Review* 92 (December 1978): 353–409. A more extended response to Professor Fuller's account can be found in my essay, "The Forms of Justice," *Harvard Law Review* 93 (November 1979): 1–58.

8. John H. Ely, *Democracy and Distrust: A Theory of Judicial Review* (Cambridge: Harvard University Press, 1980).

9. See, for example, Donald Horowitz, *The Courts and Social Policy* (Washington, D.C.: The Brookings Institution, 1977).

10. The phrase is taken from Lino A. Graglia's book, *Disaster by Decree: The Supreme Court Decisions on Race and Schools* (Ithaca, N.Y.: Cornell University Press, 1976).

11. For an analysis of the desegregation process which suggests it is far from a disaster, see Jennifer L. Hochschild, *The New American Dilemma: Liberal Democracy and School Desegregation* (New Haven: Yale University Press, 1984).

12. These issues are addressed more fully in a recently published essay of mine, "The Bureaucratization of the Judiciary," *Yale Law Journal* 92 (July 1983): 1442–68.

13. See, for example, Curtis J. Berger, "Away from the Court House and into the Field: The Odyssey of a Special Master," *Columbia Law Review* 78 (May 1978): 707–38.

14. *United States v. Morgan,* 298 U.S. 468, 481 (1936).

15. The phrase is from Robert Nozick, *Anarchy, State and Utopia* (New York: Basic Books, 1974).

# VI

# THE REGULATION OF MEDIATING STRUCTURES

★

## Bruce C. Hafen

I have been thinking the last few years about a declining, if not vanishing, breed among American institutions: the private, church-related college. In addition to serving recently as the president of such a college, I have been interested in the implications for private higher education of legislation introduced in Congress in 1984 and 1985 in reaction to the Supreme Court's 1984 decision in the case of *Grove City College v. Bell*.

The desire of a college such as Grove City to remain independent of governmental control can apparently be perceived to stem from a desire to avoid public disclosure of some inappropriate activity, such as sex discrimination. This puzzles me, since there was no finding of sex discrimination in the *Grove City College* case, nor has there been new evidence of sex discrimination on other campuses in recent years.

I wish to step back from the particular issues raised by *Grove City* long enough to suggest a perspective at the level of constitutional theory and public policy analysis. These comments are in the nature of a preliminary hypothesis and are subject to considerable further research and refinement. In general, however, I hope

*Bruce Hafen is dean and professor of law at the J. Reuben Clark Law School at Brigham Young University.*

to sketch some possible outlines of a pattern for understanding the purpose and constitutional place of certain unique private American institutions which help individuals find and nurture personal meaning and value in their lives. Private colleges are merely an illustration of these institutions. I hope also to suggest why the viability of these institutions is undermined by certain current legal and policy trends. I will then attempt to put the current civil rights legislative proposals into that larger context.

Professor Owen Fiss has written recently about the need for what he calls "structural reform" in certain of our institutions, especially governmental bureaucracies. The kind of reform Professor Fiss has in mind is directed by judges, who have a special responsibility under our constitutional system for defining and giving voice to the values of the Constitution. An example of structural reform is school desegregation, in which the courts have "penetrated and restructured" our public school system. This bold innovation led to the creation of new ideas and procedures, both organizationally and legally, because the implementation of the judicial mandates often required lengthy and complex supervision. Desegregation became "a total transformational process in which the judge undertook the reconstruction of an ongoing social institution," rather than merely resolving a dispute between two individual litigants. This process was driven by "the overriding commitment to racial equality," a constitutional value of such importance that it necessitated profound changes.[1]

Similar structural reforms have been undertaken in recent years in such institutions as prisons and mental hospitals, where violations of personal constitutional rights have been found on such a large scale that only a reform of the organizational structure itself would remedy existing wrongs. Professor Fiss believes similar reforms may be needed in such bureaucratic organizations as public housing authorities, welfare departments, taxing authorities, police departments, and state-owned industries. In effectuating reforms of this kind, judges "can articulate and elaborate the meaning of our constitutional values," according to Fiss, because the judiciary is in the best position "among all the agencies of government . . . to discover the true meaning of our constitutional values." For Fiss, this judicial responsibility is "the meaning-giving enterprise implicit in constitutionalism itself."[2]

I am intrigued by the use of such terms and concepts as "structure" and "meaning-giving" in this analysis, because they serve as an important touchstone for the analysis of another kind of organization, for the most part outside the governmental sphere, which is involved in a significant though different part of the "meaning-giving enterprise" within our democratic system. To introduce my description of these other organizations, I make two observations about the Fiss theory. First, in his discussion of structural reform, he carefully limits himself to agencies of government. There could obviously be similar reforms in nongovernmental agencies, but when such reform is based upon constitutional values, it is likely to be limited by the state action doctrine. The institutions that interest me today are not state agencies and for that reason are subject to different constitutional constraints from those that apply to the state. Second, the constitutional values which Professor Fiss identifies as important to structural reform are primarily process-oriented values designed to limit the power of the state in its interaction with individual citizens: "liberty, equality, due process, freedom of speech, no establishment of religion," and the like.[3]

These process-oriented values define the terms on which the state must deal with its citizens. They also seek to assure each individual citizen the governmental protection and the freedom necessary for his or her own pursuit of personal meaning and fulfillment in life. But, under our theory of constitutional democracy, the state is not the source of the substantive values that give meaning to individual lives. Indeed, the state is discouraged by such basic doctrines as the separation of church and state from establishing official value positions. Thus the guarantees of the Bill of Rights provide procedures and protections which are but a means toward the end of personal self-determination. By contrast, a totalitarian state gladly and aggressively assumes the role of imposing on all its citizens "one comprehensive order of meaning."[4] Among the most reprehensible characteristics of a totalitarian society is that the state denies its citizens the opportunity of pursuing their own sense of personal meaning and destiny as they may define it.

Yet the influence of our democratic state is so pervasive today that the process-oriented constitutional values that "inform and limit" the "governmental structure" are thought to be the "values that determine the quality of our social existence."[5] As a result, we actually live in something of a value vacuum. The "megastructures" of our society—which can include corporate conglomerates, large labor unions, and especially the governmental bureaucracies—have overpowering influence, and yet they do not typically seek to tell us what our lives really mean. In the case of governmental megastructures, our democratic theory discourages them from telling us. Moreover, corporate business enterprises are concerned primarily with economic activity. This activity obviously impacts its consumers and employees in non-economic ways, but the activity remains, in general, concerned more with means than with ends in the pursuit of personal meaning. Perhaps it is no wonder that modern society feels so much personal loneliness and alienation, as these vast, meaning-neutral agencies have grown to proportions of boundless influence at the very time when other large-scale forces have introduced widespread feelings of uncertainty and fear about both the meaning and the long-term security of our civilization.

Richard Neuhaus and Peter Berger have thoughtfully described the interactive relationship that exists between the public and private spheres. The personal, private sphere is where "meaning, fulfillment, and personal identity are to be realized" in one's life. The public sphere, which by their definition includes the institutions of the economic marketplace as well as the institutions of government, is made up of megastructures which are "typically alienating . . . [and] not helpful in providing meaning and identity for individual existence."[6] Standing between the individual and the megastructures are such "mediating structures" as families, churches, neighborhoods, and voluntary associations. These mediating structures have been called "the value-generating and value-maintaining agencies in society."[7]

For example, the family is "the major institution within the private sphere, and thus for many people the most valuable thing in their lives. Here they make their moral commitments, invest their emotions, [and] plan for the future."[8] Thus, the family interposes a significant legal entity between the individual and the state, where it performs a mediating as well as a value-generating function. We fully expect parents to inculcate in their children what we would not tolerate from the state; namely, the explicit transmission of intensely personal convictions about life and its meaning.

As part of this value-transmission role, parents have long enjoyed the constitutionally protected right to direct the upbringing of their children. Largely for this reason, the schools to which parents sent their children were traditionally regarded as "in loco parentis," meaning literally, in the place of the parents. In this sense, both private and public schools originally assumed a mediating structure role as extensions of the family.

In more recent years, the structural place of the public school system has become ambiguous. What is a public school today? Is it an extension of individual families and therefore part of the value-oriented private sphere? Or is it an extension of the state, which makes the public school part of the value-neutral megastructure? Clearly, the public schools today are by law and in practice primarily extensions of the governmentally sponsored megastructure. However, many parents and others still assume the public schools should play a value-transmission role more typical of a mediating structure. The reality is that public schools are now cast in both roles, with some segments of the public expecting them to be value-neutral while other segments expect them to take strong value-oriented positions. Such structural ambiguity has become the source of tension and ambivalence in the minds of teachers and administrators as well as in the public's perception.

This recent movement by the public schools away from the role of mediating structure toward the role of megastructure is actually quite typical of the way public perceptions and legal attitudes toward other mediating institutions have been changing. The momentum of the individual rights movement has placed such an emphasis on individual claims and needs that all institutions have become suspect, whether or not they are part of the constitutionally limited megastructures.

Consider in particular the emerging pattern that is being applied to that special cluster of institutions protected by the principles of the First Amendment, such as newspapers, universities, churches, and voluntary associations. These institutions suggest in contemporary terms what Tocqueville once called "the intellectual and moral associations of America," which he distinguished from the "political and industrial associations."[9] They give priority to such meaning-related values as free inquiry, public dialogue, artistic expression, intellectual discourse, personal religious discovery, and the building of associations that foster mediation between the individual and the all-powerful megastructures. Because of these roles, First Amendment institutions have traditionally enjoyed unusually protected status. The institutional protections are eroding, however, not because of a reduced commitment to First Amendment principles, but because those principles are seen primarily in individual as distinguished from institutional terms.

For example, one of the earliest and most celebrated descriptions of the concept of academic freedom as a constitutional principle was Justice Frankfurter's statement in the 1957 case of *Sweezy v. New Hampshire,*[10] which described academic freedom in institutional terms as the four essential freedoms of a university: who may teach, what may be taught, how it shall be taught, and who may be admitted to study. The Supreme Court relied on this language in its more recent *Bakke* case, which upheld a limited right for a university to establish admissions preferences for disadvantaged students.[11] In general, however, most academic freedom claims in recent years have been made by individual teachers and students against educational institutions. This is a perfectly understandable development, since school administrators may obviously violate individual free-speech rights. At the same time, the effect of this mounting series of cases is to cast in the role of the enemy the institutions whose very nature is bound up in the long-term nurturing of intellectual freedom. This view identifies colleges and universities more with the megastructures than with the meaning-oriented enterprise of mediation between individuals and the governmental megastructures.

My evidence for a similar change in emphasis in freedom of the press is primarily anecdotal at this stage. I was recently talking with a friend who has long been the publisher of a moderate-sized daily newspaper. He told me the newspaper business isn't what it used to be, primarily because of the constant difficulty he experiences with young journalists who are deeply committed to what he called "advocacy journalism." This attitude represents a commitment not only to investigative reporting, but to the idea that news reporting should promote causes the reporter believes in. My publisher friend said his cub reporters view the First Amendment as a personal protection, not only against governmental censorship, but against the contrary judgments of their publisher. This particular publisher considers their views wide of the mark, since he pays the bills and is held responsible for the content of the paper. Yet I think the reporters' attitudes more typically reflect contemporary assumptions.

I suspect the publishers of campus newspapers (which in most cases is the school administration) have had feelings similar to those of my publisher friend, as recent cases have established the First Amendment right of student writers and editors in public schools to print what they please, even if that means requiring the administration to fund a newspaper whose content it opposes.[12]

A similar dichotomy between individual and institutional First Amendment interests may be discerned in Supreme Court interpretations of the religion clauses. Even a representative treatment of this category must wait for another day, but the point can be illustrated by reference to Professor Mark Tushnet's observation about the impact of the liberal tradition on our understanding of the religion clauses. Tushnet believes the dominant influence of Protestantism in American society has given our view of the religion clauses a distinctly individualistic flavor, since Protestant theology typically emphasizes a direct connection between the individual and God. In the Catholic and Jewish traditions, by contrast, a greater role is played by institutional or tradition-laden communal forces.

This anti-institutional tendency is reinforced, in Tushnet's view, by the assumption of the liberal tradition that the free-market economy is most likely to flourish when personal economic decisions are made according to self-interest and without interference from such intermediate institutions as churches. The republican tradition, on the other hand, would allow more shaping of individual lives by the larger order, which creates more understanding of institutional religion. The ascendancy of the liberal tradition over the republican tradition in our history has therefore led to confusion about the meaning of religion as a category of constitutional interpretation.[13]

Another example of the shift away from protecting mediating institutions in favor of protecting individual claims may be found in changing attitudes toward the constitutional status of marriage and sexual privacy. Traditionally, the social and economic units created by formal marriage and kinship patterns were considered among the most fundamental structural building blocks of the society. As early as 1888, the Supreme Court described formal marriage as "the most important relation in life" and "the foundation of the family and of society, without which there would be neither civilization nor progress."[14] A family unit was thus seen as an entity, a mediating institution having even a political significance.

As described by the English writer D. H. Lawrence, "the marriage bond . . . is the fundamental connecting link in . . . society. Break it, and you will have to go back to the overwhelming dominance of the State. . . . Marriage has given man the best of his freedom, given him his little kingdom of his own within the big kingdom of the State, given him his foothold of independence on which to stand and resist an unjust State. Man and wife, a king and queen with one or two subjects, and a few square yards of territory of their own: this, really, is marriage. It is a true freedom."[15]

In recent years, however, the legal significance of formal marriage has diminished, as flexibility in creating and terminating intimate personal relationships has emerged as an important individual right. Not only has there been an increase in the number of cohabiting or other nontraditional relationships, but the very definition of the term "family" has become a subject of intense debate. In the 1980 White House Conference on the Family, for example, one delegate asked a regional session of the conference to define the family as "two or more persons who share resources, responsibility for decisions, values and goals, and have commitment to one another over time." This proposal lost by only two votes among 761 delegates.[16]

Professor Laurence Tribe foresees a coming liberation by the State of "the child—and the adult—from the shackles of such intermediate groups as the family." Tribe's commitment to individual autonomy as the supreme constitutional value moves him to advocate for each person a right of liberation "from domination by those closest to them" in the entity of the formal family, even though he also acknowledges in a vague and contradictory way the need for legal recognition of alternative relationships that "meet the human need for closeness, trust, and love" in the midst of "cultural disintegration and social transformation."[17] Under this highly individualistic view, the formal family unit is suspect for all the same reasons that the governmentally sponsored megastructures are suspect. Thus, all institutions, public or private, whether megastructures or mediating structures, are seen as the common enemy of individual rights. [18]

The tendency to lump all institutions together in this pejorative way not only obscures the general distinction between the public and private sector, it more specifically obscures the distinction between mediating structures (which should augment the development of self-identity and personal meaning) and megastructures (which should protect individual self-determination by maintaining a free environment). This obscurity has two adverse effects on the potentially positive—indeed the absolutely essential—influence of mediating structures. For one thing, it impairs the processes, relationships, and associations necessary to the long-term development of personal value systems. It also impairs the democratic framework itself. "Without institutionally reliable processes of mediation, the political order becomes detached from the values and realities of individual life. Deprived of its moral foundation, the political order is 'delegitimated.' When that happens, the political order must be secured by coercion rather than by consent. And when that happens, democracy disappears." [19]

This conceptual framework is one general way to describe why an independent college or university (especially a church-related institution) must be protected against those massive forms of governmental intrusion that uncritically assume any institution is part of the megastructure. These colleges are not part of the state megastructure. They were created and are maintained on totally different assumptions from the assumptions on which state institutions rest, because they are extensions of the private sphere of personal identity and family life, not extensions of the public sphere of government.

Against this background, I wish to consider two aspects of the federal civil rights legislation proposed in 1984 and 1985. I will focus primarily on Title IX, which prohibits sex discrimination in federally assisted educational programs. First comes a consideration of the jurisdictional theory on which the legislative proposals are based. That theory is the constitutional spending power. Simply stated, Congress may condition grants of governmental financial assistance on the willingness of a recipient to comply with certain federal requirements or policies. The underlying legal doctrine here is that Congress should not allow the expenditure of governmental funds in ways that run counter to legitimate governmental objectives. The Supreme Court has interpreted the spending power broadly, so long as the conditions accepted by recipients are "reasonable and unambiguous,"[20] and "narrowly tailored" to the achievement of the legislative goal.[21]

Much could be said about spending power issues in civil rights legislation, but for my immediate purpose, I call primary attention to the willingness—indeed, the determination—of some sponsors of the current legislative efforts to be unconcerned about reasonableness, ambiguity, or narrowly tailored standards in determining how far the spending power should carry federal jurisdiction. Some of the sponsors would clearly prefer to avoid a concern with constitutional limits altogether. They would apply Title IX as broadly as legal enforcement could, as a practical matter, be accomplished.

Specifically, both the 1984 and 1985 versions of the legislation seek broad new extensions of federal authority, based on the general idea of extending jurisdiction beyond institutions or activities that are directly benefitted by federal assistance to those that are indirectly benefitted. There are two particular manifestations of this notion in the legislation. One is the language of the 1985 bill, which would define the original Title IX term "program or activity" to mean "all of the operations" of an "entity" receiving federal assistance. The assumption behind this change in statutory language is that if one part of a large organization receives federal aid, the entire organization is indirectly benefitted, which is a sufficient basis for regulation. As suggested by one student of the legislation, if the sewer department in the City of Los Angeles receives a federal grant, the police department in the City of San Francisco should become subject to federal regulation, since the two departments are part of a common "entity"—the state of California.

A broader shift from direct to indirect benefits as a jurisdictional test may also be seen in the legislation's approach to defining "recipients" of federal assistance. The 1984 proposal defined recipients to include virtually any entity having business dealings with an actual recipient. This proposal was merely expanding the student-aid analogy, which had been held by the Supreme Court in the *Grove City College* case to establish recipient status for a college enrolling students who were themselves recipients of student aid. The 1985 bill uses different language but is motivated by the same expansive intent.

Suppose a student who receives a Pell Grant pays for education-related rent and automobile repairs with a portion of his grant funds. Does that make "recipients" of the landlord and the repair shop? If a hospital becomes a "recipient" of federal assistance by accepting fee payments from individual Medicare patients, does that also create recipient status for an independent contractor who provides respiratory therapy services for the hospital? A federal appeals court recently concluded that the independent contractor in the hospital example is a recipient, relying heavily on the student aid analogy.[22]

By comparison, the legislative history of Title VI of the Civil Rights Act of 1964, an important foundation for the interpretation of later civil rights statutes, shows that Congress at that time rejected the indirect benefit theory. As stated, for example, by Senator Humphrey, "It is irrelevant, to the purpose of these acts, what the recipient does with the money he receives. His employees, the customers of his business, or other persons with whom he deals, are in no sense participants in or beneficiaries of these Federal programs."

Our sense of the distinction between the public and private sectors will be difficult to maintain if the concept of "indirect benefit" becomes a standard basis for federal jurisdiction. All private sector entities are benefitted indirectly by federal tax exemptions and spending patterns. In an earlier era, legislative and judicial policymaking was sensitive to the need for maintaining some theory of limits on the reach of governmental power. But the contemporary individual rights movement now has such momentum that any theory of limited state power is unlikely to be taken very seriously, because such limitations appear as little more than roadblocks in the path toward achieving particular social goals. It is curious that an individual rights movement would favor unlimited governmental power, but that now seems to be the case.

For instance, some advocates today argue that the elimination of actual sex discrimination is an insufficient goal of federal civil rights policy. Rather, they stress the need to eradicate what they call all "structural" or institutional characteristics in society that have the effect of reinforcing gender-based distinctions of any kind. Only in this way, it is believed, will the ultimate sources of discriminatory attitudes be reached and controlled. Surely, our national policy must provide remedies against actual discrimination in employment, education, or in other environments; but larger questions are raised by the challenge to eliminate all private cultural sources of distinctions based on gender.

Political theorist Robert Nisbet has written that "earlier women's rights movements were . . . efforts to achieve for women a larger share of economic, educational, and cultural benefits—but within the family structure; or at least without seeking to alter that structure seriously. What gives present manifestoes, political actions, and movements toward legal reform their revolutionary character is the degree to which the substance of the family is changed. For with sure revolutionary instinct, the women's liberation movement—at least in its radical expressions—goes right to the heart of the matter, which is the historical nature of the role of each of the sexes."[23]

The commitment to eliminating attitudes about sex-based roles is illustrated in a recent report on the status of women in higher education, which discusses the "crucial role" of campus "atmosphere, environment, or climate," along with "familial and social expectations" in retarding the personal and professional development of women students. The influence of religion has also long been regarded as a major "structural" factor in perpetuating cultural assumptions that reinforce male-female distinctions. Said nineteenth-century feminist leader Elizabeth Stanton, "the religious superstitions of women perpetuate their bondage more than all other adverse influences."

It is therefore natural for aggressive advocates to look to tax policies, civil rights laws, the spending power, or any other federal source to penetrate as far as possible into religion, family life, education, or other elements of the private sphere in order to influence the sources of individual value orientation. Indeed, the pervasiveness of federal spending makes the spending power an attractive vehicle to extend the regulatory authority of the state into any realm where the privately held beliefs that encourage gender-based distinctions can be reached at their roots.

I note, parenthetically, that the Equal Rights Amendment would not reach as far as the proposed civil rights legislation in establishing gender-neutral values, since the ERA would apply only to state—not private—action.

Returning now to my earlier theme, the inclusion of indirect benefits within the spending power gives the appearance of strong linkage between the governmental megastructure and mediating structures. By this means, these mediating institutions can be subjected to meaning-neutralizing and value-neutralizing control as if they were in fact part of the governmental megastructure. The idea of transforming a private, church-related institution into a public institution in this way carries with it a special irony, because it tends to impose all of the tangled contemporary assumptions about separating church and state upon—of all places—the campuses of church-related colleges. One result of this change is that the mediating role of such institutions is undermined, thus contributing to the general decline of meaning-generating and value-maintaining processes in society and the decline of pluralistic values.

There is a sense, of course, in which such attempts by gender-neutrality advocates seek the opposite structural effect of converting the state-controlled and value-neutral megastructure into a value-oriented mediating structure. Attitudes about gender neutrality are at least arguably more a matter of personal values than they are a matter of constitutionally mandated equality, particularly because they direct their attack at the private root sources where beliefs and attitudes are generated, not merely at the more public place where actual discrimination exists.

It may therefore be appropriate to inquire whether the gender-neutral view of society is more entitled to a constitutional preference than competing views. For example, as mentioned earlier, American society has experienced in recent years a steady erosion of social and legal support for the concept of formal marriage, which has contributed directly and indirectly toward increasingly unstable family structures. The most serious harm caused by this instability is inflicted on children, whose developmental needs for continuity and stability are well documented. A plausible case can be made that a serious public policy reorientation is needed to restore support for stable marriage and kinship patterns in the legal, economic, and social environment. This case could identify instances in which cultural attitudes are subtly changing in both institutional and social contexts, with the effect of undermining the attitudes and patterns essential to stable social structures. Such developments could be shown to have a long-range impact on democratic institutions as well as social stability.

Were such a reorientation to be undertaken, its goals and interests would probably conflict with those of the current campaign for gender neutrality. In cases of conflict, which view should be entitled to governmental sponsorship? Society's interest in upholding stable family patterns is not a trivial concern. Nor can that concern be easily dismissed as a camouflage for prejudicial attitudes. Of course, serious differences in perception exist regarding the actual relationship between family stability and sex role differentiation. But the very existence of strong, unresolved differences on matters of such profound social consequence is enough to warrant a cautious approach in allowing the state to prefer one view over the other as a matter of dominant public policy.

The second issue I wish to address in the 1984 and 1985 civil rights legislation is that of religion. Religious organizations, whether churches, church-related colleges, or otherwise, deserve particular attention in this general discussion, because their role as mediating structures is protected by the free exercise clause of the First Amendment. The original language of Title IX recognized the importance of explicit protection for church-related education by including a modest statutory exemption for cases where application of the law "would not be consistent with the religious tenets" of "a religious organization" which "controls" a school. However, the 1985 Civil Rights Restoration Act has been bogged down in the House of Representatives because the bill's sponsors have been unwilling to add language designed to make the law abortion-neutral and to make the religious exemption available to religious institutions not "controlled" by churches.

This skittishness about protecting the civil right of religious liberty in a civil rights bill has puzzled some strong supporters of the general thrust of the proposed new law, such as the U.S. Catholic Conference. In fact, it was the insistence of the Catholic Conference on an abortion-neutral amendment that finally caused enough controversy to move the 1985 version of the legislation off its fast track before committee action had been taken in the House. It is curious to me that only an issue as emotional as abortion could attract enough attention to compete with an issue as emotional as civil rights. This phenomenon suggests that we are not likely to see a very rational approach to the balancing of important competing interests in future regulatory efforts of this kind. Many significant religious interests, of which abortion is only the most visible example, are affected by governmental intrusion in civil rights enforcement.

A number of recent cases have pitted religious interests against other civil rights claims. For instance, in the 1983 case of *Bob Jones University v. United States*,[24] the Supreme Court upheld the denial of federal tax exemptions to church-related schools which maintained racially discriminatory school policies. The fundamental public policy interest in eradicating racial discrimination in education was held to outweigh whatever burden the denial of tax-exempt status would impose on religious liberty interests.

The denial of a tax exemption in this case was an extraordinary step. But race has been a most unusual category in constitutional adjudication. Rules established in the racial context have often broken with longstanding traditions and legal standards simply because the national interest in eliminating racial discrimination has been so deeply felt and so widely shared. However, it has become a common pattern for the advocates of nonracial causes to lay claim to those extraordinary rules, even when their claims most probably would not have been taken very seriously if heard by a court prior to seeing the trail blazed in the racial context.

For example, a local court in the District of Columbia recently applied the *Bob Jones* test to require Georgetown University to grant official recognition to a student gay-rights organization. The university argued this result would violate its religious liberty interests in view of clear Catholic teachings against homosexuality. But the court found a "compelling governmental interest" in the elimination of discrimination on the basis of sexual orientation that "substantially outweighs the burden placed on the exercise of religious beliefs."[25] The court did not address whether the public policy interest in eliminating this form of discrimination stood on any foundation different from the interest in eliminating racial discrimination.

The Supreme Court recently heard another case which pits the national interest in eradicating sex discrimination against the national interest in preserving religious liberty related to attitudes about childrearing. In *Dayton Christian Schools v. Ohio Civil Rights Commission,* the lower court had upheld the right of a church-related school to refuse to renew the contract of a teacher who wished to continue teaching after having a child. The school's policy was based on religious teachings which counseled mothers of young children against employment outside the home. Citing procedural grounds, the Supreme Court deferred consideration of the school's religious liberty argument.[26] The *Dayton* case represents a clear conflict between the two competing policies mentioned earlier: the arguable need to eliminate all public and private sources of distinctions based on gender versus the arguable need to reinforce the interest of society and children in child-oriented family structures. This is an important problem because both interests are important.

In dealing with this policy conflict, it is worth remembering that, as important as is the need to eliminate actual sex discrimination, ideas about sex roles and family life are central to the religious beliefs of many people and many private institutions. Even apart from those religious beliefs, society's interest in our cultural patterns of marriage and childrearing is also a matter of legitimate public policy concern. It is not possible to enact everything on the agenda of gender neutrality without undercutting not only certain religious beliefs, but also the mediating role of both families and churches.

There are also important differences between sex and race as legal classifications. It is therefore risky uncritically to transfer legal doctrines developed in the racial context to problems existing in the gender context. This is particularly the case when religious values are involved, because of the potential impact on matters of personal morality.

For example, the Fair Housing Act, one of the original race-discrimination laws, was amended a few years ago by simply adding "or sex" to the statute. Shortly afterward, a single female was refused rental accommodations in a student apartment building because of a requirement by a church-related university that single students living off campus reside in sex-segregated buildings. After reviewing the woman's complaint, the Justice Department announced its intention to bring suit. However, when the public media realized that such enforcement of federal sex discrimination laws appeared to require single men and women to share apartments and bedrooms, the roof of public outcry fell in on the Justice Department. An agreement was finally reached which allowed sex-segregated housing at educational institutions, if established "on the basis of religious or moral principle." It is clear that widely supported religious and moral values can be undermined by the indiscriminate mixing of race and sex as legal categories.

One senses in today's society a general and growing uncertainty about the very issues of value and meaning with which mediating institutions have historically been concerned. Historian Barbara Tuchman has observed, for instance, an extensive loss of confidence in human judgment in Western society through the wrenching experiences of this century, one result of which is "a widespread and eroding reluctance to take any stand on any values, moral, behavioral, or aesthetic."[27] In the context of education, Gerald Grant concluded from his field research among private and public schools that "in many places we no longer have any agreement on what . . . provisional morality ought to be, or we feel that any attempt to provide it is a form of indoctrination. Hence, we [are] . . . prematurely declaring—even insisting— that children are adults capable of choosing their own morality as long they do not commit crimes. . . . Where [the informal trust created by shared agreement about provisional morality] does not exist, I think we are headed for ever greater stress, instability, and perhaps the eventual abandonment of the public schools."[28]

This kind of moral ambivalence is caused by many large-scale cultural influences. But pervading all of these crosscurrents is a loss of confidence in public and private institutions of all kinds. Mediating structures have traditionally stood between individuals and the governmental megastructures. Now they are under assault from the individual side because of their institutional character at a time when all institutions are suspect. They are also under assault from the megastructure side, partly because of constitutional doctrines that favor individual over institutional values, and partly because financial pressures are forcing their absorption by the governmental megastructure. In addition, the megastructure is responding to continuing pressure from the advocates of egalitarian value positions who want the megastructure to absorb mediating institutions in order to control them.

The *Grove City College* case offers an interesting study of these problems. I mentioned earlier that public education is in an ambiguous place along the spectrum between mediating structures and megastructures. The *Grove City College* situation introduces the additional factors of private education and a background concern with religious values. It also asks for consideration of the limits to which we should stretch our concept of federal assistance, because only student aid was involved in the case. In addition, as a religious institution that is not controlled by a church, Grove City College is not protected by the present Title IX religious exemption.

In the midst of this complex environment, the nature and mission of the college remains squarely within a mediating role sustained by the values of the First Amendment. For its students and their families, as well as for its financial supporters and other constituents, the college is a classic illustration of a value-generating and value-maintaining agency devoted to augmenting the individual quest for personal meaning and purpose in life. It is thus an extension of the private sphere of individual and family life, even though its role as an institution of higher education also allows it to share its perception of issues of meaning and value in the public marketplace of ideas. In this way the mediating role extends in both public and private directions.

In general, Title IX, as broadened to apply campus wide by the currently proposed legislation, seeks to establish an official orthodoxy about value questions relating to the roles of the sexes in society, matters of sexual morality, and attitudes about marriage and family life. The imposition of these views on the campus of Grove City College is unsettling, not only because of the chilling effect thereby imposed on the college as a mediating institution, but also because the value-neutral megastructure of government is being cast in a value orientation of its own, having been captured by a particular viewpoint in the name of value-free egalitarianism.

Consider the historical diversity which has characterized American higher education. We have had single-sex colleges, religious colleges, secular colleges, vocational institutes, and pure liberal arts institutions. This diversity manifested a deeply held idea that individuals and institutions should be permitted to pursue the goals of education in their own way, thereby giving meaning to the belief that each man or woman should be free to define the purpose of his or her own life, in association with the distinctive family, religious, or educational ties he or she might seek in the process of working out that purpose. The government of the United States does not know which of these educational approaches is most correct, nor should it try to decide.

When the state asserts a value-laden orthodoxy in so threatening a way that any contrary view is marked as illegitimate, the core sense of being in an institution such as Grove City College is threatened. In a broader sense, the nation's meaning-giving enterprise is threatened, at a time when we may need a reaffirmation of the pursuit of personal purpose and values as never before.

# Notes

1. Owen Fiss, "Foreward: The Forms of Justice, The Supreme Court 1978 Term," *Harvard Law Review* 93(1979): 1, 2–3.

2. Ibid., 57, 59.

3. Ibid., 1.

4. Peter L. Berger and Richard J. Neuhaus, *To Empower People: The Role of Mediating Structures in Public Policy* (Washington: American Enterprise Institute for Public Policy Research, 1977), 3.

5. Fiss, 1.

6. Berger and Neuhaus, 2.

7. Ibid., 7.

8. Ibid., 19.

9. Alexis de Tocqueville, *Democracy in America,* ed. R. D. Heffner (New York: New American Library, 1956), 2:201.

10. 354 U.S. 234, 263 (1957).

11. *Regents of the University of California v. Bakke,* 438 U.S. 265, 312 (1978).

12. See Bruce C. Hafen, "Developing Student Expression Through Institutional Authority: Public Schools as Mediating Institutions," *Ohio State Law Journal* 48 (1987): 663.

13. Mark V. Tushnet, "The Religion Clauses," paper delivered to the Section on Law and Religion, Association of American Law Schools Annual Meeting, New Orleans, 5 January 1986. In one recent case, however, the Supreme Court acknowledged explicitly that "religious organizations have an interest in autonomy in ordering their internal affairs," in part because a religious community is "an organic entity not reducible to a mere aggregation of individuals." *Corporation of the Presiding Bishop of the Church of Jesus Christ of Latter-Day Saints v. Amos,* 107 S. Ct. 2862 (1987) (Brennan, J., concurring opinion).

14. *Maynard v. Hill,* 125 U.S. 190, 205, 211 (1988).

15. D. H. Lawrence, "A Propos of Lady Chatterley's Lover," in *Essays on Sex Literature and Censorship* (New York: Twayne, 1973), 35–36.

16. "All in the Family," *Time,* 16 June 1980, 31.

17. Laurence H. Tribe, *American Constitutional Law* (Mineola, N.Y.: Foundation Press, 1978), 974–80, 987–90.

18. See generally, Bruce C. Hafen, "The Constitutional Status of Marriage, Kinship, and Sexual Privacy—Balancing the Individual and Social Interests," *Michigan Law Review* 81 (1983): 463.

19. Berger and Neuhaus, 3.

20. *Grove City College v. Bell,* 104 S. Ct. 1211, 1223 (1984).

21. *Fullilove v. Klutznick,* 448 U.S. 448, 480 (1980).

22. *Frazier v. Trustees of Northwest Mississippi Regional Medical Center,* 777 F.2d 239 (5th Cir. 1985).

23. Robert Nisbet, *Twilight of Authority* (New York: Oxford University Press, 1975), 82–83.

24. 103 S. Ct. 2017 (1983).

25. *Gay Rights Coalition v. Georgetown University,* 496 A. 2d 587 (D.C. Ct. Appls. 1985).

26. 766 F. 2d 932 (1985), revised 106 S. Ct. 2718 (1986).

27. Barbara Tuchman, "The Missing Element: Moral Courage," in *In Search of Leaders,* ed. G. Kerry Smith (Washington: American Association for Higher Education, National Education Association, 1967), 3 (selected papers from the 22d National Conference on Higher Education held in Chicago, Illinois, 1967).

28. Gerald Grant, "The Character of Education and the Education of Character," *American Education* 18 (1982): 135, 146.

## Discussion

**Hawkins:** * It seems to me the presentations by Owen Fiss and Bruce Hafen have had interesting points of convergence and divergence. I think they start from an interesting convergence on dissatisfaction with the kind of atomistic view of society and law that sees all rights as individuals and all ends as being privatized. There is a possible divergence here, though it is more difficult for me to state in terms of what are or should be the mediating forces in teaching social responsibility and achieving values that are addressed more to the side of public values or social values, with Professor Fiss emphasizing the judicial branch of government as a mediating institution and Professor Hafen concerned about what an activist government, I suppose in any of its branches, threatens in terms of the vitality of the private mediating institutions.

**Fiss:** I think your perception of the common starting point is correct. What unites us is a movement away from an atomistic view of society. But I think there is an important difference. Dean Hafen builds from the bottom up. He starts with individuals who are, to use his phrase, value-generating and value-maintaining, and then adds on top of them these mediating structures, which are also value-generating and value-maintaining. What I would do is to add another tier. For me megastructures are value-maintaining and value-generating as well. Megastructures like the Constitution are an important source of values. Thus, although I agree that we must move above atomistic individuals to mediating structures, I would disagree with Dean Hafen in his

---

*Carl Hawkins, professor of law at the J. Reuben Clark Law School at Brigham Young University, was the moderator of this panel of the conference.*

168

characterization of megastructure as just being value-neutralizing or value-destructive. I would also see the megastructure as a source of values and as a means of maintaining values as well.

Take the issue of racial equality. The Constitution has been value-generating and value-maintaining on the issue of racial equality. It has, to use Professor Hafen's phrase, been a source of individual meaning and personal development for me and I think for many people in society. It is not the only source, but it has been an important source of values for individuals. Megastructures can work in the way Dean Hafen envisions for mediating structures.

**Lowi:** I'd like to make a couple of points in order to stress the differences between the two as much as the convergences. One, I would like to observe that there's a kind of false dichotomy made here that to me is made mainly to serve an argument, or to gain a goal, or put in a good word for, goodness of certain kinds of things rather than an extending of an analysis. In this instance the false dichotomy or false separation is between mediating institutions and mega-institutions. I think it is more of a continuum. I don't know where the break comes. Marriage, after all, is as much a fiction of the law as it is anything else, a reflection of law that imposes and protects a certain pattern. I could argue that family instability wasn't caused by the laws, but the laws were changed to accommodate a changing family pattern that reflects itself in instability. It can go both ways. All these things are continuing. I don't think truth or productive controversy is served at all by making distinctions that are made primarily to achieve certain argumentative goals.

Now a second point I'd like to make that would bring the two essays together around their common concerns, although they differ very greatly in the bottom line. Owen Fiss raised a sort of rhetorical question I'd like to disagree with. He said that legitimacy can—it doesn't always, but *can*—depend very heavily on the instrumental factor that if an institution doesn't produce its legitimacy is undermined. It depends on what the contract was, what the sort of implicit understanding was. I think one of the things that happened in the 1960s was that a kind of implicit new social contract was established whereby institutions gave us the expectation that they could provide certain results whether they were regulatory results, or service results, or stability, or whatever. After that, when they failed to produce those results, people began to lose their faith. Certainly, that was one of the factors among the under-thirty segment of the population.

I don't want to make too big a point of this except to say that it leads me to an observation that is common, not only to the essays by Professors Fiss and Hafen, but to other comments and presentations here—especially by Professor Wildavsky—about the declining trust in institutions, from which a lot of things follow. I don't disagree with Professor Wildavsky on a number of his interpretations of that. Yes, there is declining trust, whatever produced it. But having observed that, I would simply say, "Let's not be so damned apocalyptic about it." This is not the first time that has happened, and it's not the last time it's going to happen. We go through a period when we feel down, a period when bigness or remoteness or power becomes the enemy. I think that in the Progressive period, though it was made up of several dimensions, one of the very important ones was an alienation from big institutions. It wasn't against capitalism; it was against anything big— the church; the government, even local government; Wall Street; any such institutions. Some of the great alienators or mega-institutions people at that time were people like Theodore Bilbo in the South, because rural radicalism shared the same kind of distrust.

And so what happens when people now, as in previous times, lose their faith in institutions? Here are three things. First, when people lose their faith in an institution, whether they are mediating institutions or whether they are mega-institutions, they are likely to turn to the state. They are likely to turn to some governmental institution that seems to be larger and more incorporating than the institution in which they have lost their trust, something more inclusive. If they've lost their trust in the United States they'll go to the U.N.—as the Indians have done, for example. But as a citizen you must try to go to something more inclusive to restore or to gain, or, as Schattschneider once said, "to expand the scope of conflict," or to try to gain more friends than you feel you have in the given context.

Second, people are likely to revert to individual private goals. If they lose their faith in larger institutions, they're likely to lose their faith in what those institutions stood for—equality, for example, or religious values. They are likely to privatize because they don't have enough faith in those things that had once been a reinforcing environment. It has happened before, it's happening now, and probably once we stabilize ourselves it's going to happen again. And we'll have forgotten; so when it happens again it will come as a surprise.

And third, people resort to rights. That's not the same thing as privatization, but it's related to it. The resort to rights is a very interesting phenomenon, because when you assert a right to something, you set it above the normal decision-making process. It is in a sense antidemocratic. What is a right? I silence lawyers every time I ask them this question: "Define for me what a right is, and don't give me any nonsense about what courts say." I have tried to formulate a definition as a political scientist. This is a political view of a right: To me a right is a claim made for a remedy that cannot be denied except by an extraordinary decision-making process. I assert it as a right, meaning you must give it to me or else show some very extraordinary reasons why you don't give it to me.

So we naturally, if we lose our faith in institutions, whatever they are—mediating ones, mega ones, little ones, moderate ones—we are going to assert a right to something in the hope that the elevated language will give us what we want.

**Wildavsky:** I think the Fiss and Hafen essays quite well and quite fairly represent the major division of our time over the meaning of democracy, that is, over who is to exercise power over whom. When, in this country, we were more agreed about the character and legitimacy of our institutions, we were able to say that if we only could agree on the processes and procedures of democracy, we need not agree on the ends. And that would make it easier to carry along democratic life. Following the civil rights movement and other movements, people have become less comfortable with the institutions of American political life, feeling them biased in the sense that they reinforce an institutionalized pattern of inequality. They have come to what I call the reverse sequence, that is, to believe that unless there is much greater substantive equality there cannot be equality of opportunity or indeed equality before the law.

I would just say flat out, hoping I will hear some contradictory comment, that, if Owen Fiss did not believe that lawyers from Yale, Harvard, and even Berkeley would agree that what this country needs is to redress imbalances, that is, inequalities in power, he would not be in favor of structural reform. As I read his essay, what structural reform means is that since our institutions do not produce sufficient equality to suit him, lawyers and judges, now, at this moment in time, desire for equality should provide greater equality.

Consider this from the point of view of deliberation in society. Generally, following Sheldon Wolin, when we talk about democratic life we think of people making choices and having an ethic of responsibility and of taking the consequences of those choices. This would mean that on the death penalty you and I would have to grab hold of one another and we would have to sway one another. This would be extremely difficult, if not obnoxious and stultifying, because there are deep disagreements. Perhaps we could not agree. If we did agree one way or the other, one side would have been more persuasive and the other somewhat less, but all would have had some feeling that they had a chance to participate.

However, if one feels, for example, that blacks are disproportionately executed or that poor people have much less opportunity (I won't go into the facts of the matter, but I think it's clear that some people believe this), one does not follow what one otherwise would as a democratic norm, that is, the procedure through which I persuade you and you try to persuade me. Instead, some little fellow sits in a closet. He is a graduate of a law school. He writes a brief. He sends that brief to a little bigger fellow. He is called a judge. He sits in his chambers and reads that brief. All of a sudden we discover that the Framers never intended to have capital punishment, that in our time, because of evident inequalities, it has become cruel and unusual. That is why Owen Fiss can say that judges are in a better position to derive the texture of true meaning (i.e., greater equality) than other people.

Now it may be, as Ted Lowi says, that the disagreements we have today are quite similar to deep disagreements we've had in the past. Of course, once in our history these led to the bloodiest war of that century. But if there is a distinction between our disagreements today and those of other times, I think they are quite nicely mirrored in these intelligent, lucid, and well-moderated papers that nevertheless encapsulate quite different visions of the good life. What is different is that the criteria for democracy are certainly being redefined. If one part of our people thinks you have to have greater equality of condition before you can legitimate institutions as democratic and the other thinks that democracy is what people can agree on after following certain procedures, it will not be easy to reconcile these views.

**Fiss:** I admit that I believe in substantive equality. I admit that the moving force of a lot of what happened in the 1960s in terms of the judicial process and the evolution of the "new procedure" was tied to the notion of substantive equality. I also believe, however, that a general conception of law and of procedure emerged from that period and the struggle for substantive equality, and that this general conception of procedure stands independent of the substantive issue. I would believe in the "new procedure" even if I did not believe in substantive equality. If I started on another premise, not of substantive equality but one that reflected, for example, a commitment to liberty or to democracy, I still think that I would welcome structural reform and the effort of the judiciary to protect the values in question. You may say, "Well, wait and see 'til you get a real case." That skepticism might be justified, but I hope that it is not. Race is special, I admit, but one of the extraordinary things of that period of our history is that the struggle with this special issue produced ideas and institutions that have more general and more transcendental value.

**Sorensen:** I think that the difference between Professor Lowi and me has to do with basic assumptions concerning the nature of values and the role values play in the very formation of a person. One of the things that can and should be done is to examine some of the logical features of values to see if it's not true that some of them are fundamental in the creation of the person and that, in the absence of those values, personhood itself might collapse.

The second thing on which we disagree, I think, is a hidden assumption on the part of Professor Lowi concerning whether or not there is an ultimate method by which you can show that one set of values is somehow preferable to another. It has to do with a kind of relativism that I find shared more by old-style social scientists than by philosophers. That is, I think I find more relativists, naive relativists, in the area of social science than I do informed relativists among philosophers.

I have some trouble with the distinction between private ends and public values that are used by Professor Fiss, even though I enjoyed very much reading his essay, and his other works as well. The problem I have is that, when I think about examining the model of adjudication that involves the privatization of values, I can't imagine myself analyzing that without revealing the public values built into it, that there are both public values and private ends and some of the public values built into it are various interpretations of, say, liberty and equality. So I have the impression that the debate is not between public values and private ends so much as it is a debate between one interpretation of public values connected to private ends, namely a set of common assumptions on the basis of which we can seek those private ends, on the one hand, and on the other hand, another view of public values for the seeking of private ends.

It seems clear to me, at least as a political observer, that the people who are taking the model of structural reform are changing the basic assumptions that create the structure of opportunities through which individuals seek private ends and that, really, private ends themselves are at stake in the end. So, I am concerned that the distinction between private ends and public values is, in some way, a way of disguising the fact that it's a battle between different views of both public values *and* private ends.

**Shapiro:** I think what Professor Sorensen has just said is essential to this whole discussion, and it really does divide us into two groups and make some rather strange bedfellows. It puts Lou Gawthrop and Don Sorensen and Owen Fiss on one side, and it puts me, Bruce Hafen, Ted Lowi, and Aaron Wildavsky on the other. I'm going to let Professor Wolin speak for himself because I don't know what his position is on this question. Yes— Professor Lowi's over there saying there may be a third group.

And I think it is worth explaining a little of the background to this division. As of the time of World War II, the dominant moral philosophy in the Western world was utilitarianism, the notion that the only good was the greatest good for the greatest number. Subsequent to the war and probably because of the war in a large part, there has been a great dissatisfaction with the notion that the only ethic is the greatest good for the greatest number, and a great dissatisfaction with the notion that ethics are a matter of purely personal taste. Those who believe in such purely personal ethics are insisting that when a person makes an ethical statement he is simply saying, "I like chocolate and you like vanilla," which in effect is what Lowi keeps saying to us.

In the post–World War II period, some moral and legal philosophers have tried desperately to reconstruct moral philosophy, to create a new moral philosophy which says, in effect, that it was a big mistake to say earlier, "If you can't prove a moral value scientifically in a test tube, then it is a matter of pure personal preference." They argue that scientism, that is, a naive notion of science, was highly destructive of ethics, and that if you adopt certain procedures for thinking about morality you can arrive at moral statements which are very true even though they may not be absolutely true in the sense that a mathematical equation is true—logically correct—or even in the sense that some scientific laws are said to be absolutely true. They argue that we can make some moral statements that are far more true than other moral statements. And indeed, not only can an individual arrive at some moral statements that are more true than others, but if we use the right procedures we can get a relatively high degree of consensus on what things are more morally true and what moral statements are preferable to others.

Don Sorensen has shown us a technique, that of the analytical philosopher, for arriving at moral truths that he is persuaded are more morally true than some other moral propositions. And he has great confidence in his technique for arriving at better moral statements. I think Owen Fiss is right when he says even if he wasn't sure that Harvard-, Yale-, and Columbia-trained lawyers think the way he thinks, he would still vest authority in the courts because he's confident that the dialogue between lawyers is like Professor Sorensen's analytical philosophy—a way of arriving at moral truths that are superior. That is, both the philosopher and the lawyer believe strongly that there are procedures, that is, ways of thinking and engaging in discourse, that will give us moral truths that have a superior claim of some sort.

Those whom Professor Sorensen has referred to as naive social scientists have not been persuaded that we have seen procedures that give us moral truths that have a better claim than some other moral propositions, or moral truths that can command a general consensus as to their superior moral position. It is for this reason that many of us here oppose regulation. For if regulation is the imposition of moral truth by government on individuals or groups, then until we are much more persuaded than we now are that there are such superior moral truths, we tend to be highly suspicious of regulation. That's why I put Bruce Hafen in my camp. I think the argument of his essay is that until we are all much more sure that government can arrive at superior moral truth, we are very reluctant to have moral truths imposed by government on mediating institutions. He may believe that those mediating institutions have superior techniques for finding moral truth, but he doesn't believe yet that lawyers and philosophers could guide government to embody those moral truths in regulation. I think we have a fundamental disagreement about how certain we can be about ethical truth. That disagreement underlies much of our discussion.

**Fiss:** I think there is a lot of truth to what Professor Shapiro says, but I would just divide the two camps differently and give a different label to each. One would be called rationalists and the other could be called prudentialists.

**Wolin:** Since I haven't been assigned to a camp, I am waiting for an offer. But let me make three brief, interrelated points. One pertains to Dean Hafen's remarks. And I agree to a degree with Ted Lowi's criticism in which he disputes the distinction between megastructures and the value-generating structures of mediating institutions. Professor Lowi sort of put it from the point of view (and Professor Fiss did as well) that megastructures themselves can generate values. And I would certainly, to some degree, subscribe to that. But it seems to me there is another problem. And the other problem is that mediating structures have themselves historically absorbed and reinforced the values of the megastructure. In other words, at times Dean Hafen fell into the language of calling the megastructures value-neutral. But they really aren't value-neutral. And if we think of values like patriotism or loyalty, we can see how important many of the mediating institutions have been in transmitting megastructural values through their own media. And this, it seems to me, therefore, raises questions that go beyond the dichotomy between mediating and megastructures. This means that we are not dealing with innocent mediating structures which simply are in the business of values. Mediating structures are also, in their way, institutions of power. Educational institutions shape, religious institutions shape, family institutions shape; all of them are not only transmitting values, they are also reinforcing values in very strong ways.

Now to the question of the resolution between megastructures and mediating structures, we all, I suppose, are uncomfortable with that kind of dichotomy, but we intuitively realize that there are important stakes in the difference between the two. I don't think it's very easy to resolve in any kind of permanent way what the proper relationship should be between them. I think we would all probably agree that it is healthy to the society that there be tensions and conflicts between mediating institutions and megastructures, but I also think that for that conflict to be substantive, there has to be more discontinuity in value between megastructures and mediating institutions. And my fear is that mediating institutions are themselves becoming more and more uniform in the values in which they seek to instruct students and believers. Therefore, the real problem comes back to the question—it's a very old question—concerning diversity and the range of diversity and what I consider to be its diminishing character. As I go about (the experience of my colleagues here is probably the same) the country talking to student groups at institutions as different as a small liberal arts college, the denominational college, the large state university, and the Ivy League institution, I am struck by the similarity in values. I don't find a great deal of difference among students from very different intellectual contexts and social classes. I find that some are more facile and some are slicker and some may be more sophisticated, but what they basically believe is not very greatly different. And what I miss is the variety and the crankiness that one would hope would be there.

There is a distinction that has been made here between two versions of democracy. One version rests on deliberation and discussion, which I take to be a form of democracy in which agreement on means is the distinguishing feature. The other is a democracy that imposes substantive solutions, say, on matters of racial equality or of gender discrimination. But again, I'm not so sure that that dichotomy holds. Discussion, after all, is not just a value-neutral form. Everyone may have a right to a defense counsel, but their economic means make a difference. Some can buy better defense counsels than others. And I think the same is true of conditions of discussion. Conditions of discussion today are those stipulated by John Stuart Mill. Some groups own the media of discussion; most groups have no access whatsoever; some groups are able to hire sophisticated people to speak a certain discourse that persuades. Other people don't know that discourse. They don't know anything about economics, they don't know anything about Wittgenstein, they don't know anything about any of the authoritative modes for framing problems.

That brings us to other aspects of democracy. The very things Wildavsky fears so much I see as means for equalizing the possibility of discussion, for making it possible for individuals from very poor and deprived backgrounds to acquire the education necessary to be able to participate in authoritative discourses and discussions or at least be able to comprehend them. So, again, I think we are relying on dichotomies that conceal more than they produce.

The third and final point I want to make refers to something Professor Shapiro said where he expressed his kind of skepticism about moral values. Again, it occurs to me that skepticism itself is not a value-neutral notion. Skepticism is something I think we can afford if we are more or less satisfied about things; and if we are more or less satisfied about the way things are going and about the arrangements that are in existence and the kinds of decisions that are coming out, and we feel very dubious about possibilities for significant change, we can afford skepticism. Skepticism can be a mode of self-indulgence if circumstances make it easy to say, "Well, values can't really be resolved in any way that we find persuasive or conclusive; therefore, we are skeptical."

Now, not only do I philosophically disagree with that position, I believe that moral values are susceptive to rational defense or criticism and that there are better reasons for believing or disbelieving some things rather than other things. There have been several allusions to a serious crisis in legitimation. The crisis, in my view, has to do with fundamental doubts regarding the rightfulness of authority and the decisions that are being made in the name of authority. Under those circumstances it seems to me that skepticism is, in a very real degree, self-defeating as a political response to a political situation.

**Lowi:** I want to recall one of the great philosophers of the twentieth century, Robert Benchley, who said that there are two kinds of people in the world: those who divide people up into two kinds of people, and those who don't divide people up into two kinds of people. I don't know where that puts me, but I want to place myself in neither of the two dichotomies here.

While I agree with Professor Shapiro's characterization, and think it was well worth saying to all of us, his dichotomy isn't satisfactory. Liberals, and let me just take myself as an example, do have a moral code; to the liberal, human beings are distinct from animals by their possession of a moral code. But the problem for liberals is that there are many different moral codes. And since one cannot be sure, even with an elevated process of rhetoric, what the hierarchy of values is, the best thing you can be is skeptical. Not because that's a luxury you can afford; it's because it is a condition you can't avoid. If you are unsure of what is the only good, and are unsure of what are the hierarchies of values, then you can have your own; but you would be loath to impose yours on anybody else. And you'd be loathe to have anyone else impose theirs on you. Now that's not the same thing as having none. And I think this is the part that has been overlooked as far as where I find myself placed among these two or three different dichotomies.

So the question is not whether you have values but what you do with the values you hold. There is a particularity about liberalism, which is that you must have values but not impose them—or do what you can to avoid imposing them—on others. Now, liberals may verge on substantive morality because we are not perfect. All doctrines, including liberalism, are built on contradictions. That point in liberalism is where it verges on the substantive: Liberalism embraces the right but does not want to give up the good altogether. We might as well recognize that contradiction in liberalism and do the best we can to keep ourselves from the full embrace of the substantive. Recognition of contradiction is in itself something of a solution. And this enables us to fall back on the liberal's true virtue, which is procedural, and political: Since I cannot establish my moral code as the public philosophy, I must support the principle of no moral code as public philosophy. That frees no one from the personal shame of unequal distribution. This is precisely what has been lost in the conservative epoch of the current decade, a sense of shame for inequalities. It may seem ironic, but once conservatives feel they're right with God, they can be very complacent about things around them. Liberals say, "By God, we ought to be ashamed of ourselves," even though they know institutions cannot reach all of it. We then try to push rights as far as they can go, and we may go beyond the liberal line to substantive outcomes. I think a substantive rights concept is justified as long as it is recognized as inconsistent with the core of liberalism and is employed only after procedural and political rights approaches have been exhausted. It is hypocritical for conservatives to insist now on a purely procedural, "color-blind" approach, after having been so opposed to that twenty-five years ago when it was promising to revolutionize the society.

# VII

# BUREAUCRACY AND CONSTITUTIONAL DEVELOPMENT: THE DUTY TO RISK

★

## *Louis C. Gawthrop*

Too frequently we are advised that the only facts social science can advance involve trivial insignificancies. In keeping with this cynical perspective, which is, incidentally, patently false, let me begin by advancing an axiomatic law that is deceptively simple if not outrageously trite in its substance—namely, every policy is no policy until it is implemented. Or, stated differently, the best or worst intentions are idle intellectual indulgences unless and until they are linked to specific acts designed to achieve what is intended. In the experience of our republic, we have had nearly two hundred years to experiment with the relationship between policy formulation and policy implementation, between political intentions and administrative acts; and the manner in which this relationship has evolved provides us with a valuable perspective of some of the strengths and the weaknesses of our constitutional democracy.

To administer the affairs of governance, in whatever fashion such affairs were conducted, is a time-honored tradition based on

*Louis Gawthrop is a Research Fellow at the Weston School of Theology, Cambridge, Massachusetts.*

an extremely limited set of prerequisite qualifications. In all instances, trustworthiness, loyalty, and obedience is required, with the additional requirement, under certain circumstances, of greater than average learning and/or specialized knowledge. In all attempts at social organization, from the clan or the tribe to the nation-state, three basic functions have been variously manifested in all efforts at governance: first, some form of defense against external aggression; second, some system designed to maintain internal order; and third, some manner in which the resources necessary to carry out these functions were obtained and allocated.

From the very rudimentary beginnings of social organization to the present day, public policy and public administration have been inseparably linked. To attempt to understand either without a relational reference to the other is futile. Admittedly, the precise shape of this immutable policy-administration relationship may vary quite significantly depending on the specific context in which the notion of governance is formulated and applied; but the relationship itself is invariably fixed. Thus, in the sections which follow, I focus on the linkage between policy and administration as it has developed in the formal context of our constitutional democracy.

Constitutional development in the United States should obviously be examined by a study of the law—the law as promulgated by Congress and as explicated by the Supreme Court. After all, we are a government of laws, not of men. However, in recognizing the obvious significance of these two branches of government in the two-hundred-year developmental process of our democracy, it is the role of the third branch of government, the executive branch, that has proved to be the most decisive in both positive and negative terms. Although the permanent institutionalization of presidential power throughout the executive branch in the policy process is a relatively recent phenomenon, the relationship between intentions and acts is the most elemental of all human behavior, just as the integration of policy and administration is the most fundamental and basic of every ordered network of social governance that has ever prevailed.

To be sure, many of our presidents have assumed passive if not decidedly negative roles in the expansion of the powers of the Constitution; but others, beginning with Washington, have exerted a dynamic and positive impact on the process of constitutional development. As has already been suggested, however, policy intentions cannot be separated from policy implementation and, thus, the growth of federal power in the United States can, in no small measure, be traced through the administrative apparatus of the federal executive branch. Just as the presidency—broadly defined to include all top-level policy officials (i.e., all political appointees)—has been directed in active pursuit of or passive withdrawal from the impulse of national policy power, so, also, the administrative cadre responsible for the implementation of policy has demonstrated its own capabilities to enhance or impede the policy process. Clearly, the Congress, president, and Supreme Court enjoy constitutional recognition; Articles I, II, and III focus explicitly on each, respectively. But to ignore the policy role of the vaguely defined and amorphous body of career administrators known collectively as the "bureaucracy" is to ignore the critically important fourth player in an intensely competitive and intricately complex four-cornered game.

Admittedly, this assertion is based on nearly two hundred years of cumulative experience. It is an *ex post facto* assessment that undoubtedly would have been categorically rejected if presented as an *ex ante facto* proposition at the start of the republic. Although Jefferson, Hamilton, and Madison might be intrigued today by the recent developments of the presidency, Congress, and the Court, the Supreme Court would still be a recognizable body in a familiar setting; Congress would be larger, of course—less polished, perhaps—but still the primary deliberative body, operating under familiar rules of parliamentary decorum; and the White House, despite its barricades, security forces, and banks of electronic wizardry, would still be at the other end of Pennsylvania Avenue and the president could still be found in the Oval Office. Could they, however, comprehend the Departments of State, Health and Human Services, or Energy; the commissions, agencies, or government corporations; the complex networks of regional, district, and field offices; the intergovernmental systems or the transnational complex; the National Aeronautics and Space Administration? Given what these three Framers collaborated to put into the Constitution concerning the administrative infrastructure of the executive branch, and given the overall sentiments which then prevailed concerning the role of bureaucracy in the new government, it seems reasonable to suggest that, from the Framers' perspective, the status of the bureaucracy today could only be viewed as phenomenal. From approximately three thousand civilian employees in 1800, the federal career service has expanded to approximately three million. How can such growth and complexity be explained in terms of the Constitution? Perhaps the best way to start is to let the Constitution and the intentions of its framers speak for themselves.

A close reading of Article I, sections 3, 6, 8, and 9, reveals that federal offices other than the president, vice-president, senators, representatives, and federal judges were anticipated; but the language is decidedly fuzzy, its focus hazy. Article II, section 2, is little more specific. There will be executive departments in the new government but they are left unnamed and unnumbered. These departments will be directed by individuals who at one point in this section are referred to as "the principal Officer," and at a later point in the same section are referred to as "the Heads of Departments." These individuals shall be nominated and appointed by the president with the advice and consent of the Senate. Moreover, this section provides for "other . . . inferior Officers" who may be appointed, with prior congressional approval, directly by the president or by the heads of departments.

With two important exceptions, the seeds of the federal bureaucracy can be found in the 224-word statement contained in Article II, section 2. The key words for structuring a public administrative support system for the new government are: executive departments, principal officers (heads of departments), and inferior officers. All else that has developed over the past two hundred years has been derived from these three phrases. Upon reading this article, one can truly begin to appreciate the astuteness of Tocqueville, who perceived that the most amazing feature of our Constitution was "the variety of information and the amount of discernment that it presupposes in the people whom it is meant to govern."[1] This was a telling insight insofar as the administrative structure of the new government was concerned.

As noted above, all constitutional language concerning the federal administrative support structure may be derived from Article II, section 2, with two important exceptions. The first is contained in Article II, section 1: "The executive Power shall be vested in a President of the United States of America." One could easily glide past this seemingly innocuous line were it not, as

Corwin reminds us, for the explosive potential that this simple declaratory sentence repressed.[2] In the first place, it settled the heated debate in the Constitutional Convention as to whether the chief executive was to be singular or plural in number. In the second place, it gave the holder of this position a precise title. If one then skips down to the next-to-last statement in Article II, section 3 (the article contains only four sections), buried below a series of enumerated presidential clerkship duties can be found what Hamilton would have described as the source of the energetic impulse of the presidency and of the entire executive branch: "[H]e shall take Care that the Laws be faithfully executed." To emphasize the seemingly casual manner in which this phrase was presented, perhaps this clause should be bracketed by that which immediately precedes and follows: "[H]e shall receive Ambassadors and other public Ministers; he shall take Care that the Laws be faithfully executed, and shall Commission all the Officers of the United States."

One can only wonder why this operative phrase was not linked to the opening sentence of Article II. The result would have been a dynamic, action-forcing statement: "The executive Power shall be vested in a President of the United States of America [who] shall take Care that the Laws be faithfully executed." Certainly by linking the two intentions together and by positioning them prominently at the beginning of Article II, the office and its primary function would have been strategically emphasized. Conversely, of course, if the intention was to deemphasize deliberatively the obvious linkage, then the strategy of choice could well have been the one followed. Some clue to this disjunctive phrasing may be gained by reference to another debate that arose in the drafting of Article II.

During the draft stage, Madison suggested wording that explicitly identified the establishment of a Department of Foreign Affairs headed by an individual "to be called the Secretary of the Department of Foreign Affairs who shall be appointed by the President with advice and consent of the Senate, and to be removable by the President."[3] The Framers split on this clause with the result that Madisonian crispness was replaced by the more generally acceptable fuzziness of Article I, section 2.

That the Constitution speaks to the bureaucratic support structure of the new government in *sotto voce* is no accident. Rather, it reflects a commonsense solution to the kind of group decision making we have all experienced; that is, when dealing with primary issues of major significance, avoid controversies over secondary issues that may subvert agreement on the former. This is particularly true if the secondary issues involve elements that are so obvious to all that they do not have to be made explicit. As split as the fifty-five Framers may have been on the fundamental issues and methods of governance, the necessity of some kind of administrative cadre was taken as a given. The scope and magnitude of the new government was a debatable issue, but law in action is administration and there was certainly no question that the new regime would promulgate laws. Hence, the necessity for an administrative support staff was a nondebatable issue. It was an obvious, commonsense fact of political life. Indeed, this issue had almost completely worked itself out by the time the Constitutional Convention was convened.

Bear in mind that the historical reality and necessity for "inferior officers" were well established by 1787. For the preceding 150 years, America was internally administered by civilian personnel working in the service of either the colonial governors or the colonial legislatures. As the colonies grew in number and size, policymaking became more complex just as administrative practices became more permanent. As Robert Goldwin reminded us several years ago, "Considering how long Americans were on this continent before 1787, it is perfectly intelligent to speak of what the American constitution was before the Constitution of the United States was written."[4] One important part of that colonial American character involved the administrative implementation of policy intentions. Clearly, this caused various individuals to become involved in administrative methods, techniques, organizational structures, rules, and procedures. It may not be fair to say that the new government "hit the ground running" on this issue of an administrative support staff, but it certainly did not have to start from point zero.

Leonard White argues that while the art of self-government flourished during the colonial period, the art of management hardly existed. Moreover, he notes that the art of evading government assumed major proportions, becoming something of a "high art."[5] But perhaps White's standards are set too high. To judge that which passed as administrative implementation by the criterion of management is somewhat unreasonable. Public management as a science was beginning to take formidable shape in Europe at this time, and the administrative form that emerged in the colonies certainly paled by comparison. Nevertheless, colonial budgets were put together, records were kept, public projects were undertaken, and public order was maintained. But was it with managerial artistry? no; with administrative sufficiency? unquestionably yes.

Certainly by 1787 the development of colonial administration had progressed to the point where a body of experience had developed beyond the primitive stage. Moreover, one should not overlook the fact that administrative experience was not derivable solely from the public sector. The successful operation of banks, businesses, and even large farms required some degree of competent judgment and administrative skill, even if manifested in rather unsophisticated and elementary form. For example,

> Symbolic of the state of the administrative art in early American business was the preference for committees rather than single executives. The directors of the Massachusetts Bank confided even the smallest matters to committees of the board—the alteration and repair of the building, the procurement of a bell in case of fire or robbery, the erecting of a lightning rod. . . . The direct supervision of banking transactions was the duty of a "sitting director" selected in turn by the alphabet, to be in charge for a week.[6]

In addition to the cumulative body of experience gained from the colonial years that caused the administrative function to be taken for granted in the Constitution, the experience derived from the Continental Congress and the Articles of Confederation was also instructive. The constitutional reference to "departments" has to be read in light of the fact that, under the Articles of Confederation, Departments of Foreign Affairs, Treasury, War, Navy, and the Post Office had been established and their continuation seemed prudent. Similarly, the genesis of the singular phrases "principal Officer" and "Heads of Department" can also be traced to the experience obtained under the articles. For instance, committees of the Continental Congress initially attempted to perform directly the administrative functions of the established departments, but the committee members were quick to realize the heavy burden of carrying out both legislative and administrative functions. Private citizens were then selected and organized into boards accountable to the Continental Congress to perform the implementation function. But operational ineffectiveness persisted. Under these plural bodies, considerable time was lost and administrative efficiency was seldom even closely approximated. Thus, the next logical step was to create the position of secretary to serve as the principal operating officer of each department. Just as it was assumed that the departmental structure would be carried over into the new government, it was also assumed that each would be headed by a principal officer known as the secretary.[7]

Thus, the new republic was launched, complete with the basic elements of an administrative system; and while it may not be said that this bureaucratic enterprise flourished, neither may it be said that it floundered. Indeed, the policy and administrative challenges were formidable, and, although the demands and responsibilities for running a nation were, in 1787 as in 1988, an endeavor that dwarfed all others by comparison, the values of individual initiative, courage, and self-responsibility seemed to be the dominant manifestations of the newly formed administrative class. For those who did make the transition to the public sector, these values served as a base on which operational competency was subsequently developed. The new government was infused with intentions and moved by actions; purpose clearly preceded process. The intentions were explicitly value-based; the purpose was viewed as a transcendent national good, fuzzily defined but intuitively felt.

Both the original set of intentions and the original sense of purpose are viewed by many today as quaint and prosaic remnants of our past, ill-suited to meet the complex challenges of the twenty-first century. The almost linear decline of such sublime faith and hope in the administrative mission is, we are told, inversely related to the seemingly linear rise of a politicized bureaucracy that extended throughout most of the nineteenth century. Such a view does not lack for persuasive evidence, but such evidence is not without a competing counterforce. Throughout the nineteenth-century cycle of political degeneration, one can also trace the persistent strain of a commitment to those eloquent values that yield a deeply entrenched faith in an imminent transcendent good. Both sets of these contradictory values infused the spirit of bureaucracy as it matured during the formative years of the nineteenth century. Both sets of values are central to an understanding of our own particular bureau-democratic ethos and need to be examined in some detail.

## II

When Andrew Jackson began his presidency in 1829, he inherited what he perceived to be an impossible, schizophrenic bureaucracy. The first twelve years of the republic were carried out under the governance of the Federalists. The artful guidance of Washington yielded a fairly high degree of operational cohesion with a relatively low degree of ideological fervor. This did not remain for long, however. Policy and political differences, often bitter and intense, started to divide the nation into Federalist and Republican camps, and in 1801, with the election of Jefferson, the spirit and tone of democracy began to reflect a notably different tenor than that which had characterized the Federalist years. From 1801 to 1829, the policy and programmatic intentions of Jeffersonian republicans contrasted sharply with those of the early Federalists, and the two periods—one of twelve years' duration and the other of twenty-nine—must be viewed as philosophically and politically discrete. Viewed in terms of specific programmatic policy activity, however, the two periods were much less sharply delineated; and, most significantly, the administrative apparatus established at the outset by the Federalists remained essentially intact during the entire forty-year period. Thus, when Jackson entered office in 1829, he inherited a policy philosophy that was infused with the values of Jeffersonian republicanism. He also incurred a forty-year heritage of Federalist values deeply embedded in a substantially enlarged administrative structure. Jackson found the tenets of Jeffersonian republicanism essentially congenial to his own way of thinking but he viewed the Federalist values as revealed in the administrative structure as a totally unwarranted and illegitimate subversion, not only of his own brand of democratic republicanism, but of his constitutionally imposed responsibility to insure that the laws be faithfully executed.

Paradoxically, Jackson's views of presidential leadership were much more akin to those of Hamilton than Jefferson, and his presidency provided a benchmark in the emergence of a strong, forceful, and dynamic chief executive. But aside from this stylist link to the Federalists, Jackson's personal ethical and moral values were reflected in the spirit of a new democracy which was totally antithetical to the Federalist perspective. As a consequence, Jackson provided our constitutional and political history with not one but two lasting imprints: a model of a strong chief executive and the champion spokesman for the democratization of the public service, that is, the federal bureaucracy.

The infusion of a new "publicness" into the spirit and mechanics of democratic government that started with Jackson extended more than fifty years to the administration of Cleveland. Depending on one's predilections, it was a period that could be characterized as the Dark Ages of American government. Congress, the presidency, the administrative branch, and the courts were all scarred and scathed by the partisan political holocaust that swept through the nation. In the name of a new spirit of democracy, the federal establishment became politicized to the point where, democratic values aside, the basic notions of human decency were placed in grave jeopardy of survival. The true significance of the contributions by the early Federalist administrative system to the stability and the civility of the democratic policy process became visibly apparent when compared to that which stood in its place fifty-five years later. The purported elitist criteria of the Federalist notion of public service were abandoned in favor of political endorsements. The notion of career permanence was rejected in favor of rotation in office. The idea of professional expertise was dismissed in favor of political loyalty. The concept of quality education as a prerequisite for public service was discounted in favor of partisan obedience. Each of these factors, it must be emphasized, represented the manifest tendencies and general inclinations evidenced in government at the time. Although they were not the only forces that prevailed, the overall effects of this attitude and its concomitant values had a decidedly negative impact on the administrative system. Viewed by virtually any objective criterion, the period was predominantly a disaster for the career public service—with one important exception. During this period, national expansion and complexity accelerated in virtually every dimension and, as the nation expanded dramatically in both population and area, the federal administrative apparatus was forced to expand as well. Jackson was no nationalist; but national expansion, as Jefferson and his cohorts were quick to learn, could not be abated or ignored. If the Constitution follows the flag, can the bureaucracy be far behind? From 1800 to 1880, the federal bureaucracy increased by a factor of 33.33 in personnel. By comparison, between 1900 and 1982 that bureaucracy increased by a factor of 11.76. However, despite the phenomenal growth not only of the federal bureaucracy but of social complexity in general, the federal policy machine operated during this period at a relatively passive level.

Although Jackson was dogmatic in his vision of a strong chief executive, the power he attempted to centralize was designed to guard against government control rather than to extend federal policy regulation. Throughout the Jacksonian period, and beyond, "the strongest argument in justification of broad constitutional powers in the federal government was aimed at preventing regulation by the states."[8] According to President Van Buren, such a laissez-faire government would "leave every citizen and every interest to reap under its benign protection the rewards of virtue, industry, and prudence."[9] In keeping with this attitude, President Pierce vetoed, in 1854, a bill that authorized the granting of public lands to the states for the benefit of indigent insane persons.[10] Pierce reasoned that to extend such preferential treatment would logically lead to extending the same consideration to the indigent but sane, and he refused to move the federal government in that direction. Pierce, however, was not without a charitable bent. From 1850 to 1857 he combined with his predecessor, President Fillmore, to sign into law the appropriation of twenty-five million acres of federal public land to the states for the construction of more than fifty railroads. Indeed, it was on this policy issue that Congressman Justin Morrill based his land grant college bill which passed both the House and the Senate in 1857. On this issue, however, it was President Buchanan, not Pierce, who had to make the tough decision; and his veto endorsed, as "undeniable," the proposition "that Congress does not possess the power to appropriate money . . . for the purposes of educating the people of the respective states."[11] In the post–Civil War years, President Grant was, at one point, inclined to use federal funds to alleviate the depression of 1874 through the means of proto-WPA projects. James Garfield, then a congressman, and Grant's secretary of the treasury, Benjamin H. Bristow, combined to have him reconsider such a perilous policy. Garfield subsequently announced, "It was not part of the functions of the national government to fund employment for people." This attitude carried through to President Cleveland, who noted, in connection with the economic recessions that plagued his administration, "that while the people should patriotically and cheerfully support their government, its functions do not include the support of the people."[12]

The period of constitutional and political history covering the pre–Civil War Jacksonian Democracy and the post–Civil War Republicanism began on a note of high-spirited democratic humanism. It progressively degenerated, however, into an ugly mood of political nihilism and social despair. In the waning decades of the nineteenth century, the federal regulatory power did begin to assert itself, but only slowly. The objective reality of the corrupting effects of unregulated social complexity reflected the complementary emphasis of the social Darwinism of Herbert Spencer, the Protestant ethic of Calvinism, and the "invisible hand" of Adam Smith. The federal administrative system was caught in the vicious vortex of these countervailing forces, and although it was not crushed, it emerged from the vise badly bruised. Caught in the midst of a turbulent social reality that was fundamentally altering the American character from rural agrarianism to urban industrialism, and a turbulent political reality that was fundamentally altering the democratic character from the artistry of citizen participation to the craftiness of citizen manipulation, the federal bureaucracy was much more the victim than the victimizer. And yet, despite the predominant mood of political corruption that pervaded the federal establishment, the noble side of the democratic spirit of bureaucracy was never completely snuffed out. Perhaps goodness in the form of energetic courage, initiative, and self-responsibility is the *sine qua non* of a constitutional democracy and a democratic bureaucracy. On the other hand, perhaps such characteristics were evidenced solely on the basis of chance. In any event, the nineteenth century was not a total wasteland as far as the growth of bureaucratic competence, wisdom, and virtue was concerned.

## III

Viewing the foundation established by the early Federalists, Morison and Commager observed, "seldom has a class acted more wisely for the good of the whole than the Federalists."[13] Integrity and firmness became the guiding principles of President Washington, and he bequeathed good faith and justice to the nation in his Farewell Address. Even the Antifederalist Jefferson pressed for a trained cadre of career officials endowed by "genius and virtue." Washington may have been the guardian of federalist democracy and Jefferson may have been democracy's republican prophet; but, in many respects, it was Ralph Waldo Emerson who became democracy's high priest. Moving beyond Jefferson, Emerson sought to expose the existential being of democracy. Thus, it was Emerson, not Jefferson, who saw that free institutions would never liberate a body politic which was not, itself, free of blind prejudice, hatred, and corruption—that is, not free to think out the full consequences of democracy.[14] As Morison and Commager noted, "Transcendentalism was a movement to liberate America spiritually, as independence and democracy had liberated her politically; an attempt to make Americans worthy of their independence and elevate them to a new stature among mortals."[15]

By the same token, however, it was probably Jefferson rather than Emerson who had the better insight into the inherent nature of our Constitution. The neat and orderly rationalism that served to frame Emerson's transcendentalism could hardly have fit into Jefferson's more pragmatic republican idealism. Transcendentalism, to paraphrase an analogy offered by Fisher Ames, "is like a merchantman. You get on board and ride the wave and tide in safety and elation but, by and by, you strike a reef and go down. But democracy is like a raft. You never sink but, dammit, your feet are always in the water."[16]

To keep the raft afloat required hard work, ingenuity, common sense, and a high degree of personal integrity—characteristics much more closely associated with the pragmatic deists of the early Federalist period than with the transcendental Unitarians who followed. Democracy's prophet and high priest together inspired the new republic and infused its theoretical underpinnings with a sense of moral consciousness; but the craftsmanlike artisanship of governmental operations was drawn more directly from the practical wisdom of Benjamin Franklin than from either Jefferson, the prophet, or Emerson, the high priest. Indeed, the imprint of Franklin seemed stamped deep in the psyche of the federal bureaucracy from the very beginnings of its operation. Hard work, ingenuity, common sense, and personal integrity were the fundamental values employed in the administrative implementation of public policy.

Reflecting this practical wisdom, Washington wrote, "In every nomination to office I have endeavored . . . to make fitness of character my primary objective."[17] The notion of fitness of character, however badly it may have been abused in the subsequent years, was, nevertheless, consistently evidenced in the forms of administrative genius and virtue, integrity, and firmness. Hamilton, as the secretary of the treasury, set the early benchmark for administrative vision and wisdom; and during the period 1817 to 1825, the War Department, under the direction of John C. Calhoun, replaced the Treasury Department as the dynamic center of government operations.[18] The high standards of integrity, responsibility, and accountability imposed by Calhoun on his subordinates were duplicated by John McLean, who served as postmaster general from 1823 to 1829. Moreover, for each of these three early department heads, policy implementation was viewed in a positive and dynamic context. Calhoun and Hamilton undoubtedly would have concurred with McLean when he observed: "I say now as I have always said on the subject, that I do not consider an efficient administration of the department is shown by an annual balance in its favor. Its funds should be actively employed in extending the operations of the mail."[19]

Clearly, the first forty years of the new republic were shaped by the gentlemanly public service virtues of the Federalist tradition. But, to a very real extent, even the dismal pox-pits of political corruption that infected the nation during the remaining years of the nineteenth century were offset, in part, by putting the old elixir in a new bottle. George Bancroft, as secretary of the navy under President Polk, wrote that he would be guided by two maxims: "First, regard to the public service; and second, to act as if the eye of the whole democracy watched every motion and its ear heard every word I shall utter. Duty and publicity will be my watchwords."[20] A strong sense of publicness infused the Treasury Department again when President Pierce appointed James Guthrie as its secretary. Honesty, integrity, vigilance, fidelity, and economy were the guiding virtues employed by Guthrie, who, according to White, took to his task "with all the zeal of a ruthless reformer." As seen by Guthrie, the public was to be treated by all Treasury employees with frankness, courtesy, and kindness. "Thus, by dignity of deportment and an accommodating spirit, [each clerk would] serve to conciliate . . . the confidence and respect of the people for the government."[21] Moreover, other basic public service values such as expertise and responsiveness were incorporated in an emerging new professionalism that was located in the newly created Department of Agriculture.

Organized originally in 1862 as a subcabinet department headed by a commissioner, and elevated to full cabinet status in 1889,[22] this department was destined, for approximately the next hundred years of its existence, to become the trend setter for many of the best (and some of the less-than-best) features of our bureau-democratic ethos. From its very beginning, the department was permeated with a sense of mission that White describes as an undercurrent of devotion to the qualitative improvement of farm life in particular and to human life in general. Deeply steeped in political astuteness from the outset, the department, nonetheless, was predominantly concerned with science, not politics; with experimental programs, not partisan campaigning; and with long-range planning, not immediate payoffs.[23]

Agriculture was the first client-oriented department in the federal establishment, but it was also the first science-oriented department; and these two conditions combined to serve very nicely the steadily expanding regulatory inclinations of Congress. Unlike the Departments of the Treasury, Post Office, or Interior, which were organized around clerks engrossed in the implementation of highly structured, routinized program activity, the Agriculture Department, with its cadre of highly diversified scientists, was effectively utilized in countless ways to extend the constitutional presence of the federal government into virtually every hamlet in the nation. To be sure, in the twilight years of the nineteenth century, the expansion of federal regulatory policy was certainly not limited to the mandates assigned the Department of Agriculture by Congress.[24] However, the patterns of federal regulatory activity associated with the independent regulatory commissions, for example, differed significantly from those assigned to the Agriculture Department. The portents of the positive state that emerged full force in 1933 are not to be found in the value assumptions that underlie the independent regulatory commissions; rather, they are to be found in the public-service commitment that infused the Department of Agriculture.

The tone and tenor of this commitment were set quite simply, but explicitly, by the department's first full-fledged secretary, Jeremiah Rusk: "Everything that leads to a more intimate acquaintance between the department and the farmers throughout the country must be mutually advantageous."[25] It is doubtful that any of the early Federalists would have concurred with a literal rendering of Rusk's pronouncement. There can be no doubt, however, that their respective purposeful intentions would have been the same. The administrative vision of a transcendent purpose could apply equally to both periods, with traces being consistently revealed in between. Indeed, the sense of administrative ethics that wends its way through our entire constitutional history suggests a norm of material life that has been consistently portrayed in art, literature, and the Bible. In Shakespeare's *The Tempest,* Ferdinand speaks of the hope of "quiet days, fair issue, and long life," a theme that is repeated by Juno: "Honor, riches, marriage blessing/Long continuance and increasing." In citing these passages, it is Lionel Trilling who then notes that "it has to do with good harvests and full barns and the qualities of affluent decorum."[26] This same symbol of virtue is reflected in Proverbs in the form of a simple causal proposition: "[If you] Honor the Lord with your substance and with the first fruits of all you produce, then your barns will be filled with plenty and your vats will be bursting with wine."[27]

The notion of prosperity was linked to freedom in forming a key element of our democratic heritage, and although the Founding Fathers were not unmindful of a material prosperity associated with good harvests and full barns, Jefferson's notion of the pursuit of happiness (linked though it may be to Locke's notion of property) does suggest a prosperity that is much more normative and spiritual in its symbolic content. The Greek concept of *eudaemonism,* or happiness, when linked to the biblical notion of obligation (Honor the Lord) becomes, in our democratic ethos, the foundation from which virtue is to be derived. The pursuit of happiness, along with the freedoms of life and liberty, will yield good harvests and full barns; but they also will yield a spiritual and an ethical plentitude that will insure a government designed solely in response to the needs and wants of the governed. To paraphrase Rusk, an intimate acquaintance must bind government and the governed—and especially the bureaucracy and the citizenry. The notion of intimate acquaintance suggests an element of sincerity, and the richness gained from sincerely founded interpersonal relationships creates a prosperity of happiness that becomes energized by an inner sense of obligation. Thus, as a result of this deeply rooted sense of happiness and obligation, the abject political immorality that threatened the inner nucleus of democracy was never totally successful in destroying the integrity that is inherent in the sound craftsmanship of public administration, particularly as that craft is applied in its bureau-democratic form. In its many subsequent manifestations—whether energized by the tenets of scientific management, partisan mutual adjustment, or analytical optimization—the operational competence of public administration has always been held accountable to the more fundamental and transcendent values of our bureau-democratic tradition. As Abigail Adams long ago advised her young son, John Quincy, "Great learning and superior abilities, should you ever possess them, will be of little value and small estimation unless virtue, honor, truth, and integrity are added to them."[28] What can be learned from this experience is that unyielding individual integrity, moral rectitude, and ethical maturity—the core elements of a democratic *civis, civitas, civilitas*—simply cannot be taken for granted, but, rather, have to be applied, practiced, and cultivated—nurtured and nourished—in a purposeful environment that is conducive to the free and open—the unashamed and unabashed—expression of such values.

The effects of Jacksonian democracy and partisan politics on the federal administrative complex were many and varied, but one seemingly paradoxical pattern appears most pronounced. In both centripetal and centrifugal fashion, the federal bureaucracy was simultaneously pulled *into* the body politic as a result of the politicization of the public service, and driven *away* from the body politic as a result of the prevailing laissez-faire philosophy of public policy. Ironically, it was these counteracting forces that provided the fertile seedbed for the subsequent growth of a democratized merit system on the one hand, and the clearly demarcated policy/administration and value/fact dichotomies on the other.

The political reform movement that swept across the nation during the closing decades of the nineteenth century became fixed on the concepts of procedural fairness, equity, and impartiality, and, in no small measure, the impressive organizational achievements of the Department of Agriculture significantly influenced the thrust of this reform movement. Unfortunately, however, only half of the Agriculture Department's success formula was embraced: the lustrous brilliance of an undiluted, undefiled, and unadulterated science of management became the new hope of the twentieth-century policy process. But in this instance, that which was overlooked proved to be much more important than that which was embraced, and the words of Abigail Adams assumed even greater prophetic proportions—"Great learning and superior abilities . . . will be of little value and small estimation unless virtue, honor, truth, and integrity are added to them."

The science of agriculture was immutably linked to a critically conscious sense of a salutary public mission. This resulted in the emergence of an ethics of responsible citizenship. By contrast, the science of management that evolved in the federal bureaucracy during the first third of the twentieth century was linked to the notion of detached objectivity. The administration of public policy during this period was driven, as Max Weber would say, *sine ira et studio*—without passion or enthusiasm. And, once again from the past, we hear the transcendental whispers of Ralph Waldo Emerson, reminding us that nothing great was ever achieved without enthusiasm.

## IV

What emerges from this all-too-brief and sketchy examination of the development of our constitutional democracy, the public policy process, and the federal bureaucracy in America during the nineteenth century is a combination of elements that somehow must be captured and linked together to form the essence of a bureau-democratic ethic consistent with, and supportive of, the basic tenets of our democratic creed. Learning in the form of intellectual competency, virtue in the form of ethical maturity and moral integrity, and enthusiasm in the form of purposeful democratic objectives are all essential elements that form the basis of an effective bureaucratic system. Such effectiveness, however, cannot be derived in a vacuum or on a unilateral basis; it can only be developed and maintained on the basis of reciprocal relationships.

First, policy impulses must flow reciprocally between career administrators and policy officials; second, such impulses must also flow reciprocally between career administrators and the citizenry. Thus, the infusion and expansion of intellectual capabilities, ethical maturity, moral integrity, and democratic purposefulness are possible only where interpersonal relationships are marked by some common bond. Indeed, in regard to all three of these sets of participants in the policy process—policy officials, career bureaucrats, and individual citizens—reciprocal lincs must be drawn linking each to the other in a common bond of trust and loyalty. Each learns to trust in response to evidence of loyalty; each is loyal in response to evidence of trustworthiness. Such trust and loyalty form the basis of a constitutional faithfulness which is the generative source of an intellectual, ethical, and purposeful mutual interdependence between policy officials, career bureaucrats, and individual citizens.

Loyalty and faithfulness are two of the basic biblical themes that permeate our entire democratic tradition. The Old Testament directs our loyalty and faithfulness to the supreme authority of God, as when the Book of Proverbs tells us, "Let not loyalty and faithfulness forsake you; bind them around your neck, write them on the tablet of your heart."[29] From the Greeks, loyalty and faithfulness to authority were reflected in the notions of *hieros* (sacred) and *archos* (leader) from which is derived the early Christian concept of *hierarchia* (hierarchy) and *hierarches* (one who is a hierarch). Similarly, it is also from the Greek of the early Christian church period that the notion of love is given a specific theological connotation that serves to bind all citizens, regardless of official rank or social position, into a common fellowship based on the mutual reciprocity of loyalty and faithfulness to each other. It is this loyalty and faithfulness as encapsuled in the notion of love of God and love of neighbor that is the dominant theme of the New Testament, and which is subsequently reflected in our own democratic tradition in the form of Jefferson's social ethic. Life, liberty, and pursuit of happiness are totally vacuous concepts unless viewed in terms of the loyalty and faithfulness of a love that binds citizen to citizen, neighbor to neighbor. What may be derived from our biblical tradition is a holistic synthesis of loyalty *and* faithfulness, obligation *and* love, purpose *and* being; and it is just such a synthesis that is reflected in the democratic ethos which permeates our constitutional character.

Perhaps it is too much to suggest that this is exactly what Hamilton, Jefferson, and Madison had in mind as they guided the formation of our Constitution and subsequently lent their efforts to the actual responsibilities of making the new government work. But it is certainly not too much to suggest that, despite their radically different perspectives of the central government's policy and regulatory responsibilities, as well as the role of the federal bureaucracy in carrying out these tasks, they were in complete accord over the unquestionable fact that the intrinsic elements needed to make a constitutional democracy work were essentially ethical and moral in character. Viewed in terms of democratic theory and political rhetoric, this intrinsic ethical and moral "goodness" of the American character has never escaped our attention over the past two hundred years. But the paths that guide theory and rhetoric on the one hand and actual day-to-day operational decisions on the other have diverged more frequently than they have converged over the same period. And the major premise that is advanced here is that the critical variable affecting the degree of convergence or divergence between these two forces (i.e., theory and practice, or intentions and acts, or policy and administration, or even, if you will, morality and ethics) is the role of the federal bureaucracy in the policy process.

Some years ago, Norton Long wrote: "Accustomed as we are to the identification of election with both representation and democracy, it seems strange at first to consider that the nonelected civil service may be both more representative of the country and more democratic in its composition than Congress."[30]

On the surface, this proposition appears to rest solely on an empirical base, and it would be totally unwarranted to suggest that Long intended any conclusion other than the empirical observation he advanced. Nevertheless, if Long's observation is juxtaposed to another, more avowedly normative proposition advanced by David Levitan, some four decades ago, an interesting ethical speculation concerning the role of bureaucracy in our constitutional system can be advanced. "An outstanding government administrator once remarked," Levitan wrote, that "administration must have a soul." . . . It needs to be added, however, that administration should contribute to the fuller development of the soul of the state. I have tried to point out that the administrative machinery and the political and philosophical principle together determine the system of government; that a democratic state must be not only based on democratic principles but also democratically administered, the democratic philosophy permeating its administrative machinery and being manifested in its relations both with the citizen outside the government and the citizen inside the government, the public servant; that administrative procedures are more important in effectuating the basic principles of government than is substantive law; and that these procedures must therefore be constantly reexamined in terms of the ends they serve and changed when the changing social and economic milieu requires different means to attain these ends.[31]

The notion that "administration must have a soul" is an interesting proposition despite its confounding implications. In the medieval merger of church and state, the imprint of the human soul became a matter of central significance as the divine right of kings doctrine, complete with papal anointment, carried with it not only the divinely ordained right to rule, but also the divinely ordained responsibility for the protection and respect of even the lowest vassal's inner being. Ostensibly, the Reformation cleaved a nominal dichotomy between church and state, and the Enlightenment cut an even deeper swath between the metaphysical and physical worlds. Thus, concern about individual human worth presumably could be ignored by all purely secular political institutions. In actual fact, of course, we know this not to be the case. The nation-state, from its emergence to the present day—and that is to say *every* nation-state—has been forced to address this immutable and implacable phenomenon. As ingeniously as it has attempted for the past five hundred years to finesse the theological implications of this concept, no nation-state has been able to ignore the ontological system of ethics that is associated with the notion of human worth or being. Our own revolutionary document, the Declaration of Independence, rests on the premise that the divinely ordained soul of a people had been profaned by a despotic and tyrannically evil king. Moreover, in anticipating the Preamble of the Constitution, the Declaration of Independence concludes by "appealing to the Supreme Judge of the world for the rectitude of our intentions."

If the notion of the human soul comes to us from the Greeks as filtered through the medium of the Middle Ages, still another theological concept that has previously been mentioned, if only briefly, relates directly to our democratic experience—namely, the New Testament notion of love *(agapē)* as reflected in the Greek *eros* and in the Latin *caritas.* From ancient Rome, the concepts of *civis, civitas,* and *civilitas* flow forward to form the underpinnings of the U.S. Constitution; but it is the notion of *caritas* that is certainly seen by Jefferson as creating a democracy not just of the people, by the people, and for the people, as Lincoln phrased it, but a democracy of one individual self always as related to another individual self through the impulse of *caritas.* Indeed, the democratic character of America incorporates both concepts in the sense of a love or deep and genuine respect for the intrinsic dignity of the divinely ordained human worth. Thus, although all of our chief executives, legislators, and jurists are sworn to uphold this implicit premise of our constitutional system, it is the career public servants—the bureaucracy—who are most directly, and most personally, confronted by its challenge. Viewed in this context, Levitan's provocative observation—"administration should contribute to the fuller development of the soul of the state"—can begin to assume practical significance.

For example, such an attitude was expressed in the very early years of our republic by one political commentator who wrote:

> Good government manifestly depends much more on the goodness of the men who fill the public offices, than on the goodness of the form of government, constitution, or even laws of the state; for the errors of all these, under the administration of good men, will be mended or made tolerable . . . but weak and wicked men will pervert the best laws to the purposes of favour or oppression.[32]

A similar attitude was also reflected by Jefferson, who on one occasion observed, "On great occasions every good officer must be ready to risk himself in going beyond the strict line of the law when the public preservation requires it; his motives will be a justification."[33] Later, following the purchase of the Louisiana

Territory, Jefferson found the need to apply his own advice to himself, and his response was resoundingly eloquent.

> The legislature in casting behind them metaphysical subtleties, and risking themselves like faithful servants, must ratify and pay for it, and must throw themselves on their country for doing for them unauthorized what we know they would have done for themselves had they been in a situation to do it. It is the case of a guardian investing the money of his ward in purchasing an important adjacent territory, and saying to him when of age, I did this for your good; I pretend to no right to bind you; you may disavow me and I must get out of the scrape as best I can. I thought it my duty to risk myself for you.[34]

"I thought it my duty to risk myself for you." With these words Jefferson illuminated the intrinsic link between policy implementation and a deep affection and respect—or, simply, love—for the sanctity of democracy. This sense of responsibility was reflected by Secretary of Navy Bancroft when he said, "Duty and publicity will be my watchwords"; by Secretary of Treasury Guthrie, who insisted that frankness, courtesy, and kindness be extended to the public by his clerks with a dignity of deportment and an accommodating spirit; and by Secretary of Agriculture Rusk who proclaimed, "Everything that leads to a more intimate acquaintance between the department and the farmers . . . must be mutually advantageous." From these comments, one can, perhaps, glean just what is involved in assuming the duty of risk in the administrative implementation of public policy. At the very least, it means incurring empirical risks by demonstrating initiative in creative, imaginative, and innovative problem solving. It certainly means incurring ethical risks associated with openness, sharing, trust, and loyalty. And, most significantly, it means incurring the dangerous risks of excessive zeal, blind obedience, and myopic purposelessness.

Given the very serious consequences associated with risk taking, perhaps we should be wary of urging our bureaucratic cadres to risk themselves for us in the name of democracy. History provides too many examples of administrative villainy borne in the cradle of virtuousness. Thus, our constitutional tradition strongly emphasizes the notion that ours is a government of laws, not of men; responsible constitutional democracy is founded on collective rational deliberation and not on impetuous individual risk taking. Indeed, it can be persuasively argued that, no matter how deeply rooted the principles of *caritas* and human dignity may be in our democratic system, they can amount to naught in the wake of a bureaucracy committed to the nihilistic values of political expediency hidden behind a facade of empty virtue.

As valid as this perfectly legitimate fear may be, however, the fact remains that the luster of these precious democratic concepts can no less be corroded by an administrative service that has been intellectually, ethically, and motivationally neutered by the canons of objective impersonality in the name of efficiency, economy, impartiality, or procedural justice. The sense of authentic mission that characterized much of the nineteenth-century bureaucratic experiment in learning to cope with the multiple complexities associated with an expanding public policy process was, to be sure, grossly contorted and corrupted by the machinations of an ogreish patronage system. But, as noted above, in attempting to restore the bureaucracy's purity of mission, the reform efforts of the late nineteenth century stripped the public career service of its duty to risk itself for the qualitative enhancement of the citizenry.

According to Lionel Trilling, George Eliot, the British author, once confided to a friend that God was inconceivable and immortality was unbelievable. But, she said, it was beyond question that Duty was "peremptory and absolute."[35] Duty, so perceived, would seem to assume the character of a cause or, if you will, a categorical imperative which, according to Trilling, could validate the personal life that obeyed it. A categorical duty, thus viewed, creates for the individual his or her own inner imperative which guides the individual with a sense of purposeful direction or cause and creates within the individual a sense of personal coherence and selfhood.[36]

As seen in this context, duty carries an individual far beyond the realm of mere compliance, obedience, or even objective performance. Rather, it suggests an energetic, albeit existential, enthusiasm to experience the purely inner satisfaction, personal affection, or genuine love that is realized when duty provides purposeful direction to a transcendent cause. Nevertheless, a duty to a cause which is peremptive and absolute must be infused by an impulse of *caritas* if it is to avoid degenerating into a dutifulness that is mechanistically contrived or situationally expedient. If one is to say, "I thought it my duty to risk myself for you," such duty clearly has to be found in a love for some other human being, or, in a less personalized sense, in a sincere affection or genuine respect for some transcendent cause or sense of purposefulness. "The cause sustains and feeds the relation," H. Richard Niebuhr once observed, "and a community . . . can be a community only by virtue of such a common and binding cause."[37]

Our constitutional democracy rests on the basic notion of the inviolability of human dignity, and the justifications for our governmental system and the public policy process rest solely on the extent to which this categorical imperative of democracy is defended and enhanced. While every public official can legitimately be held accountable to this peremptory and absolute duty, it is the public administrator for whom this notion of duty has particular importance since it is the individual bureaucrat who stands opposite the individual citizen on a face-to-face, day-to-day basis as the actual implementation of public policy unfolds. If individual public administrators are to move beyond the role of boundary guarding agents, engaged solely in the transfer of quantitative goods and things, they must—in the fashion of the early Federalist and early Agriculture Department administrators—become motivated by a commitment to a purposeful cause and a sense of duty which transcend the specific situational circumstance and extend beyond to the categorical imperative of democracy—that is, the enhancement of the quality of life of the individual citizen.

George Eliot could speak of God as inconceivable, immortality as unbelievable, but Duty as peremptory and absolute. In a strikingly similar fashion, H. Richard Niebuhr noted:

> To deny the reality of a supernatural being called God is one thing; to live without confidence in some center of value and without loyalty to a cause is another. . . .
> We cannot live without a cause, without some object of devotion, some center of worth, something on which we rely for meaning.[38]

The notion of duty as a love or an intense inner commitment to a cause that extends beyond the exigencies of the moment would seem to constitute a specific attribute of the public administrator as agent of the citizen. Lionel Trilling provides an interesting insight that may be relevant in this regard. Jane Austen, he notes,

> was committed to the ideal of "intelligent love," according to which the deepest and truest relationship that can exist between human beings is pedagogic. This relationship consists in the giving and receiving of knowledge about right conduct, in the formulation of one's character by another, the acceptance of another's guidance in one's own growth.[39]

Trilling is correct in noting that life perceived as an aspect of instruction is scarcely a new vision; but its relevance for our current predicament seems nonetheless real, particularly at a time when rapidly accelerating social complexity makes right conduct highly problematical. Certainly, insofar as the effective implementation of public policy is concerned, it is the federal bureaucracy that enjoys the most advantageous position *vis-à-vis* the citizenry to inform and to be informed, to guide and to be guided. The cause that binds the citizen and the public administrator in our constitutional system is a shared respect or love in the democratic ideal of intrinsic individual goodness. The attainment of this ideal is directly related to the "intelligent love," the pedagogical love which potentially exists between the citizenry and the bureaucracy. It is this binding force that makes interpersonal trust possible, and it moves democracy beyond the banalities of a mechanistically contrived constitutionalism to the transcendent position of a dynamic, holistic process guided by a "living," organic document.

To be sure, for those who tend to perceive public-sector career bureaucrats as ominous, murky gray forces who operate somewhere on the other side of midnight, the argument I am advancing will surely be discomfiting. Even those who have a more benign view of public administration and administrators may be inclined to echo Glaucon, who says to Socrates that his heavenly city is too ideal and does not exist "anywhere on this earth." But Socrates' answer to Glaucon should not be summarily dismissed; it holds particular relevance for administrator and citizen alike if the ideal vision of American democracy is to carry into the twenty-first century. "Glaucon, whether such a [city] exists or ever will exist in fact, is no matter; for he will live after the manner of that city, having nothing to do with any other." But, Socrates adds, "In heaven there is laid up a pattern of it, methinks, which he who desires may behold, and beholding, may set his own house in order."[40]

Indeed, it is the tone and temper of Socrates speaking here that seems to be also reflected in the oath of the Athenian city-state which, for public administrators, is known simply as the Athenian Code.

> We will ever strive for the ideals and sacred things of the city, both alone and with many; we will unceasingly seek to quicken the sense of public duty; we will revere and obey the city's laws; we will transmit this city not only not less, but greater, better, and more beautiful than it was transmitted to us.[41]

Crisis and complexity are relative and relational terms; no age has a monopoly on either and virtually every decade of our history has been infused with both. The explosion and enormous expansion of public policy activity by the federal government during most of the twentieth century have imposed an almost intolerable burden on those who bear the responsibility to insure that the laws are faithfully executed. In the early nineteenth century, the responsibility of political faithfulness was viewed by most public administrators primarily as a peremptory and absolute duty to realize the true sense of *caritas* inherent in democracy. Perhaps this can be attributed to the unsophisticated naiveté that characterized our political process at that time with a dynamic hopefulness. By the end of the nineteenth century, democracy, and the federal bureaucracy, were spared from the ravages of the spoils system by the combined energies of the reform movement. Nevertheless, the long-term consequences of this movement, which have manifested themselves throughout the second century of our constitutional enterprise, have had some serious, debilitating effects. The categorical imperative of the federal bureaucracy has steadily diminished during the twentieth century with the exception of its heightened revival during the crisis years of the Great Depression. The earlier sense of duty seems now, as we attempt to recall it, a nostalgic anachronism. And yet, the search for excellence in management circles, public and private, is proceeding in directions which are strikingly reminiscent of a past that may not, in fact, be so distantly removed from our present reality. The qualities of organizational and managerial excellence which are currently being "discovered" are, in reality, qualities of human interpersonal relationships which are profoundly ethical and moral in character.

At the present time, some very exciting and challenging changes are taking place inside public-sector organizations, especially at the subnational levels. At the local level, for example, public administrators in numerous communities throughout the nation are operating—perhaps out of the stark necessity for sheer survival—with a very clear and pronounced sense of duty to risk. As a consequence, in many instances the notion of citizen is being reclaimed as the notion of the democratic ideal becomes revived. The situation that relates the citizenry to its national government, however, is not as bright. There is more than sufficient evidence to indicate that the policy outputs of the federal establishment are still being treated variously by the body politic with boredom, distrust, and/or futility. The constitutional sense of duty at this level of government seems hopelessly enmeshed in a webwork of the mechanistic constitutionalisms of dutifulness. Certainly there is little to suggest that the categorical imperative of democracy is currently at work at the national level, preparing us to broach the twenty-first century. Are the elements for such an ethic irretrievably lost or are they simply lying dormant? The premise I advance is that they exist in the ethos of a profession that has survived the millenniums; but, more directly, these elements exist in the ethos of a bureaucracy especially fitted to the contours of our democratic constitutional tradition. Let me attempt to capsulize the essence of this premise as it has been developed in the preceding sections.

The prime virtue of our constitutional democracy is derived from two basic sources. First, it is based on the Greek notion of happiness, as modified by the Old Testament dictum of love of God, and, second, on the Old Testament convenantal notion of obligation or duty, as amplified in the New Testament as love of neighbor. These two themes, happiness and duty, form the keystone of our democratic archway. Happiness, as in Jefferson's "pursuit of happiness," is a love—an absolute and unwavering faithfulness—in the divinely inspired, transcendent goodness of democracy. Integral to this notion of happiness or goodness are the concepts of the absolute sanctity of individual human worth and dignity (life) and of individual human reason and choice (liberty). Thus, the Constitution of the United States can be viewed as the positive document designed to insure, protect, and guarantee the "natural law" intention of its framers—that is, the inalienable rights of life, liberty, and the pursuit of happiness.

The Constitution, including the Bill of Rights, implicitly embodies the notion of the transcendent purposefulness and goodness of democracy; but its primary métier is in its explicitly articulated sense of duty or obligation as, for example, the explicit obligation of the president to insure that the laws are *faithfully* executed. If one integrates the sense of happiness or transcendent purposefulness with the sense of duty or obligation, it becomes apparent that the primary function of government is to maintain a sociopolitical environment which is fully conducive to the qualitative enhancement of the life of the citizenry. It is this purposeful function and duty which constitute the categorical imperative of democracy; and the proposition advanced in the preceding pages rests on the assumption that the extent to which this categorical imperative of democracy can be even approximately realized depends, in turn, on the extent to which individual career public administrators who comprise the bureaucracy can internalize this imperative as their own mandate for the democratic implementation of public policy.

The transcendent goodness of constitutional democracy depends on the manner in which its specific policy goals and objectives are implemented by our cadre of professional managers and administrators. Given a high degree of rational-intellectual competency, ethical maturity and integrity, and a shared vision of the transcendent purposefulness of democracy, the bureaucracy stands as the agency of the citizen; it stands as the primary problem solving and problem dissolving policy mechanism in our system; it stands, in the final analysis, as both our first and last line of defense in making democracy "work." However, given a low degree of rational competency, ethical maturity, and/or transcendent vision, the world's most sublime experiment is bound to diminish the faithful hopes engendered by the ratification of the

Constitution. As the preceding sections have attempted to demonstrate, individual bureaucrats can be infused with a sense of transcendent purposefulness or with a sense of egoistic self-interest generated by a politicized pragmatism. Both value perspectives have been manifested in the course of our constitutional development; but the implications of each perspective, as related to the categorical imperative of democracy, are as different as the vision of light is from the vision of darkness.

To be sure, administration is politics, the bureaucracy is an integral part of our political system, and politics in a democratic context is clearly the art of the possible. We would have it no other way. But a commitment to the art and artistry of the possible incurs an inherent tension between the conflicting forces of "the possible" as energized toward a transcendent hopefulness of that which is, is good, and "the possible" as impelled toward a pragmatic expediency of that which is good enough, is good enough. Bureaucracy stands as the critical intervening variable in determining the outcome of this complex equation, and, in this regard, even a high degree of intellectual competency, ethical maturity, and purposeful direction cannot be taken as determinative. This cluster of critical values can be decidedly skewed by a conscious choice between risk-incursive and risk-aversive behavior. Either strategy can be pursued in the name of professional competence, ethical integrity, and purposefulness but, again, the relational value impact of risk-incursive as opposed to risk-aversive behavior on the categorical imperative of democracy is, itself, fundamentally and categorically different.

Thomas Jefferson certainly seemed to sense the dynamically different import attached to these contradictory attitudes of risk. It was Jefferson who led us through our first dark age, and the astute foresight he evidenced at that time seems particularly appropriate when applied to our bureaucratic context today as we attempt to manage and control the vast complexities of our current condition. "I thought it my duty to risk myself for you." This, in itself, captures the total essence of the purpose of bureaucracy as it relates to the categorical imperative of our constitutional democracy. Nothing less will do; nothing more is needed.

# Notes

1. Alexis de Tocqueville, *Democracy in America* (New York: Vintage Books, 1964), 172.

2. Edwin S. Corwin, ed., *The Constitution of the United States: Analysis and Interpretation* (Washington: U.S. Government Printing Office, 1953), xix.

3. Carl B. Swisher, *American Constitutional Development* (Boston: Houghton Mifflin, 1954), 52.

4. Robert A. Goldwin, "Of Men and Angels: A Search for Morality in the Constitution," in *The Moral Foundation of the American Republic,* ed. Robert H. Horwitz (Charlottesville: University Press of Virginia, 1977), 8.

5. Leonard D. White, *The Federalists* (New York: Macmillan, 1961), 470–71.

6. Ibid., 472–73.

7. Swisher, 23, 51.

8. Ibid., 272.

9. Leonard D. White, *The Jacksonians* (New York: Macmillan, 1956), 6.

10. Swisher, 372.

11. Ibid., 374.

12. Leonard D. White, *The Republican Era* (New York: Macmillan, 1963), 4, and William. B. Hesseltine, *Ulysses S. Grant: Politician* (New York: Dodd, Meade, 1935), 339.

13. Samuel E. Morison and Henry Steele Commager, *The Growth of the American Republic,* 5th ed., rev. (New York: Oxford University Press, 1950), 1:278.

14. Ibid., 522.

15. Ibid., 520.

16. Esmond Wright, *Fabric of Freedom, 1763–1800* (New York: Hill and Wang, 1978), 216.

17. White, *The Federalists,* 258.

18. Leonard D. White, *The Jeffersonians* (New York: Macmillan, 1961), 246, 248–49, 264.

19. Ibid., 303.

20. White, *The Jacksonians,* 102–3.

21. Ibid., 184–85.

22. The establishment of the U.S. Department of Agriculture with full cabinet status in 1889 followed a nearly 100-year gestation period. In the early days of the republic, when the Patent Office was part of the State Department, the commissioner of patents was designated as the receiving clerk for all exotic seeds and cuttings American consuls in distant lands were instructed to send back to the United States. This obviously industrious

and imaginative federal clerk, operating only on a departmental directive and with no funds, enlisted the cooperative support of various congressman who began distributing free seeds to their constituents. In time, this makeshift operation began to flourish and, in 1839 Congress made its first $1,000 appropriation for seed distribution, conducting agricultural investigations, and gathering agricultural statistics. In 1849 the Patent Office was transferred to the newly created Interior Department while still maintaining jurisdiction over this mini-agriculture "program." In 1862 the "program" itself was transferred to the newly established subcabinet Department of Agriculture, at which time the annual appropriation for agricultural activities, including the free-seed program, had expanded to $60,000. See Swisher, 376–77, and White, *The Republican Era,* 238.

23. White, *The Republican Era,* 243.

24. Ibid., 247–51.

25. Ibid., 242.

26. Lionel Trilling, *Sincerity and Authenticity* (New York: Harcourt Brace, 1980), 38.

27. Proverbs 3:9–10 (RSV).

28. White, *The Jeffersonians,* 549.

29. Proverbs 3:3 (RSV).

30. Norton Long, "Bureaucracy and Constitutionalism," *The Polity* (originally appeared in *The American Political Science Review* 46 [September 1952]: 808–18; Chicago: Rand McNally, 1962), 71–72.

31. David M. Levitan, "Political Ends and Administrative Means," *Public Administration Review* 3 (Winter 1943): 359.

32. White, *The Federalists,* 268.

33. White, *The Jeffersonians,* 6.

34. Swisher, 122.

35. Trilling, 109.

36. Ibid.

37. Libertus A. Hoedemaker, *The Theology of H. Richard Niebuhr* (Philadelphia: The Pilgrim Press, 1970), 70; see also H. Richard Niebuhr, *The Responsible Self* (New York: Harper and Row, 1963), 118.

38. H. Richard Niebuhr, *Radical Monotheism and Western Culture* (New York: Harper, 1960), 25, 118.

39. Trilling, 77.

40. *Plato's The Republic,* trans. B. Jowett, 3d ed. (Oxford, England: Clarendon Press, 1888), 9:306.

41. Gustav Gilbert, *The Constitutional Antiquities of Sparta and Athens* (London: Swan Sonnenschein & Co., 1895), 220–22, esp. n. 1, p. 222. See also Lewis Packard, *Morality and Religion of the Greeks* (New Haven: Tuttle and Taylor, 1881), 20–21.

# VIII

# PRUDENCE AND RATIONALITY UNDER THE CONSTITUTION

★

*Martin M. Shapiro*

I n the United States the study of constitutional law has involved a continuous discussion of the nature of politics in the broadest sense, that is, a discussion of how to achieve the goal of the good person in the good state given existing conditions and the qualities of human nature. The Constitution is so important to us that, while in Europe constitutional law is conceived of as a subset of public law, for us public law—that is, the law governing the relations between government and the individual—is conceived of as a dependency of constitutional law. So all of our public law provides an occasion for the debate about politics.

A second realm for the same political discussion is public administration. But thinking about the nature of public administration from a political perspective has been far less continuous than has the exercise of that same perspective in constitutional law. The United States is the first nation in which large-scale government enterprises arose at the same time as large-scale private enterprises. In Europe, institutions and techniques for managing the large endeavors, first of the Catholic Church and then of the royal and imperial dynasties, had developed long before the Industrial Revolution created large private entities. Thus, public

*Martin Shapiro is a professor at the School of Law, University of California, Berkeley.*

administration existed long before business administration. In the United States, government and business corporations grew up at the same time. So business administration and public administration tended to be conflated. Given our vast capitalist energies, business administration was the dominant flavor in the conflation. In France, middle-range government managers are recruited to run the corporations. In the United States corporate managers are recruited to run the government. When we are not thinking especially hard about government, we say we want to make the government "businesslike." Because we tend to either forget or denigrate the "public" in public administration, we tend to forget or denigrate the politics in public administration.

In certain times of crisis, however, American thinking does focus on the public in public administration and then public administration does become a vehicle for political debate. The first of these crisis periods was that of the Federalists and the Antifederalists and their Jacksonian successors. In that period, two rival models of public administration, based on two rival political theories, were debated. The Hamiltonian model, based on theories of mixed government that combine elements of rule by the one, the few, and the many, called for public administration by a few long-serving experts under the hierarchical authority of the president.[1] The Jacksonian theory, based on theories of direct democracy, called for the "spoils system" and "rotation in office."[2] As the people gave their votes to one party or the other, the common men who were partisans of the winning party should come into office to run the government until changing electoral fortunes replaced them with the common men who were partisans of the other.

By about 1840 this debate was settled largely in favor of the Jacksonians. Americans did not think deeply about public administration again until the Progressive movement of the 1880s and 1890s. The Progressives attacked the dominant Jacksonian style of administration not by explicitly offering an alternative political theory but by denying that politics should have a place in public administration.[3] There was, they said, no Republican or Democratic way to pave a street; public administration should be apolitical management by experts. Progressivism gave us the politically neutral civil service recruited by examination. It also gave us nonpartisan, expert city managers to replace the elected mayors who ran wicked city political machines.

There was little debate in the Progressive era. A great deal of Jacksonianism survived, but less as a principled opposition articulating an alternative democratic theory than as an inertial tradition of political practices that resisted and outlasted the Progressive reform movement.

The third great period of concern with public administration was the New Deal. The New Dealers expounded an explicit theory of public administration by the technologically expert. Sometimes when under attack they spoke the Progressives' language of a politically neutral body of experts. In their franker moments, however, it was clear that the theory was one of technical experts under the direction of New Deal political leaders and loyal to New Deal visions of social justice.[4] That a Republican might someday inherit President Roosevelt's mantle as leader of the experts was unthinkable.

What the New Deal saw as technical expertise in the service of democracy, its opponents saw as big government, bureaucratic red tape, Socialistic central planning, and management by people who had never met a payroll. Their solution was not to rotate Jacksonian common people into office but to substitute businesslike, efficient government for big government and to rotate business managers into public administration. The political theory of the welfare state underlay the New Deal theory and the political theory of the laissez-faire, minimalist state underlay that of their opponents. Both wanted public administration by experts, but they defined expertise differently. For one, the expert was the dedicated specialist in poultry science or social welfare using his or her knowledge to bring more government help to more people. For the other the expert was a manager *qua* manager whose only goal was reducing the costs of delivering whatever governmental services political decision makers required him or her to deliver. The Hoover Commission Reports[5] and the appointments of the Eisenhower years are monuments to this view of administration.

If constitutional law/public law continuously, and public administration intermittently, are major arenas for discussion of the basic nature of American politics and government, then we would expect administrative law to be an especially notable arena for such discussions. For it is the place where the domains of public law and public administration overlap. Indeed we do find such a debate enjoying a central and shaping position in the development of administrative law. This debate has been waged between two different views of politics, one rationalist, the other prudential. These two opposing visions are not neatly derived from two opposing world views, moral philosophies, or political ideologies. Neither is necessarily liberal or conservative nor does either necessarily imply that human behavior or human history is either governed by specific laws or essentially contingent. Rather, the two constitute differing preferences or styles of political discourse and action. The rationalist seeks to constitute political life as a set of general principles, however derived, from which particular political decisions can be derived logically. The prudentialist seeks to constitute political life as a set of particular political decisions that are derived in the light of past experience, current conditions, and expectations about the future. Each decision is tailor-made to the past, present, and future of the particular situation rather than logically derived from a preexisting general rule. Both prudentialists and rationalists may entertain or reject deontological moral philosophies and both may have open or fixed views about the ultimate nature of the good person in the good society. Both may believe that fixed principles exist. Rationalists believe that single correct solutions to particular problems can be derived from those principles. Prudentialists believe that such principles, if they exist, only suggest a range of acceptable solutions rather than dictating a correct one. Obviously, the terms *rationalist* and *prudential* do not capture all of the dimensions of political, legal, and moral thought and neatly order them into mutually exclusive and internally consistent watertight boxes. They are used here to suggest that there are two major American "family circles" of thought about constitutional law, administrative law, and public administration and that each serves to provide a fairly coherent picture of the way in which the practice of American public administration is to be legitimated by reference to administrative law and ultimately by reference to the constitutional law from which administrative law is derived. Let us look briefly at these two visions, first as they express themselves in constitutional law and in public administration, and then as they appear in administrative law.

The rationalist vision in constitutional law treats the Constitution as a contract of government of the sort described by John Locke. It is entered into by rational individuals each of whom seeks to maximize his individual freedom and utility. The Constitution is a blueprint of the machinery of government. Each part of the machine—Congress, the executive, and federal courts—is distinct in structure and function from the others. The three great parts are meshed together by a system of precisely shaped gears— our famous checks and balances. One major activity of those who write about the Constitution is to expound the structure of this machine and clearly define and differentiate the unique tasks of each of its parts.[6]

Under this rationalist vision the Constitution is also a text in which neutral principles of constitutional law can be discerned.[7] From these principles constitutional rights logically can be derived.[8] The task of the Supreme Court is to discover these principles and rights and protect them by law no matter what the costs to other social interests and no matter what the opinion of the people or their representative officials.[9]

The prudential vision does not begin with an abstract agreement by abstract individuals but a coming together of real individuals and groups of individuals to found a political community. That community is not constructed to a blueprint but grows; and its growth encompasses the various overlaps, confusions, redundancies, contradictions, and even pathologies that characterize the real growth of real human beings and human organizations. The Constitution breathes vitality into three such organizations—Congress, the executive, and the courts—but what they do and how they relate to one another is determined by the contingencies of their growth.[10]

The Constitution contains not fixed principles and rights to be logically determined but a melange of values and aspirations. The task of the Supreme Court is to act prudently in furthering whatever vision of the good person in the good state it discerns. Prudence consists of taking sufficient account of our constitutional traditions and current beliefs in seeking to influence the directions of our future political development.[11]

This same dialectic of rationality and prudence also takes place in our thinking about public administration. The rationalist tradition of the Federalists, Progressives, and New Dealers stresses government by experts, and scientific management. Just as the rationalist tradition in constitutional law seeks to separate law from politics through a notion of "neutral principles" of constitutional law, that tradition in public administration seeks to separate administration from politics through a "neutral" civil service and scientific principles of public administration. By the 1930s dozens of political science departments and public administration programs taught a science of public administration reducible to a few basic principles that could be memorized by students on their way to jobs in local, state, and federal government created by the programs of the New Deal.[12]

The prudential tradition has seen public administration not as technique but common sense—"common" in at least two different meanings of that word. American public administration should depend on the preferences of the common people, not an expert elite. Successful public administration must be informed by technical facts but ultimately consist of making commonsense or prudential choices among imperfect alternatives.

In the prudential tradition, politics could not be separated from administration. Public administration was instead a subset of politics. For even the implementation of major policy choices made by others necessarily entailed a host of smaller policy choices made by the administrator. These smaller choices add up to a major share of the ultimate public policy actually achieved. There was indeed a Republican and Democratic way to pave a street so long as some administrator had to choose whether a Republican or Democratic contractor got the paving job and whether a particular street in a particular neighborhood was to get expensive concrete or cheap asphalt paving.

At the time of the New Deal this prudential tradition was represented by a different political science.[13] This other political science was neatly symbolized by the founding of the Littauer School of Public Administration at Harvard, whose faculty consisted not of separate specialists of public administration but simply the regular faculties of the Harvard government and economics departments. What was important for public administrators to know was politics in general and economics in general, not a special science of public administration, for administration was basically political and economic choice.

I have focused on rationality and prudence at the time of the

New Deal because American administrative law for the first time began to take on an identifiable quality and ideology only in response to the New Deal.

The New Deal theory of administrative law was that Congress, rather than passing detailed statutes telling the executive branch what to do, should delegate large amounts of policymaking authority to agencies staffed by experts. Courts should defer to agency expertise. In short, the administrative agencies should be largely free of legal controls and be governed instead by their own professional standards and the political leadership of the president. Anti–New Dealers wanted more legal controls. A grand compromise was struck in the first major congressional statute on administrative law, the Administrative Procedures Act of 1946 (APA).[14]

The APA divided what the administrative agencies did into three parts. Administrative decisions that focused on the particular actions, legal rights, and legal duties of particular private individuals or firms were labeled administrative adjudication. The agencies were required to adopt courtlike procedures in making such decisions, and their decisions were subject to rather rigorous judicial review. Agency decisions that took the form of general rules or regulations that sought to prescribe the future conduct of large numbers of individuals or firms were labeled rule making. With certain exceptions, rules were to be made by an informal process of "notice and comment" rather than a formal trial-like proceeding. The agency was to give notice that it was considering making a rule, to receive comments from interested parties about what the rule should be, and then to issue the rule along with a brief statement of its basis and purpose. Such rules were subjected to some judicial review but less than administrative adjudications. Anything that was neither adjudication nor rule making was to be left to agency discretion for which no procedures were prescribed and only the minimum of judicial review provided.

The great debate between rationality and prudence has occurred in the realm of informal rule making.[15] At first the rationalists had their day. Statutes did delegate broadly to expert agencies. Reviewing courts deferred to the agencies' interpretation of those statutes embodied in the rules they made. Judges presumed that the agencies had adequate factual support for their rules. The APA required that courts invalidate "arbitrary and capricious" rules. Courts conceived this requirement as a kind of lunacy test, striking down rules only in those few instances in which it appeared that no reasonable person could have arrived at the rule the agency had made. Thus, rules were treated as the objectively correct product of expert knowledge.

Beginning in the mid-fifties and rapidly accelerating in the sixties and seventies, things changed. Congress and the courts came to fear that agency experts were being "captured" by special-interest groups and turning out rules that favored those special interests over the public interest. In response, courts stepped up their level of judicial review. They made it far easier for a far broader range of people to participate in notice-and-comment proceedings and to seek judicial review of rules. They demanded that the agencies listen and respond to all the comments made by all the participants. Instead of presuming that the agencies' rules were supported by facts, the courts demanded that the agencies compile "rule-making records" that presented the facts, comments by participating parties and agency responses to those comments, and the agencies' reasons for the rules they made. The courts struck down many rules as arbitrary and capricious because the agencies had not responded carefully to outside comment, or had not gathered sufficient facts, given good enough reasons, or correctly interpreted statutes.

This heightened level of judicial activity was guided by the judges' belief in the dominant political theory of the day, a theory called pluralism. This theory was in part derived from the prudential tradition. It taught that the basic units of political action were not John Locke's abstract individuals but groups of real people, each of which had special interests that it sought to achieve. Politics was group struggle and public administration was a part of politics in which groups sought to get agencies to serve their interests.

Although the pluralists rejected any concept of rationally correct substantive political outcomes, they did have a way of specifying objectively correct outcomes. This way was derived from utilitarian political theory. The utilitarians believed that there was no rational or objective good but only the subjective preferences of each individual. Each individual knew his own interests best. It followed that a democratic political process in which each person pursued his or her own self-interest would lead to the only kind of good that there really was, "the greatest good of the greatest number," that is, the greatest amount of what the most people wanted. Thus, while there was no objectively correct, substantive good for politics to achieve, there was an objective process definition of the good in politics. Whatever came out of a democratic process that allowed equal participation by everyone was by definition good. To decide whether any given government policy was truly good, we need only look at the process by which it was made. If the process was democratic, we could all agree that the policy was good even though we all had different and purely subjective views on whether the particular policy was sub-stantively good or bad. I might believe that a rule against high-rise buildings was a good thing and you might believe it was a bad thing. But if a majority of individuals had voted for it, you and I could agree that the rule was legitimate because it had been arrived at by a democratic process.

If we simply substitute groups for individuals, we have the pluralist theory of politics and public administration. The govern-ment agency should be an arena to which *all* groups have maxi-mum *access*. The rules that emerge from such an agency are, by definition, good if they are responsive to the interests of all the groups. If an agency is "captured" by one or some groups and so does not respond to others, its rules are, by definition, bad. Utilitarians may be considered part of the rationalist rather than the prudential tradition to the degree that they believe that a political system can be so carefully contrived that it will be able to correctly register the exact preferences of every individual and generate public policies that achieve the single, correct optimiza-tion of the sum of all of the individual preferences. Even though their basic position derives from utilitarianism, pluralists tend to fall into the prudential camp because few of them believe that politics can ever be arranged so as to register exactly the precise preferences of all groups or that a single correct policy that would optimize the sum of the preferences of all groups is ever really discernable. Instead, pluralists tend to see politics as proximate solutions thrown up by group struggle that are constantly changed by more group struggle. At any moment a number of different policies seem plausible in the light of group interests, and there is a need for prudent choices among them with more prudent choices coming later. There are no rationally correct solutions to the policy problems thrown up by group politics. Instead there are only more or less prudent compromises that better or worse reduce intergroup tensions for the moment and better or worse pave the way for more prudential decisions in the future.

Pluralism provides a perfect blueprint for what the courts were doing in the sixties and seventies. By liberalizing "standing" rules, they were providing maximum access for groups to the rule-making process. By elaborating notice-and-comment requirements, they were requiring the agencies to listen and respond to every group. And they were labeling each rule good or bad on the basis of whether or not it was the product of such group struggle. In this process the experts within the agency became just one of the groups whose interests should be reflected in the final outcome. Administration became a form of group politics.

This heightened judicial review of the rule-making process almost unconsciously imported another crucial dimension of the prudential tradition. Congress and the courts elaborated the rule-making record requirement so that reviewing judges would have before them a complete record of what had been said to the agencies and what they had said back. Such a record allowed judges to make sure that the agencies had engaged in the "dialogue" with interest groups that pluralism demanded. Once the record was before them, however, how could the judges prevent themselves from asking, "In the light of all the facts, arguments, and analyses in this record, did the agency make a good rule?" Courts began by demanding that the agencies take a "hard look" at what was presented to them. Courts ended up proclaiming that judges would take a "hard look" in "partnership" with the agencies. In other words, the judges were expressing most of their disagreements with the agencies in terms of finding fault with agency procedures, but they were also invalidating rules that just didn't seem substantively right to them. In the end judges simply could not resist striking down rules that they thought were really bad public policies even when those rules were the product of group struggle.

The connection with the prudential vision immediately becomes clear once we remember that the agency is a set of technical experts and the judge is not expert at the things the agency is making rules about—atomic energy or air pollution or soybeans. Thus judicial "partnership" and "hard look" consisted of the review of the technological expert by a nonexpert embodying the common sense of the community.[16]

Heightened judicial review thus combined two prudential insights. The first was that public administration was part of politics and therefore should not be done in isolation by experts. Once the political nature of administration is confronted and the real nature of politics as the pursuit of particular interests recognized, then the pathology to be feared is capture of the experts by some groups to the exclusion of others. The cure is providing equal access to all groups. The second insight was that, whether or not the experts have been captured, expert judgment ought to be checked by common sense.

Heightened judicial review of informal rule making ought not, however, to be seen as the open, unalloyed triumph of prudentialism. Both prudentialists and rationalists saw the danger of capture. The prudentialist cure for this incursion of interest-group politics into administration was more interest-group politics. Let's make sure that all groups get access so that none can capture and each can get some of what it wants. The rationalists can hardly accept such a cure because they want to separate politics from administration. Instead they see the judge as insisting that all groups have access so that each can counteract the excessive claims of every other, thus freeing the expert to be expert, that is, to make the correct decision. Similarly, the judicial "hard look" is seen by the rationalist not as the subordination of expertise to the commonsense judgment of the community, but as intervention by a disinterested neutral person to insure that particular special interests have not corrupted expert judgment.

Thus, in the sixties and seventies, prudentialists and rationalists could unite in support of judicial review. The prudentialist saw review as completing the proper politicization of public administration by insuring that administration would consist of the competition of groups. Moreover, the prudentialist saw review as the subjugation of expertise to common sense. The rationalist saw review as insuring expert neutrality by establishing a system of countervailing group pressures that would cancel one another out. Moreover, where the system failed for some reason, judicial review allowed a neutral person to veto the rule because it was insufficiently expert. When a court invalidated a rule as arbitrary and capricious, it was often hard to tell whether the agency's process had insufficient dialogue or the agency had not provided a sufficiently technological rationale for its decision. Courts often flunked agencies on both counts at once.

In the 1980s, almost unconsciously and accidentally, judicial review of informal rule making has moved on and the inherent tension between prudence and rationality that was masked in the sixties and seventies is reemerging. To understand what has happened, we must look more carefully at the Janus-faced nature of our concept of rules.

Aside from common law rules, which are very strange things indeed, we usually mean by a rule a kind of sub-statute made by a court or administrative agency. It fills in or amplifies the language of the statute but, like the statute, is general in character rather than applying to a single individual. Let us suppose Congress passes a statute that says no one "shall operate a vehicle in a wilderness area." The agency that administers the area may then make a rule that provides among other things that "horse-drawn sleds shall be considered vehicles." There are two fundamentally different ways of viewing such rules. One is essentially prudential and sees rule making as comparable to legislation. The other is essentially rationalist and sees rule making as comparable to adjudication.

Most federal rules occur because Congress has delegated part of its law-making powers to an agency, specifically authorizing it to make rules. The English actually call such a situation "delegated legislation," and we normally call such rules legislative rules. Congress was of course free to choose among alternative basic laws. It could have banned all vehicles or only trucks or no vehicles at all. If it delegated part of that law-making power to the wilderness agency, then presumably the agency has the same kind of legislative discretion—that is, the power to choose among alternative rules—that Congress itself had. Of course, the agency will not have as much discretion as Congress did. Its discretion will be bounded by the words of the statute. It can choose to issue a rule against horse-drawn sleighs or rule that only things with motors will be considered vehicles. But it probably cannot issue a rule against horseback riding because hardly anyone would agree that the word *vehicle* in the congressional statute was meant to include horses.

If rule making is a kind of subordinate lawmaking, it would seem to follow that the rule-making agency need not follow rigorous, courtlike, adversary procedures any more than Congress had to in passing a law. Moreover, a court reviewing such a rule presumably would not ask whether the rule is right or wrong but only whether it is within the range of alternative rules allowed by the statute. A rule banning horse-drawn sleighs would not be invalid as far as a reviewing court was concerned. Neither would a rule permitting such sleighs. But a rule forbidding horses would be wrong. Thus, under this vision of rules, reviewing courts would not review either rule-making procedures or the substance of rules very strictly. They would only intervene when the agency had gone beyond the boundaries to its discretion set by Congress.

The other vision of rules is quite different. It sees the statute as containing a full and complete set of choices already made by Congress. Congress authorizes the agencies to make rules not so that the agencies can make choices but only so that they can fill in the details of the choices already made by Congress. When Congress banned vehicles, it either did or did not intend to ban horse-drawn sleighs. The job of the agency is to determine whether Congress did or did not intend to ban sleighs. If Congress did, then a rule banning sleighs is right. If Congress didn't, then a rule banning sleighs is wrong.

Under this vision the agency is doing what a court is supposed to do in a lawsuit involving the application of a statute. In such instances, courts always at least pretend that they are discovering the true meaning of the statute, not making policy choices of their own within limits set by the statute. It would follow, therefore, that a reviewing court would require the agency to use adjudicative procedures in making a rule and that a reviewing court would have to decide whether the sleigh-banning rule was right or wrong. It could hardly say that either a rule banning sleighs or one not banning sleighs would be legally valid because it cannot say that Congress intended both to ban them and not to ban them. Thus, under this vision, courts would strictly review both the procedures by which rules were made and their substance.[17]

The first vision is prudential in that it empowers the rule-making agencies to make policy choices bounded by Congress but based on a wide range of policy and political considerations. The second vision is rationalist in that it empowers the agency to make only the single correct rule demanded by the statute.

At the time the APA was passed, there is no doubt that Congress entertained the prudential vision for what we normally call informal notice-and-comment rule making. It authorized such rule making in Section 553 of the APA. In two other sections, 556 and 557, it specified that certain legislative rules were to be made by adjudicative procedures. So it knew about both visions and chose the prudential one for most rules and the rationalist one for a few exceptional rules. That is why reviewing courts did so little real review of rule making in the forties and fifties.

In the course of the sixties and seventies a strange, paradoxical, and almost unnoticed shift in the vision that federal courts entertained of rules gradually took place. As noted previously, the courts were busy transforming administrative law according to pluralist prescriptions. The pluralist view of public administration was essentially prudential. At first, the courts attempted to solve the perceived problem of expert administrators politically captured by interest groups with the orthodox pluralist solution. That solution was not to isolate the administrator from politics. A little politics was a dangerous thing leading to capture. The answer was more politics. If every group had equal access, the agencies would become full political arenas accurately reflecting public preferences. So the courts concentrated on group access. They constantly demanded from the agencies more and more evidence that they had invited every group; listened to every group; seriously considered every fact, argument, and alternative offered by every group; and responded to everything said by every group.

This process was governed, however, by one overwhelming American psychocultural phenomenon. American lawyers and judges think they are wonderful and believe their way of doing things is the best way. And most of the rest of us tend to believe them. Perhaps every profession thinks its ways are best, but none other than law has the political power and the cultural dominance to enforce its way as a model of governance. Indeed, lawyers in very few other countries have such a position.

As a result of this lawyers' vision, when lawyer-judges sought to assure the pluralist vision of equal access of all groups to notice-and-comment rule making, they invented a new rule-making procedure. The procedure amounted to a pseudotrial wherein every interest group would be a party and each would litigate against every other in front of an agency official who acted as a judge. In spite of the clear structure of the APA, courts came to insist that notice-and-comment rule making proceed by essentially adjudicatory rather than legislative procedures.

This evolution of law was natural enough because it was lawyer- or judge-made law. In a lawsuit, no matter what the disparities of power, wealth, and influence among the litigants, each party is formally treated as equal and given an equal chance to argue his or her case. The judge is assumed to be neutral, and the trial is an arena in which the parties struggle equally against one another. This trial model is central to the training and experience of lawyers. It is little wonder then that when judges seized upon the pluralist model of public administration (the agency serving as an arena in which interest groups struggle equally), they turned it into a trial in which every group litigated against every other group before an agency acting as judge.

As notice-and-comment rule-making procedures turned into trial procedures in the public law and administrative procedures of the sixties and seventies, something else happened that is clearer by hindsight than it was at the time. It is hard to import part of the lore of trials without importing it all. Although we all know that in many instances judges have a great deal of discretion and can arrive at a number of alternative solutions to the factual and legal problems presented in a particular case, the lore of trials is otherwise. In nearly all societies, courts gain their legitimacy and the consequent consent to their judgments by pretending that they discover the single correct outcome to every lawsuit. Courts claim there is no Republican or Democratic decision to a law case, only a correct decision—the just decision dictated by the law, not chosen by the judge. In short, the lawyers' version of the trial is a part of the rationalist tradition of legally objective principles, rights, and duties and single, correct solutions to problems of governance.

Thus the great paradox of contemporary administrative law. The courts used an essentially rationalist institution—trial—as their device for enforcing an essentially prudentialist vision—pluralism—on the administrative agencies. This contradiction could not be maintained indefinitely. In the sixties and seventies the courts pursued pluralism; but by the eighties, without fully understanding what they were doing, courts began to insist that rule making be rational. If the agencies had to pretend to be courts in their procedures, it became inevitable in the lawyer-dominated world of judicial review that eventually they also would have to pretend to be like courts substantively as well, that is, to announce single correct answers at the end of their procedures.

This shift from pluralism to rationalism is visible along a number of dimensions. One is a shift in the judicial vision of the statutes under which rules are made. They are seen less as delegations to the agencies of the discretion to make law and more as the creators of statutory rights vested in individuals, groups, and the public—and statutory duties imposed on the agencies. In making rules, the agency is seen far less as legislating and far more as doing what courts do, making a just decision according to preexisting law. Rule making becomes part of a rationalist regime in which the agency seeks to find exactly what rights and duties have been imposed on it and others by the congressional statute under which it operates.

A second dimension involves the standard for judicial review. The words of the APA have not changed, but the courts have shifted to other words. Instead of saying that they strike down a rule when the agency has been arbitrary and capricious, courts now say they strike down a rule when the agency has made a "clear error of judgment."[18] The words "arbitrary" and "capricious" clearly implied that an agency had a range of discretionary choices none of which were right or wrong and that courts would intervene only when the agency went beyond that range—when it chose not the wrong alternative but an alternative that no reasonable person could have chosen. The word *error* "in clear error of judgment" implies something quite different—that there is a right answer and the agency has chosen the wrong one. Of course, if the court is not quite sure that the agency is wrong it will approve the rule. That is what the "clear" in clear error means. But if the court is sure the agency is wrong, then the rule falls. The issue is right and wrong. The clear-error rule is actually a transfer to administrative law from criminal law of the "clearly erroneous" standard under which appeals courts review the decisions of trial courts. And of course in such situations the issue is not whether the trial court exercised its discretion prudently but whether it reached the right or wrong verdict.

The most important dimension of the recent shift from a prudential pluralism to rationalism involves only the dropping of a few words. The ultimate pluralist standard announced by courts was that agencies should consider and respond to every fact, policy alternative, and value or policy goal *raised by every interested group*. Such a standard insured equal access by all groups and prevented capture. It recognized that rule making was political choice and demanded a full and fair political struggle. If, however, we simply drop the underlined words, *raised by every interested group,* a magical transformation occurs. The judicial demand is no longer that the agency grant political access to everyone but that it know everything—that it gather every fact, conceive every alternative, and weigh every value.

There is a special decision-making-theory jargon that helps to make this shift clearer. Decision theorists speak of two models of decision making, the incremental and the synoptic. The incrementalist gives great weight to what we are currently doing, only moves away from the status quo if it is causing a lot of complaints, and only considers a few alternatives very close to the existing policy. The incrementalist gathers a few new facts, relies on the feedback that will come after a small change to tell him whether more changes are necessary, and is content to be guided by a set of goals that have not been put in any order of priority. The incrementalist aims for a policy that "satisfices," that is, gives every interested person enough of what he wants that he will go along. The synopticist constantly considers moving from the status quo, gathers all facts, clearly states and establishes value priorities, and generates every possible alternative policy for getting from the existing facts to the ultimate goals. Then he chooses the correct alternative—that is, the one which will optimize the achievement of his goal priorities at the least possible cost.[19]

When the courts dropped the few magic words "raised by every interested group," they were shifting away from the incremental demand that agencies respond to complaints, react to feedback, consider what people want, and try to satisfice them. Instead the courts were now making the synoptic demand that the agency know everything and arrive at the correct policy. Incrementalism is, of course, a formal statement of prudence, and synopticism is a formal statement of rationalism.

The judicial shift from incrementalism to synopticism[20] did not appear abrupt to the judges who made it for two reasons. First, in the sixties and seventies the so-called public interest law movement flourished. There were so many groups doing so much research and saying so many things that the demand that an agency listen to all groups seemed functionally equivalent to the demand that it know everything. Second, if one didn't understand the utilitarian basis of pluralism very well, it was easy to get a basic pluralist tenet backward. Pluralists defined a right answer as whatever answer resulted from a struggle of all the groups. It is only one wrong step from this conception to asserting that if you listen to all the groups you will get the right answer. Judges frequently took that step.

No matter how small and easy and natural it seemed, however, the step from incrementalism to synopticism was momentous. It was the step from administrative politics to administrative science—from rule making as prudence to rule making as the neutral, rational formulation of correct legal rights and duties. For synopticism ultimately merges procedure and substance into a single shining whole, the right answer arrived at in the perfect way.

Of course, no movement of the sort I have described is as simple and uniform as I have made it seem. Courts continue to speak the New Deal language of deference to expert discretion and the pluralist language of group access along with the newer language of synopticism. The Supreme Court has cut back a little on "standing"[21] and on the propensity of the Court of Appeals for the District of Columbia to invent more and more procedures.[22] Thus it has slightly reduced pluralist prescriptions. But only slightly. It has consistently affirmed the basic notion that all interested groups must be listened and responded to. Two recent well-known cases, *Chevron v. NRDC* and *MVMA v. State Farm* (Seatbelts)[23] reveal the Supreme Court's current thinking about discretion and synopticism.

In *Chevron,* the Court wrote a New Deal hymn to expert discretion. The case involved Environmental Protection Agency use of a "Bubble" concept in regulating air pollution. The EPA's statute requires the agency to make rules that forbid an increase in air pollution from any stationary "source" and forbid any new sources that would significantly increase air pollution. One way to look at a large industrial complex like an oil refinery, chemical plant, or steel mill is as a place of many sources. Each cracking tower, blast furnace vent, or smokestack is, in this view, a source. If a new furnace were built at an old mill, that would be a new source. In order to encourage technological development and economic growth, EPA fashioned rules that put a bubble over any large complex. So long as total pollution within the bubble stayed steady or declined, the EPA ruled the statutory standard was met. New production facilities could therefore be added to a particular plant even if they caused new pollution as long as some old facilities at the plant were shut down or made less polluting. The pollution the company "saved" by shutting down or fixing up its old equipment, it could "spend" in installing new equipment that was not totally pollution free.

The Supreme Court agreed that the basic antipollution purpose of the Clean Air Act might be better served by interpreting the word *source* as meaning each individual industrial process. To do so would have created great incentives for industry to develop nonpolluting processes because firms would have been forbidden to install any new production processes unless they were totally nonpolluting. The Court emphasized, however, that Congress had given the EPA the responsibility for achieving clean air and the agency had used its expert judgment in deciding that a bubble rule would be a good way of meeting its responsibilities. The Court deferred to the EPA's discretionary judgment.

In *Seatbelts,* the Supreme Court ruled that the Agency could not rescind an existing rule that required airbags or nondetachable seatbelts in cars even though the agency concluded that the rule would not work to achieve greater safety. The Court said the Agency might not rescind the old rule until it had undertaken new research and considered new alternatives and either come up with a better rule or shown that no rule would work. In short, the Court demanded that the Agency act synoptically.

*Chevron* and *Seatbelts* symbolize the current state of administrative law. The courts do not always require synopticism of the agencies, but the courts do reserve to themselves the final decision as to when the agencies must be synoptic. And when they defer to agency discretion to make rules, the judges are not deferring to

prudential administrative politics but to what they see as technological expertise. What the courts have not confronted and
worked through is that their continued insistence on pluralist
group access is incompatible with their emphasis on expert discretion and synopticism. For this emphasis flows from a vision of
administration as perfect scientific enquiry and solution. The
experience of the last few years makes clear that the rationalist
vision of pluralism does not correspond to what goes on in the real
world. More open access for all groups does not lead to a perfect
group process in the sense of one that results in a single, correct
optimal satisfaction of the sum of group interests. Nor does such
access result in groups countervailing one another so perfectly
that experts are freed to make a simple correct technical decision.
Instead, court insistence on pluralism has in reality been an insistence on administration as group politics leading to prudential
choice among a range of compromising, satisficing, incremental,
and thus never absolutely correct or "rational" solutions. As so
often in the history of American public law, prudentialism and
rationalism are unreconciled neighbors.

From this failure to acknowledge, choose between, or reconcile
our two competing models of law and administration come two
political and institutional problems. These problems are now
becoming increasingly acute because courts are increasingly insisting on neutral, scientific, right rules embodying *the* correct fulfillment of the exact rights and duties created by the statutes.

The first of these problems is a dilemma created for the agencies by judicial review. In reality there is a great deal of discretion
in rule making, and there is a Republican and Democratic way to
make a rule. Even when Congress has expressed its intent clearly
and consistently in a statute, a choice among interpretations is
usually open to the agency. And many congressional statutes are
in fact lotteries into which various goals and values have been
tossed by contending congressional factions that expect that the
rule-making process will be the place where the actual priorities
and the trade-offs among them will be established.

Even aside from statutory ambiguity, rule makers often confront high levels of uncertainty. In writing a rule or standard for
airborne carcinogens, for instance, there may be three or four
equally plausible models of how the air circulates in a particular
location, widely varying estimates of how much exposure to how

much of the particular pollutant causes how much risk of cancer, and a number of different techniques of statistical analysis available to interpret the data. Various combinations of models, estimates of potential cancer incidence, and statistical techniques may yield a spectrum of scientifically defensible, permissible emission standards. The spectrum may range from forbidding industry to release into the air any of the material in question to allowing them to release the amounts they are releasing now. Somebody must choose between using the largest, smallest, or some intermediate estimate of cancer risk as the basis for arriving at the final standard. Often, arriving at a successful conclusion is severely complicated by having to consider several uncertain risks in combination. Consistently choosing the high-end estimates for all these risks will lead to a result that differs wildly from that arrived at by consistently choosing low-end estimates. In cancer rules for instance, those who are especially concerned about cancer may legitimately use the high end consistently to arrive at very strict antipollution rules. Others who are less concerned about cancer, and very concerned that the increasing cost and intrusiveness of government regulation will adversely affect the American economy and standard of living, can legitimately use consistently low-end estimates to arrive at antipollution standards that are easier for industry to attain.

These choices of models, statistical techniques, and risk estimates are legitimately within the discretion of the agency. But what should agencies do when confronted by courts that sometimes admit and approve agency discretion and at other times insist that the agency make the single correct decision in the single correct way? During rule-making proceedings themselves, and in defending rules before reviewing courts, should the agencies carefully identify where they have made discretionary choices and say that they have made the ones they have because they hold a certain set of value priorities or because at the time of rule making the administration was Republican or Democratic? That is the truth, and it might be a good idea to encourage government to tell the truth. But if an agency official tells the truth before a reviewing court bent on synopticism, it is likely that he will be defeated utterly. As courts tend to become increasingly synoptic, there is greater and greater pressure on the agencies to disguise political value *choices* as scientifically or technologically dictated,

correct *answers*. Political discretion is turned into expert discretion. In order to survive, agency officials must increasingly say
that the prudential vision of administrative politics is wrong and
what they are doing fits the rationalist vision of administrative
science. The natural tendency of the agencies to hide behind
screens of expertise is intensified by their need to do so in order to
survive judicial review.

This problem is particularly intense for the Reagan deregula-
tors. Often what they want to do is tell the truth. The truth is
that the existing rules were made by agencies dominated by
enthusiasts of government regulation who consistently made
those choices, particularly in terms of high-end estimates of risk,
that would result in the highest levels of regulation. Those
choices were legitimate and the rules that resulted from them
were legitimate. But now it would be equally legitimate to re-
write the rules on the basis of different estimates and different
choices. The fact that one set of choosers got there first should not
be decisive forever.

Reaganites, however, today frequently confront courts, including the Supreme Court, that treat rules made in the past by
notice-and-comment legislative rule making as if they were the
kind of rules made by law courts. The old agency rules are treated
by courts as if they were the kind of rules that we must pretend
are the single correct answer to the legal question posed by the
statute. Where courts treat agency rules this way, it is not enough
to say, "Yes, they were free to make a Democratic rule and we are
free to make a Republican one," or "They were free to choose the
highest level of regulation that the statute contemplated and we
are free to choose the lowest one." Instead, the Reaganites have
learned by bitter experience that they must say, "The old rule is
incorrect and our rule is correct." Or better yet, "New evidence
and better methods of analysis have now revealed that, no matter
how correct their rule seemed then, our rule is really correct
now." Even aside from the enormous cost in time and money
expended in constructing technical smoke screens, we ought to
deeply regret that judicial review today so often defeats one of its
own major purposes. For in order to protect themselves against
synoptic review, agency officials today often have strong incentives not to give a clear and truthful explanation of what choices
they have made and why.

The second major problem that arises from the newest style of judicial review is that this new review not only distorts what the agencies do but ultimately destroys what courts do. Remember that from a prudentialist perspective the greatest value of judicial review is that it allows the judge as a lay person to impose common sense on agency expertise. The paradox of synopticism is that, as courts think they are increasing the rigor of judicial review by demanding correct answers, they are putting themselves out of the review business and thus decreasing the commonsense supervision of expertise. For the world is not static. As agencies learn that they do better in court by asserting expert correctness than by admitting political choice, they devote more and more of their effort to erecting screens of expert correctness. The rule-making records that go to courts for review get longer and longer and more and more technical. Nonexpert judges find it harder and harder to pretend that they can understand the proliferating technological agency presentations that they themselves have demanded. At stage one of synoptic review, courts strike down agency rules because they have not been sufficiently well defended as technologically correct. At stage two the courts have to uphold agency rules because the judges can no longer pretend that they can penetrate through the endless layers of technological garments in which they have demanded the emperor be clothed. Once courts refuse to admit and applaud the prudential element in rule making, laymen, including those laymen called judges, must yield to the technological superiority of the agency rule maker.

While I decry the substance of my own prediction, I believe we now stand somewhere over the threshold of another one of those long periods in the history of American law and administration that are dominated by rationalist visions. As courts demand that agencies be rational rather than prudential, the agencies will work harder and harder to disguise their prudence and proclaim their rationality. Administrative politics will masquerade as administrative science. And administrative law will once again be dominated by judicial deference to a pretended administrative expertise. The judges are already beginning to bow low to an idol they have made with their own hands.

# Notes

1. See Leonard D. White, "The Federalists," in *A Study in Administrative History* (New York: Macmillan, 1956).

2. See Paul Van Riper, *History of the United States Civil Service* (Evanston, Ill.: Row Peterson, 1958).

3. See Woodrow Wilson, "The Study of Administration," reprinted in *Political Science Quarterly* 16 (December 1941): 448–506; Frank Goodnow, *Politics and Administration* (New York: Macmillan, 1900).

4. See U.S. President's Committee on Administrative Management, *Report of the President's Committee on Administrative Management* (Washington, D.C.: Government Printing Office, 1937); U.S. Attorney General's Committee on Administrative Procedure, *Final Report of the Attorney General's Committee on Administrative Procedure: Administrative Procedure in Governmental Agencies* (Washington, D.C.: Government Printing Office, 1941), Senate Doc. 77–8.

5. See U.S. Commission on Organization of the Executive Branch of the Government, *Report to Congress* (Washington, D.C.: Government Printing Office, 1949).

6. The most famous of these approaches is Thomas Cooley, *A Treatise on Constitutional Limitations* (Boston: Little Brown, 1871 and succeeding editions). A typical modern example is Edward S. Corwin, *The President: Office and Powers,* 4th ed. (New York: New York University Press, 1957).

7. Herbert Wechsler, *Principles, Politics and Fundamental Law* (Cambridge: Harvard University Press, 1961).

8. Ronald M. Dworkin, *Taking Rights Seriously* (Oxford England: Oxford University Press, 1977).

9. This view permeates the major contemporary constitutional law treatise by Lawrence Tribe, *American Constitutional Law* (Mineola, N.Y.: Foundation Press, 1978).

10. See Martin Shapiro and Rocco Tresnolini, *American Constitutional Law,* 6th ed. (New York: Macmillan, 1983), 10–12.

11. Alexander Bickel, *The Supreme Court and the Idea of Progress* (New York: Harper & Row, 1970). See Anthony Kronman, "Alexander Bickel's Philosophy of Prudence," *Yale Law Journal* 94 (1985): 1567–1616. Professor Kronman is engaged in a major work on prudence. His vision of prudence entails a far more determinate ethical component than does mine.

12. See e.g., Luther Gulick and L. Urwick, eds., *Papers on the Science of Administration* (New York: Institute of Public Administration, 1937).

13. See e.g., E. Pendleton Herring, *Public Administration and the Public Interest* (New York: McGraw-Hill, 1936).

14. See Walter Gellhorn, "The Administrative Procedure Act: The Beginnings," *Virginia Law Review* 72 (1986): 219–34.

15. Detailed accounts of the administrative law developments summarized here may be found in Richard Stewart, "The Reformation of American Administrative Law," *Harvard Law Review* 88 (1975): 1667–1781; Martin Shapiro, "Predicting the Future of Administrative Law," *Regulation* (May/June 1982): 18–25; Merrick Garland, "Deregulation and Judicial Review," *Harvard Law Review* 98 (1985): 505–91; Cass Sunstein, "Deregulation and the Hard-Look Doctrine," *Supreme Court Review* (Chicago: University of Chicago Press, 1983), 177–226.

16. Martin Shapiro, *The Supreme Court and Administrative Agencies* (New York: Free Press, 1969), 44–47, 52–54.

17. The rationalist vision as set out here and in succeeding paragraphs is presented in detail in Garland, "Deregulation and Judicial Review," and in Cass Sunstein, "Factions, Self-Interest, and the A.P.A.: Four Lessons since 1946," *Virginia Law Review* 72 (1986): 271–97. Cf. Martin Shapiro, "A.P.A.—Past, Present and Future," *Virginia Law Review* 72 (1986): 447–92.

18. See *Citizens To Preserve Overton Park v. Volpe,* 401 U.S. 402 (1971); *Motor Vehicle Manufacturers Association v. State Farm Mutual Automobile Ins. Co.,* 463 U.S. 29 (1983).

19. For a summary of these approaches, relating them to judicial review of administrative action, see Shapiro, *Supreme Court and Administrative Agencies,* 73–91.

20. The shift is charted in detail in Colin Diver, "Policy-making Paradigms in Administrative Law," *Harvard Law Review* 95 (1981): 393.

21. See *Simon v. Eastern Kentucky Welfare Rights Organization,* 426 U.S. 26 (1976).

22. *Vermont Yankee Nuclear Power Corp. v. NRDC,* 435 U.S. 519 (1978).

23. *Chevron U.S.A. v. NRDC,* 467 U.S. 837 (1984); *Motor Vehicle Manufacturers Association v. State Farm Mutual Automobile Ins. Co.,* 463 U.S. 29 (1983).

*Discussion*

**Wildavsky:** We cannot have the virtue placed in the bureaucracy that Lou Gawthrop would wish for, this for a very strict reason, namely, that, alas, those who like small government dishonor the bureaucracy because it's large; those who like big government because they wish it to redistribute, not only money, but power from men to women, from parents to children, from people to animals, and so on—*they* wish greater equality of result; they dislike authority. A major problem for the Democratic party, for example, is that most of the people who keep pushing bigger government find authority distasteful because authority is a prima facie case of inequality.

In the dawn of our republic, the people Professor Gawthrop was talking about in some respects—the Antifederalists, Jeffersonians, and Jacksonians—believed that the central government was the source of artificial inequality in society. Following the great battles of the party of the king and country that you might read about, say in Lance Banning's wonderful book *The Jeffersonian Persuasion,* you will see that they feared the undermining of republican government by central authorities doing terrible things: engaging in debt, creating banks, charters, franchises. They were willing to leave life to ordinary competition, but they thought the central government would make for so much more inequality that it would render government impossible.

Today it is just the reverse, of course. Those we call left or progressive believe in the central government as a countervailing power to corporate power, and, therefore, they want to build up that authority. But they face, as all of us face, fundamental contradictions in life. I argue with "Reaganites" that if you want authority respected in society, you can't demean the bureaucracy. And I argue with left liberals that if you want to build up the government, then you must say, if you are bigger you are better, and you must give government the benefit of the doubt. If we have a situation in which the people who like social equality dislike governmental authority because it is too weak, and the people who like equality want to undermine government because it's unequal—the life of bureaucrats is very hard; they will need more than the courage that Gawthrop has.

**Wolin:** I may, perhaps, indiscriminately lump Professors Gawthrop and Shapiro's essays together, but I think there is a certain sense in which they belong together if only because I think they both fall victim to the temptation that one always has on an occasion like this, which is to become self-congratulatory and to perhaps suspend critical judgments about the subjects that we are considering.

It struck me that Professor Shapiro, in his very interesting essay, with its emphasis on the rationalist and the prudentialist strands, was not so much defining a dichotomy as stating the limits within which there are choices in the ways that we might think about public power. Moving through the essay I found less and less that distinguished the rationalist from the prudentialist; it seemed to me the prudentialist was simply a rationalist without a handy rule, and the rationalist was a prudentialist who had taken leave of his senses. But beyond that, it seemed to me that what was at stake was some kind of definition of a quest, as Professor Wildavsky said, some kind of preoccupation with authority. The problem was highlighted by his reference to the Jacksonians. He tried to place the Jacksonians with the prudentialists and to oppose them to the rationalists and the *Federalist.* But it seems to me that the Jacksonians were much more concerned with a deeper question of how to legitimize state power when its governing group is drawn from a small sector of the community. In seeking their kind of understanding of a public service—more open, more egalitarian, less dependent on formal qualifications, much more inclined to rotate office—they were trying to root government power in a popular basis. They were trying to establish the same kind of bureaucratic forms of power that the *Federalist* had attempted earlier. However, the Jacksonians sought a different legitimating principle. The *Federalist* appealed to "a new science of politics" while the Jacksonian seeks a populist principle in "the people." But I don't think this had much to do with prudentialism. Rather, it was an attempt to find a basis that could underlie both prudentialism and rationalism by seeming to give the system some kind of popular basis. When the whole Jacksonian movement eventually was undercut toward the latter part of the nineteenth century—as Professor Shapiro has pointed out—by the bringing in of what was essentially to be a meritocratic system, that is, a system in which the civil service would be based on examination, it looked like a form of democratic fairness in the sense that there would now be careers presumably open to all talents. In reality it did not strike hard at questions of power. The fact that civil servants were now to be recruited from different classes would not nullify a more fundamental consideration. Regardless of class origins, civil servants would all have to acquire similar credentials in order to qualify. They would prepare for the same exams and acquire the same skills. A democratic bureaucracy would mean only that careers were open to the same talents. The real stake in many of the puzzling developments during the nineteenth century had more to do with a crisis in the legitimation of power and authority. The crisis was bred by a growing realization in many quarters that the system seemed to be developing away from democratic principles and possibilities, and yet public rhetoric continued to claim the opposite. It seems to me, therefore, that the alleged opposition between prudentialism and rationalism obscures the congeniality between the two.

The rationalist principle gives you a claim to scientific authority that kills democratic debate. The prudentialist principle opens up a problem of discretion and the desirability of discretion and the limitations of rule-bound knowledge, but it doesn't hit at the question of power. It is simply a statement about the nature of a judgment to be made while presupposing all the structures of power remaining in place. I think, therefore, that if we take these matters further, what we've got is not so much a question of celebration but some of the elements of a crisis.

**Lowi:** I still feel strongly the association with several of the points made by Professors Shapiro and Gawthrop. I think that these two gentlemen, both good political scientists, have been unduly influenced respectively by law school and divinity school. Both are hazardous to your health, specifically to loss of sensitivity to power.

I think that the distinction between rational and prudential is a useful one, although I'm extremely suspicious of dichotomies. I think it is possible to sustain those two only if one stays within a certain kind of textual analysis. And they tend to break down under the weight of adjectives assigned to each. And Professor Gawthrop's problem seems to be taking too seriously words like virtue, truth, and love. Those are not categories; those are personal expressions of some kind of emotion that we are supposed to like. While the words themselves are extremely useful under certain circumstances, they have to be put in the context of power. What comes to mind in the case of Professor Gawthrop's essay is that the kinds of things that Washington was saying and meant (meant them sincerely just as Lou Gawthrop means the virtuous words he says) occurred at a time of state building, a dark period when those involved had to worry whether the next day there would be a republic left, whether there would be another rebellion, whether there would be a loss to another country and loss of national autonomy. Then, the notion of virtue really meant something and the assumption was that the people who uttered those words embodied them; it wasn't just that we should embody them, it was that those already there had them, or appeared to have them, and that's what the nation required at that time. There is a relationship between the kinds of things the government was having to do in the 1790s and early 1800s and the concept of "good administrator" they would espouse. I won't go through the whole history, but there is no coincidence that there was a rather dramatic shift in the sincerely held concept of a good administrator as government functions changed. Once the stability of national government was established, the demands for policies changed, and so did the concept of good administration. If you look at the history of the nineteenth-century federal government—in fact, review the annual session laws of Congress—you will find that national government did little more than give out claims, give out land, give out privileges, and so on. All the fundamental governing was being done by the states. Such a national government was fertile ground for political parties and therefore fertile ground for a type of administration consonant with political parties. What would that be? Rotation in office, of course. There is nothing sinful or virtuous about rotation. But there is something extremely consonant between rotation and party government, whether for good or for evil.

Washington's virtue was distant, having been replaced by political equality. You can go on through to the late nineteenth century and understand merit and the stress on merit in the same terms: the rise of the first national regulation, the first notion of a national military, the first notion of a permanent navy, a possibility of world presence, and so on. That is not fertile soil any longer for party government or for rotating administration. Those who stressed merit as virtue were fighting party government.

You can tie this in to Professor Shapiro's more contemporaneous distinctions. While I can't explain them one for one, the fact is that there have been enormous changes as to who is doing what: in the functions being performed by the national government, in the role of the Constitution in the national government, and in the relation between national government and the states. Professor Wildavsky's apocalyptic vision makes him more conservative than even I thought he was, but whether he is correct or not about what the national government is trying to do to make us all communistically equal, he's absolutely correct that a number of very important system-wide things were happening in the last fifty years that weren't happening before. And that's not the kind of situation in which either rotation *or* a civil service meritocracy has much meaning. The latter merely meant get rid of bad guys. We start developing very positive notions of how to develop good guys, guys who are trained and professionalized; and that's where prudence and rationalism begin to break down in terms of a more positive notion of what a good administrator is. I won't go into it any further except to say that a whole series of relationships can be established between what it is the government is doing, what are the prevailing power relationships, and what it is that administrators are having to contend with. I can't predict the outcome, but I don't think that sense can be made out of these tendencies by dealing with the words and the legal or the religious distinctions or the normative distinctions the way you two have. I think the politics part of both these things has been left out. I'm especially disturbed by Gawthrop's argument because I find it simply an appeal to "love your bureaucrat." That may be a reflection on my background rather than what he really said, but I found almost no meaning in the words because they were absolutely not tied to anything that was going on.

**Wildavsky:** Not too many years ago I would have agreed entirely with Martin Shapiro, who would have probably said more or less what he said and said it in the same way and believed it as he does now. I do think he has described what is happening, but I do not think any longer that it is sufficient to describe what is happening without some consideration of why it is happening. From all we can tell from Martin's essay, just as some are born liberals and conservatives, judges are somehow born rationalists and prudentialists. Perhaps it is a matter of fashion—some years are blue and the other years yellow—or perhaps it is sunspots. But I think not in this case.

Why would you suppose that—as I thought about these categories today, though not in other decades—all rationalists are liberals and all prudentialists are conservatives? If we ask the question of why it is that judges might want what they want so that we can make some sense out of their behavior, we might come a little closer to an understanding of this matter. As I see it, in the New Deal period, when the judges believed in what the New Deal was doing, they saw the political system flawed but the New Deal as good. They were by no means radical, but they were radical in comparison to the past. They were prudentialists, and they did what you and I would do: they took ameliorative measures to facilitate what they thought desirable. But if one comes to the post-1960s period and imagines that many of the judges feel that the American political system is seriously flawed and may not recover, that its inequalities are unconscionable, and that therefore it is their duty to redress the social and political and economic inequalities as moral men and women, then it would make a lot more sense for them to impose on the bureaucracy holistic and synoptic criteria.

An example comes to mind. I have recently spent a lot of time with the law of torts—the law of personal injuries. In the mid-nineteenth century, when capitalism was rising, if you got cut in half in an accident, neither half could collect. The circumlocutions of this kind were quite amazing. The agency doctrine might be, "If my foreman did you in, too bad. Who was he but a mere employee?" But today, system blame is rampant. It's all right if doctors and gynecologists get it in the neck because, after all, they are richer than you and me; but when midwives get hurt, now that is getting serious. Basically it's like this. If somebody takes a table and on that he puts a chair, on top of which he puts a tricycle, on top of which he puts a bicycle, then steps on all of these and falls, the courts will undoubtedly rule that the manufacturer of any of the components in the tier should have had the foresight. If you get hit by a baseball at a game, now you sue and collect. The cases are absolutely amazing. Unfortunately, lawyers don't do quantitative research, but the Rand Corporation has now stepped in so we see exactly what has happened. If I am in a terrible accident and you hit me with your car and I am very seriously injured, I collect from your insurance a certain amount. However, if you are a city government, I collect four times that amount; and if you are a corporation, I collect six to eight times that amount.

What is this about? What I understand is happening is that when courts want to implement decisions in the direction of justice, by which they mean fairness, to which only one expression exists, "greater equality of condition"—they impose criteria of proof on administrative agencies that, one, will encourage them to move in the direction the judge wants, or, two, discourage them from moving in the direction where they are going. To put it another way, no one would impose on themselves or other reasonable people such restrictions if they thought that the system of which they were a part was desirable and they wanted it to work. They don't want it to work. That's the whole point of this; they want it to be quite a different system. And, disliking it, they impose strange, convoluted, and draconian formulas.

In any event, I think we have to have some consideration of why this is occurring—whose interest it is in. If we say that life is people, that what matters to people is what they do with other people, then it makes some sense for this generation of judges to do things that were not done in other generations.

**Wolin:** It seems to me that in one of the categories that Professor Shapiro has talked about—a rationalist category—he picked up on what could be said to characterize discussion during much of the last half of the nineteenth and the twentieth centuries—the notion of a bureaucracy as a genuine repository of scientific knowledge (using that term very loosely) and the notion that scientific knowledge represented a final authority that one could appeal to, whether in the form of principles of scientific management or as the basis of public policies. This might explain why you find the courts imposing more rationalist criteria at the present time, precisely because we've reached a historical point where faith in rationalism is declining.

**Shapiro:** In two senses Wolin is right. First, our faith that the bureaucracy is the repository (the sole or major repository) of scientific knowledge is gone. Now we often think that it is the universities or the private corporations or the research groups. In a sense, what the courts are saying to the agencies is that, "We've caught you too many times pretending to have scientific expertise when you didn't have it; now you've really got to deliver." That's Wolin's narrower point.

Second, the broader issue is the point about a general reduction in faith in rationalism. The courts are suspicious of rational claims by the agencies. As a result they try to force the agencies to prove "scientifically" everything they claim. Judges often don't say to the agencies, "Tell us when you're guessing and then make your best guess." Usually they demand that the agencies be scientific. Instead of asking the agencies to put their uncertainties on the table so everybody can see that they are really making a policy choice, courts demand that agencies pretend their decisions are correct science rather than prudential guesses.

**Wildavsky:** This really won't do, and I will appeal here not to exotica, but to today's newspapers. The idea that people are for or against science is quite wrong. I will give you evidence and you will see in your daily life that this cannot be. What they are for and against is our institutions. The question of technological danger and risk are referenda on our institutions. Immense correlations exist between opposition to nuclear power and opposition to the American political system. Let's take somebody who puts his body on the line before the nuclear power plant, or somebody who is worried about some chemical carcinogen. They will derogate scientific expertise, they will tell you that the scientists are bought off by the government, that they're rotting our insides out for their profit. What do you expect from capitalists? Turn to page C in the newspaper. Now the article's about Acquired Immune Deficiency Syndrome. Gays are good because they're antiestablishment and because they reduce differences among people. The very same person who seeks deviant scientists on nuclear power will seek an established scientist on AIDS. Don't tell him about some dopey doctor in Queens who thinks you can get an epidemic by shaking hands. If you talk about residual uncertainty they will say, "Oh, doctors always talk about residual uncertainty; you have no problem putting your child in a classroom with AIDS kids." Take a look, in other words, not at how they think about science in one area, but in several.

When you like the institutions that corporate capitalism represents, then you honor its products. If the mine caves in, what do the Mormon miners say? Well, they don't blame the bosses, they don't hold them accountable. They say, "That's the risk we took for a good occupation; let's get together and compete for higher production." But when you derogate the system and think that hierarchies are coercive and that markets are inegalitarian and that both really can't be supported, then you try to show that their products make you sick. Similarly, the Moral Majority says that when you violate God's commandments He brings plague upon the people. The connection with the practice that violates your sense of morality, that is, that violates your sense of trust in institutions that generate this morality, is tied exactly to perception of danger. On the right, they want to segregate the poor victims of AIDS and they want to have nuclear soup for breakfast, and on the left they have the one-hit theory—one molecule is sufficient to give cancer. Don't be afraid about getting a blood transfusion; after all, forty million people do it, and only 476 died. Not one person died from a nuclear accident in this country. In other words, if what people care about is how they live with others, their use of science is purely instrumental. I know and have read that Sheldon Wolin thinks it might be otherwise. But what I see here is that when you like the social system that produces things, then you go with whatever scientific opinion will support that system.

**Wolin:** That says the same thing that I said in the same way— that is, if you are saying that it is obvious that we are operating on a complete understanding of science whether we recognize it or not—that one group finds it to their interest, the group that is identified with corporate capitalism, to either love or hate science depending on the context, and the left does the opposite.

I'm not quarrelling with that. What I would want you to explain, though, is what you think is the political impact on ordinary people when they see the spectacle of scientific opinion ranged on opposite sides of the question.

**Wildavsky:** In recent years I have begun to believe, following Mary Douglas's cultural theory, that what you have said is far more true than I once believed. But it is not entirely true. That is to say arguments do matter.

Let me be prejudicial here. The amount of carcinogenic material in ordinary food that you and I have eaten today, as Bruce Ames shows without refutation, is over 10,000 times larger than anything we get as pesticides from industry unless we sit down to eat the pesticides themselves instead of a peanut-butter sandwich. The people on the left have multiplied not by hundreds but by thousands the amount of danger to be feared. Why am I concerned about this? Turn to AIDS for a moment. Maitland was right: society is a seamless web. We have the great possibility in our country of an epidemic of fear concerning AIDS. How would we turn that around? It is bad enough that what they got is deadly. All we can really do is appeal to evidence; all we can really say is that with some residual area of uncertainty the best medical advice and research advice we can get tells us that, while this is very deadly and we don't know everything about it, it does not appear to be transmitted by casual contact and therefore if you don't engage in bad needles and certain types of sex, you should be okay. All that relies on is the authority of the best science we know. Our best hope for a cure or remedy is our basic research in biomedicine. If in one area of life you discredit experts, how are we going to say in another area of life this man is rotting my guts out for profit but believe your medical researchers?

**Wolin:** But how can you avoid the discreditation of the expert when the question of science becomes a political issue? I can make the arguments from the opposite side. I can say, for example, that all the scientists you have said are on the left were also the ones who years ago talked about the problems of acid rain or talked

about the greenhouse effect; and now we have the Reagan administration acknowledging, "Yes, there is an acid rain problem; yes,
there is a problem of the greenhouse effect." The point is not that
one side is right and the other side is wrong; it's that we are faced
with a situation in which scientific knowledge has itself become
part of the political controversy and inescapably so, and you can't
say, "Let's just keep our hands on the facts." Both sides are clearly
trying to keep their hands on the facts.

**Wildavsky:** Empirically, I agree with you. However, I believe
that it really is essential to try and that is what I am doing here;
my essay on risk is part of a book in which I'm trying to deal with
the more objective parts of this. If we give up civility, if we
simply say that we are ships passing in the night—I have my
ideology, you have yours—certain things will come up that are
unexpected, like AIDS, and we will not only be unable to have
discourse with each other but nobody will have credibility for
anything.

**Lowi:** Be careful. This is just like my believing in the virtue of
democracy. Beware of blaming the victim or expecting from the
victim more than you expect from the perpetrator. The fact is that
science has become a part of the governing regime. Not all scientists, but for a good part of this century and well before, starting
well after anybody had faith that bureaucracies could house these
things, sometime after that we got a sense that with pure science
you could solve certain kinds of problems. The big risk you take
when the government starts basing so much of its estimates and
its policies and its recommendations on science, is that science, in
allowing itself to do so, becomes attached to the regime. It will
suffer the ups and downs of regimes—as Tocqueville said, "The
virtue of separation of church and state is that the church doesn't
get attached to a specific regime." That is better for everybody.
We took a risk on science and we have our problems, so don't tell
me that it is the fault of believers and nonbelievers.

**Wildavsky:** It's an American problem, Ted. Once when doing a
paper, I was lucky that I found other people had done work on the
regulation of chemical carcinogens in six countries—England,
Germany, Sweden, France, the United States, and Japan. In the

other countries, when they need scientists, they talk to two or three; there is no controversy and whatever the top men suggest is what they do. While we do immense research, which is hardly ever followed, they do very little research and follow whatever opinion there is. The United States is the only country among the six that has hostile and punitive relations with the regulators. What Rita LaVelle was sent to jail for, they give medals for in Japan and England. These countries have classic hierarchies. They believe that business and the bureaucracies are all part of the same family, that they should show each other private memoranda, they should be mutually persuasive to one another. What we have to explain is not why science universally has become enmeshed in these political wars but why so much more in America than in other places.

**Lowi:** Are you suggesting that you want a set of institutional relationships in those countries whose carcinogenic policies you admire? Would you want the more credible attitudes toward science along with the rest of that fruit plate? It seems to me that vigilance toward science would be all part of the price of liberty.

**Wildavsky:** You can look at the policies actually followed toward carcinogens; every country's policy is virtually identical. If you look at the heartburn, the rhetoric, the fear, the concern, then it is remarkably different. Basically, every country regulates the things that we know how to do something about.

What is the layman to say? Silicon Valley's well water is contaminated. That's true, but so is life. It's true that there is mucky stuff in Silicon Valley but it is well water and it turns out that if you drink a glass of Silicon Valley well water, you are drinking less carcinogenic material than a glass of water in Oakland, which I do every day. But finding out about what's bad is difficult. I'm paid to pursue such matters and I have to continually ask for advice on chemicals with funny names. What's really in trouble is our institutions and what I quite agree about is the crisis of legitimacy that we have here. If we thought our institutions were reasonable and decent, we would rely on them to assuage our fear.

# Index